Acts

INTERPRETATION
A Bible Commentary for Teaching and Preaching

INTERPRETATION
A BIBLE COMMENTARY FOR TEACHING AND PREACHING

James Luther Mays, *Editor*
Patrick D. Miller Jr., *Old Testament Editor*
Paul J. Achtemeier, *New Testament Editor*

Old Testament:
Genesis by Walter Brueggemann
Exodus by Terence E. Fretheim
Leviticus by Samuel E. Balentine
Numbers by Dennis T. Olson
Deuteronomy by Patrick D. Miller
Joshua by Jerome F. D. Creach
Judges by J. Clinton McCann
Ruth by Katherine Doob Sakenfeld
First and Second Samuel by Walter Brueggemann
First and Second Kings by Richard D. Nelson
First and Second Chronicles by Steven S. Tuell
Ezra–Nehemiah by Mark A. Throntveit
Esther by Carol M. Bechtel
Job by J. Gerald Janzen
Psalms by James L. Mays
Proverbs by Leo G. Perdue
Ecclesiastes by William P. Brown
Song of Songs by Robert W. Jenson
Isaiah 1–39 by Christopher R. Seitz
Isaiah 40–66 by Paul D. Hanson
Jeremiah by R. E. Clements
Lamentations by F. W. Dobbs-Allsopp
Ezekiel by Joseph Blenkinsopp
Daniel by W. Sibley Towner
Hosea–Micah by James Limburg
Nahum–Malachi by Elizabeth Achtemeier

New Testament:
Matthew by Douglas R. A. Hare
Mark by Lamar Williamson Jr.
Luke by Fred B. Craddock
John by Gerard S. Sloyan
Acts by William H. Willimon
Romans by Paul J. Achtemeier
First Corinthians by Richard B. Hays
Second Corinthians by Ernest Best
Galations by Charles Cousar
Ephesians, Colossians, and Philemon by Ralph. P. Martin
Philippians by Fred B. Craddock
First and Second Thessalonians by Beverly Roberts Gaventa
First and Second Timothy and Titus by Thomas C. Oden
Hebrews by Thomas G. Long
First and Second Peter, James, and Jude by Pheme Perkins
First, Second, and Third John by D. Moody Smith
Revelation by M. Eugene Boring

WILLIAM H. WILLIMON

Acts

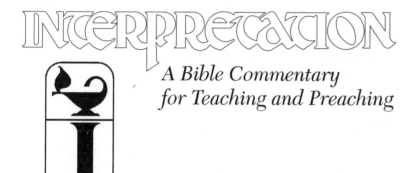

A Bible Commentary
for Teaching and Preaching

WESTMINSTER
JOHN KNOX PRESS
LOUISVILLE • KENTUCKY

2010 paperback edition
Originally published in hardback in the United States
by Westminster John Knox Press in 1988.
Published by Westminster John Knox Press
Louisville, Kentucky

10 11 12 13 14 15 16 17 18 19—10 9 8 7 6 5 4 3 2 1

Library of Congress Cataloging-in-Publication Data

Willimon, William H.
  Acts.
    (Interpretation, a Bible commentary for teaching and preaching)
  Bibliography: p.
  1. Bible. N.T. Acts—Commentaries.   I. Title.   II. Series.
  BS2625.3.W56   1988
  226'.607   87-26085

  ISBN-13: 978-0-8042-3119-0
  ISBN: 978-0-664-23625-0 (paper edition)

PRINTED IN THE UNITED STATES OF AMERICA

⊗ The paper used in this publication meets the minimum requirements of
the American National Standard for Information Sciences—Permanence of
Paper for Printed Library Materials, ANSI Z39.48-1992

SERIES PREFACE

This series of commentaries offers an interpretation of the books of the Bible. It is designed to meet the need of students, teachers, ministers, and priests for a contemporary expository commentary. These volumes will not replace the historical critical commentary or homiletical aids to preaching. The purpose of this series is rather to provide a third kind of resource, a commentary which presents the integrated result of historical and theological work with the biblical text.

An interpretation in the full sense of the term involves a text, an interpreter, and someone for whom the interpretation is made. Here, the text is what stands written in the Bible in its full identity as literature from the time of "the prophets and apostles," the literature which is read to inform, inspire, and guide the life of faith. The interpreters are scholars who seek to create an interpretation which is both faithful to the text and useful to the church. The series is written for those who teach, preach, and study the Bible in the community of faith.

The comment generally takes the form of expository essays. It is planned and written in the light of the needs and questions which arise in the use of the Bible as Holy Scripture. The insights and results of contemporary scholarly research are used for the sake of the exposition. The commentators write as exegetes and theologians. The task which they undertake is both to deal with what the texts say and to discern their meaning for faith and life. The exposition is the unified work of one interpreter.

The text on which the comment is based is the Revised Standard Version of the Bible. The general availability of this translation makes the printing of a translation unnecessary and saves the space for comment. The text is divided into sections appropriate to the particular book; comment deals with passages as a whole, rather than proceeding word by word, or verse by verse.

Writers have planned their volumes in light of the requirements set by the exposition of the book assigned to them. Biblical books differ in character, content, and arrangement. They also differ in the way they have been and are used in the liturgy, thought, and devotion of the church. The distinctiveness and use of particular books have been taken into account in decisions about the approach, emphasis, and use of space in the commentaries. The goal has been to allow writers to develop the format which provides for the best presentation of their interpretation.

The result, writers and editors hope, is a commentary which both explains and applies, an interpretation which deals with both the meaning and the significance of biblical texts. Each commentary reflects, of course, the writer's own approach and perception of the church and world. It could and should not be otherwise. Every interpretation of any kind is individual in that sense; it is one reading of the text. But all who work at the interpretation of Scripture in the church need the help and stimulation of a colleague's reading and understanding of the text. If these volumes serve and encourage interpretation in that way, their preparation and publication will realize their purpose.

The Editors

PREFACE

I began work on the Book of Acts with the fear that my challenge as an expositor would be somehow to make ancient history live for modern Christians. I knew enough about modern Christians to know that for many of us the acts of people in the past, even people of some notoriety like Paul or Peter, usually fail to move us. As a preacher, I have struggled through many a Sunday morning desperately trying to coax an unwilling congregation into the murky, stagnant waters of history by convincing them that a twenty-minute plunge into the past would do them a lot of good. A half century ago Fosdick warned us preachers against the peril of assuming that anybody in the pew wonders what ever became of the Jebusites.

As often happens when one studies Scripture, I was amazed by the contemporaneity of the Acts of the Apostles. Here is remembrance in service of the reformation of the church. The church, even when Acts was written, already needed reformation, self-criticism, bold recollection. The church in any age lives and breathes and grows by remembrance.

Remembrance is a risky venture for the church. But not always. In my library I have probably a dozen histories of local churches, most of them as scintillating to read as a telephone directory. All of them are affectionately written by some sincere local historian to insure that the contribution of dear Uncle Mortimer to the construction of the banisters on the front steps of the church will not be forgotten. Such church history is down-home hagiography, idealized remembrance with most of the messy, really interesting stuff lovingly censored. Fierce arguments over the purpose of the church—the trustees' debate over what to do with the 1948 Christmas offering, the person who stormed out in a huff in 1959 over the selection of a new pastor—are nowhere to be found, swept under the carpet. In their place we have lists of former pastors, past teachers of the Men's Bible Study Class, and fascinating data on the square footage of the new parsonage.

Now the author of Acts is not above a little hagiography of his own. But you need not spend a long time with Acts before you discover that Acts is engaged in a more significant undertaking than the writing of an official history of First Church

Jerusalem. A first encounter with Acts can be deceptive. At first one thinks, "I have come face-to-face with history," but upon further reading one discovers that Acts is a much more interesting character than even history. A pleasant, if somewhat idealized, recollection of the past becomes an assault upon present reality, a bold refashioning of the church, a critique of our current discipleship arrangements. What first appeared to be history, or apostolic memoir, explodes into a fierce argument about the nature of the church, the meaning of the Christian life, and the sustenance of discipleship. And why would you or I still take the trouble to listen and then to teach and preach from Scripture unless we were interested in effecting the same in our church today?

I am endebted to scholars and friends like Franklin Young, Fred Craddock, Moody Smith, and the editors of this series who read and reacted to this commentary as it was written. Because of the nature of the Acts of the Apostles and my vocation as a preacher, I am perhaps even more endebted to the people whom I have been privileged to serve during my two decades of ministry. They, like Theophilus before them, raised the right questions for which Acts provides many of the right answers. They are the ones today, who in their own struggles to be God's church, must answer to the interrogation of Scripture. May my efforts here help them in that faithful dialogue.

CONTENTS

For
William L. Parker
Bessie B. Parker
Carl L. Parker
Servants of the Word

Introduction

Sometime between A.D. 70 and 100, somewhere within the Mediterranean world, the Acts of the Apostles was written. We know that it was by the same creative theologian who gave us the Gospel of Luke, although Acts may not have been written at the same time as the Third Gospel. We do not know for sure who wrote Luke-Acts. Though it is doubtful that it was Paul's fellow worker mentioned in Philemon 24, let us call the writer "Luke" in accordance with tradition, the author of almost one-fourth of the entire New Testament.

In Acts Luke utilized material from a number of early Christian sources, presenting it with a variety of literary techniques, to proclaim the mighty acts of God. The story told here is open-ended, because it continues today in your church and mine. It is a story worth retelling because it deals with issues which are always in season in the church: questions about the relationships between Christians and Jews, Christians and pagans; issues related to the Christian's stance within the modern state; problems with prayer; the purpose of preaching and teaching in the church; and a host of other dilemmas which press upon the contemporary church with more relevance than the headlines of this morning's newspaper. We will undertake a fresh reading of Acts in service of those who teach and preach in today's church. We shall be curious about why Luke chose certain literary forms and what he was saying to the church by the way he presented the story. We shall try to do what people are supposed to do when told a good story—listen to the story, attempting to take the story itself a little more seriously and our "modern" questions about the story a little less so. We shall presume that our interpretive task is to hear the text of Acts questioning us, rather than to come up with questions about the relevancy, practicality, or historical accuracy of Acts.

The church in Acts exists as the church has always existed— as a people who claim to know something that we would not have known except as it was given to us. The Book of Acts opens

1

with the community waiting for something to happen, listening for a word. Presumably if God had done nothing, had said nothing, there would be no community. Your church exists today in the same situation—as the result of the dialogue between a loquacious God who refuses to be silent and a community that tries to listen. Whenever, in your church, Scripture like Acts is read and interpreted, your church is participating in the same primal activity which gave birth to the Book of Acts. When Acts listens to the Hebrew Scriptures, the only real "Scriptures" Luke knew, it asks not simply, "What does the Bible say? but also, "What is God using the Bible to do to us?" (cf. David H. Kelsey, p. 90).

When you read Acts, you immediately realize that you are reading a story, a collection of stories. Stanley Hauerwas notes that the church exists as a "story-formed community" (p. 46). The church is an imaginative construction which results from acts of imagination that we call stories. Indeed when you come down to it, you and I are imaginative constructions, because all of us are trying to make sense out of the world and out of our lives, trying to discern significant beginnings, plots, style, coherence, and worthy conclusions, the same way in which a story deals with life. Scripture is the story of a particular people to whom certain peculiar events occurred. The events are rendered in a certain way, with certain things being emphasized, other things being left out. Something happens to us as we listen to stories like those of Acts, because each of us in our own congregations, in our own lives, is trying to tell a story in a way that makes sense. Three characteristics of stories, particularly the stories of Scripture, have relevance for our interpretation of Acts:

1. *Stories make sense.* A story not only means something but also *does* something. The story performs certain actions when told, heard, and remembered. In the telling of the story in Acts we begin to glimpse that behind what happens there is an active presence who gives coherence and meaning to the narrative. As it turns out, it was not just by chance, not just blind fate, that Saul happened to be on the road to Damascus. It was not for nothing that the believers happened to be gathered in an upper room at Pentecost. They are part of a story that *makes sense,* that reveals an author who is someone more than Luke, someone none other than the one in whom ". . . we live and move and have our being" (17:28). God is not just a character in the story, rather God is the author who makes the story

possible and whose nature and purposes are revealed in the telling of the story.

2. *This story in Acts not only depicts the nature of God but also renders the promise of God to give us a new heaven and a new earth* (Rev. 21:1). The God of Luke-Acts is a God of promise who can be depended upon to be faithful to his promises (Ronald Thiemann, *Revelation and Theology: The Gospel as Narrated Promise*, pp. 110, 142). In listening to this story of God's fidelity to promises made "to you and to your children and to all that are far off, every one whom the Lord our God calls to him" (Acts 2:39), something happens to us. The reader becomes the recipient of the promise. Not only is a God depicted but a new world as well. The world rendered to us in Acts is not just a few images from the ancient Middle East or first-century Rome. What is portrayed is what is going on in the creation as a whole. This world in Acts is not a sober description of what is but an evocative portrayal of what, by God's work, shall be, a poetic presentation of an alternative world to the given world, where Caesar rules and there is enmity and selfishness between men and women and there is death. This is a world where God is busy making good of his promises. Therefore the future is never completely closed, finished, fixed. God has been faithful before (history) and will be faithful again (apocalyptic). The story is a stubborn refusal to keep quiet and accept the world as unalterably given. The "world" of Acts is what is real, what is really going in in life, the ultimate meaning and destiny of humanity. The more we talk about and tell stories of this "world," the more this "world" becomes our own. We find that we have not simply been listening to a little story about an unfortunate elderly couple named Zechariah and Elizabeth (Luke 1:5–25), but we have been changed by their story of a promise fulfilled, shaped by it, so that we can no longer think of ourselves without thinking through their story. We live in a world where God makes promises and keeps them.

Whenever we tell the story of our lives or of our church, we can be expected to engage in a good deal of fanciful reconstruction and downright cover-up and deceit. It is a difficult task to see our lives truthfully. We are frightened creatures who, in the absence of a story which makes sense and gives us hope and security, can be counted upon to make up stories about ourselves in order to get by. My world is invariably refracted through the distorted vision of my own deceit and alienation. I need some story so coherent, so dependable, so truthful, yet

3

so hopeful that it will enable me to tell my story truthfully. The Christian claim is more than that the stories of Acts are interesting, exciting, or historically valuable—which they often are. Our claim is that these stories, the ones you and I must preach and teach in our church today, are nothing less than *true*. That is, they help us see the world as it really is. The world really is a place where God's promises make a difference, and that makes all the difference to us.

3. Lest this all sound too intellectualized, let us be reminded that *Acts, like the rest of Scripture, has as its purpose the formation and equipment of disciples.* Jesus did not come bringing an interesting philosophy of life. He came calling people to a new way of living and dying. The stories in Acts not only depict an author, God, not only render a new world, God's world, but they also render a new way of living, discipleship in the church. Given who God is and the way God's world is, this way of life makes sense. When we read about the way the early church organized itself and stood with its surrounding culture, or when we read the exploits of people like Paul, we are learning what sort of pilgrimage life is, the dangers it holds for those who are faithful, the limitations inherent in this life, what sort of character is required to make it through, the rewards to be had by living faithfully. Scripture, like any good story, depicts an adventure and gives clues as to how ordinary folk like you and I can get on in this life, can be the church today, or how we can miss the whole point. When asked by unbelievers, "How do we know your gospel is true?" we must, like Acts, trot out not only our little arguments for inspection but also our little lives. The best support any of us can give these stories is the way we back them up with the lives we lead.

The stories of Luke's Gospel ended with the disciples being commanded to witness to Christ's life, death, and resurrection as the fulfillment of God's promises (24:44–47). The Book of Acts continues the story of witness which began in the Gospel and becomes part of the church's obedience to witness "in Jerusalem and in Judea and Samaria and to the end of the earth" to what a faithful and beneficent God continues to do through God's faithful people.

4 **What Is an Acts?**

What are we reading when we read Acts? The question is crucial, because if we do not know the form of a writing we do not know its function. Misinterpretation results. How could one interpret Revelation, for example, if one did not know that it is an apocalypse? Yet, in our attempt to interpret Acts, we should take care. No less a scholar than Adolph Harnack said, . . . "no other book of the New Testament has suffered so much from critics as the Acts of the Apostles. . . . All the mistakes which have been made in New Testament criticism have been focussed into the criticism of the Acts of the Apostles" (p. 122).

There have been various attempts to place Acts within the literary environments of early Christianity. Hermann von Soden noted that Luke-Acts is like the biographies, particularly what Charles Talbert calls "cultic biographies" of the Greco-Roman world. A narration of the life of the founder of a religious community is followed by stories of his successors and disciples. Luke-Acts tells the story of Jesus so that he is portrayed as the founder of a new community, a founder who makes provision for its continuation after his departure. Moreover, the story is told in such a way that the Twelve and Paul reproduce in their lives key events in the life of the earthly Jesus. The lifestyle of the new community is thus shown to be rooted in the career of Jesus himself.

The modern reader who encounters Acts for the first time may suppose that he or she is reading history—albeit rather primitive, unsophisticated history, certainly more primitive than the classical history of Thucydides or Plutarch. Acts narrates certain events set against the backdrop of identifiable names and places. But Acts is so filled with miracles, visions, dreams, and novelistic events (e.g., Paul's sea journey) that even ancient historians like Josephus might have questioned the veracity of its story as history.

Talbert's opinion that Acts is "cultic biography" suggests that Acts, like much of classical biography, has a very practical, homiletical purpose—to tell the story of Christ and his new community in such a way that the values of the founder and his immediate successors might be emulated today. The writer of Acts wants to do more than to write a chronicle of the past. Rather, the past becomes the platform from which to preach to the present.

Such writing is always of use in the church—not only as proclamation and inspiration from the past to the present but also as a defense against those who deny or modify the tradition in order to remake the community of faith in their own image.

5

Acts functions as a norm or canon: here is what is really Christian about the early church which is a measure for all later attempts to be the church.

How do we read Acts? Martin Dibelius helped us to see that if we read Acts as history we shall be disappointed, because Acts is not "history" as we often define the word—"objective," dispassionate reporting of "the facts"—nor does it claim to be. In the past many interpreters have studied Acts by comparing it to the Pauline epistles, but they studied Luke's Gospel by paralleling it to the Synoptic Gospels. By so doing, historical questions about Acts tend to be given prominence over theological ones. Acts is reduced to the level of a poor secondary resource, a mine from which to quarry a reconstruction of early Christianity, a romantic and idealized history of the early church, or a downright deceitful, selective polemic in service of some long-forgotten intrachurch feud. This approach yields little fruit for the preacher and the teacher.

The truth of Acts is not to be measured in terms of accuracy in reporting some historical incident but in its correspondence to the apostolic faith in Jesus Christ, which forms the church. When Paul speaks before Agrippa and then Felix, we note apparent historical inconsistencies in the speeches. The real audience for the speeches is not a court of Roman law but the church. This does not mean that the narrative framework of the speeches—two Roman officials—is purely fictional. Rather, the writer of Acts has allowed the theological purpose of Acts to shape the presentation of historical material.

Ezra Pound once defined a novel as "news that stays news." This is Acts. A newspaper headline which causes a brief flutter of excitement and public interest is one thing. News that continues to sway the lives of millions and give meaning to lives generations later is news worth pondering. A person is being unbelievably obtuse to ask, after attending a performance of *Macbeth*, "Now, did that *really* happen?" It is not the right question. A high school English teacher may be interested in questions of the historical veracity of *Macbeth*, the possible historical antecedents, the probable literary models. Few would gather to perform *Macbeth* today if its value depended solely upon history. Unfortunately, many of the interesting historical questions about *Macbeth* will never be solved because we do not have the data at hand.

Historical questions are not irrelevant to the study of Acts.

6

It may not make a difference whether or not a man named Macbeth really lived, but it does make a difference whether or not a man named Jesus lived. A man named Jesus lived His followers staked their lives on his life. What is the meaning of this?

The prologues say that a major purpose of Luke-Acts is to provide an *orderly* and *accurate* account of what has happened (Luke 1:1–4; Acts 1:1, 2). A rigid dichotomy between historicity on the one hand and free Lukan composition on the other is unjustified. There is much in Acts that does not conflict with the information in Paul's (earlier) epistles. Luke is writing neither theological romance nor secretly received personal revelation. He is interpreting the stuff of history, actual events. History and proclamation are not exclusive categories. To preach Christ is to preach history "that you may know the truth" (Luke 1:4) (M. Hengel).

Modern people often define history as an objective reporting of the facts. But scholarly objectivity is a myth which has been put to rest by the studies of people like Paul Ricoeur who stress that all history is written because of certain subjective interests of the historian. Without such subjective interests, historiography would be nothing more than a jumble of unrelated data without meaning. Whoever looks for nothing in history finds nothing. Luke is a true historian, even if an ancient one, who is looking for abiding meaning within "all that Jesus began to do and teach" (1:1).

This commentary benefits from the work of scholars who have studied the possible historical contexts of Acts, the literary antecedents for this type of literature, the socio-political situation of the work. We shall note some of their helpful insights in our exposition of Acts. I shall not, however, burden the reader with detailed discussion of the possible technical and historical issues related to a given text in Acts—except as they relate immediately to the task of exposition. A good technical commentary on Acts, such as the classic one by Ernst Haenchen, is of great value to the interpreter of Acts; and use of it, along with this exposition, will be helpful to the preacher and teacher alike. Yet, our concern is primarily with the theological content of Acts, and therefore we shall attempt to read Acts as a theological document.

This commentary benefits from the impact of literary criticism upon the study of Acts. Luke-Acts must be read together.

7

The Gospel helps to interpret Acts, and Acts helps to interpret Luke. In so doing we attempt to enter the narrative world of Luke, to discern the theological point of view which led the author of Luke-Acts to select material, arrange it in a certain way, and present it, using a wide array of classical literary devices, to say something of life-and-death significance to the church.

The Purpose of Acts

The specific purpose for writing this narrative called Acts is a matter of debate. The reader soon realizes that the title is not much help because *Acts is not really concerned with the acts of all the apostles.* At the beginning Matthias is selected to replace Judas and there follows not a word about the others of the Twelve. James merits only one line (12:2) and John receives little more attention. Peter and Paul are depicted as the pre-eminent disciples. Yet some of the most significant break-throughs for the spread of the gospel are attributed not to the Twelve but to Stephen, Philip, and unnamed persons of Cyprus and Cyrene (11:20). In a surprising reversal, Paul becomes the foremost spokesman for a position he once denounced, and Peter is reluctantly drafted into a mission beyond the Jews (cf. chaps. 10—11). Thus the traditional designation of "The Acts of the Apostles" fails to tell us much about the purpose of the work at hand.

Some suggest that a better designation of the work is as the *Acts of the Holy Spirit.* Jesus both preached in Nazareth (Luke 4:16–30) and was led into Galilee (4:14) by the Spirit. As in Luke, the Holy Spirit is of primary importance in Acts as the dynamic which drives the church to proclaim the gospel across great barriers. In Nazareth Jesus said that the Spirit led him to proclaim the fulfillment of God's promises *today.* In Acts the Spirit continues to be the power which manifests and effects God's salvation to each new generation of believers, the power which resists any effort to confine Jesus to the testimony of past history or to the experience of past believers. Yet it would be a mistake to infer that Acts features the Holy Spirit in the way that the Gospel of Luke features Jesus. It is the living Christ who continues what he began (Acts 1:1). Throughout Acts, there is an easy interchange between "Jesus," "the Holy Spirit," and "God" (e.g., chap. 10) demonstrating that the writer makes no sharp distinction between Christ and the Spirit.

8

There are great portions of Acts where the Holy Spirit is not mentioned or mentioned only in passing. The main concern seems to be with what the Spirit does rather than with the Spirit itself. God is the planner and actor of this mission and God's Word, empowered by the Spirit, accomplishes the plan (Haenchen, p. 98).

Perhaps Luke's concern is *to show how the gospel spread into every corner of the gentile world.* I remember well, but none too fondly, how our church youth group labored many months to construct a giant map of the Mediterranean world and, attempting to follow Acts, tried to show how Paul's journeys eventually took the gospel to Rome. Acts 1:8 does provide, as Luke was in the habit of doing, a geographical framework for the narrative (Jerusalem, Judea, and Samaria, and to the ends of the earth); but it is doubtful that Luke's concern is with geographical problems. We learn how Paul got to Rome, but not how the gospel got there. The real barriers to the gospel were national, theological, doctrinal, and economic; not geographical.

In his commentary Haenchen makes Acts *a response to the political problem between Christianity and Rome* (cf. pp. 102, 726). He sees Acts as an attempt to establish Christianity, like Judaism, as one of the recognized religions within the state. Christianity lost the toleration which Judaism enjoyed, so now Luke must defend Christianity against the charge of subversion of the state. But much of Luke-Acts would be unintelligible to pagan Romans, and it is unimaginable that some Roman bureaucrat like Felix would plow through Luke-Acts to learn about Christianity (Jervell). The Gospel of Luke begins with the proclamation that haughty politicians shall be overthrown (Luke 1:57), and Roman officials would not likely be flattered by the portraits of Pilate, Felix, and Festus. No, Acts, like the rest of the New Testament, is addressed to the *church* and not the government (see *Reflection: The Politics of Luke*).

F. C. Baur saw Acts as *a second century irenicon designed to patch up the split between the followers of Peter and Paul.* But Acts indicates that the real gap was between James and Paul, with Peter caught in the crossfire (cf. Acts 11:1–18; 21:17–26; Gal. 2:11–14). It was James who intimidated Peter about fraternizing with the uncircumcised, according to Paul. Undoubtedly Acts does speak to a cleavage in the faith community, but it is not between Peter and Paul.

9

More recently, Conzelmann finds *disappointment in the delay of the parousia* to be the setting for Luke-Acts. The hopes of faith are shifted from eschatology to a theology of history in which the church becomes the official bearer of sacred tradition and the sole means of salvation. The period of Jesus was "the middle of time" that has now given way to the period of the church. Luke reinterprets the return of Christ to be sudden but not necessarily soon. Such a theory can only be held by ignoring the textual evidence. We must disregard Luke 11:20, sever John the Baptist from Jesus, and accentuate an issue which receives scant treatment in Luke-Acts. Luke divides history, but not into three parts as Conzelmann claims (time of the law and the prophets, time of Jesus, time of the church). In Luke-Acts there appear to be two epochs of promise-fulfillment. There is (1) the time of prophetic promises and (2) the time of eschatological fulfillment in the church. Within the eschatological time of the church, there are also two great periods: (1) the mission to the Jews (9:43) and (2) the mission to the gentiles (11:18), probably divided by the conversion of Cornelius.

When one examines Luke's parables of the parousia (Luke 12:35–38, 39–40, 41–48; 19:12–27), one sees that Luke's polemic is aimed at those who would fix a date for Christ's return. The church's realization that the period before the return of Christ might be longer than was first thought has not undercut the expectation. As Luke's parables indicate, the return, though more distant than once thought, will be sudden and unexpected. There is no attempt by Luke to make the best of an embarrassing predicament. Rather, the time before the parousia is part of God's plan to visit his people with judgment and redemption that they may turn and repent. The "time of the gentiles [must be] fulfilled" (Luke 21:24). Luke has not, as Bultmann claimed, demythologized the eschatological promise nor has he domesticated it by collapsing the promise into the history of the church. Rather, Luke has reshaped the promise of return to conform more closely to the Old Testament prophecy-fulfillment pattern. Even as Israel had to endure a time of indignity until the coming of God's kingdom (Dan. 7:27), so the church must learn to wait for the sure but unexpected date of Christ's return to his people.

10

By isolating certain Lukan passages such as the birth narratives, Jesus' baptism, and possibly Acts 1:4 and 10:41, Talbert argues that Luke-Acts is *a defense against Gnosticism (Luke and the Gnostics).* While Luke could have been concerned with Gnostic tendencies, we see little trace of this concern in his Gospel and virtually nothing in Acts. The problem with many of these theories is the great difficulty of taking so complex and rich a story as Acts and reducing it to a one-factor analysis. As we have said, Luke-Acts is not only full of stories it is itself a story, a narrative of what God is up to in Christ and in his church. Any story which can be easily collapsed into one abstract idea or one specific purpose is not a very good story. Acts is a good story, as complex and rich, as varied and mysterious, as true as life itself. So we do well to be suspicious of any claim for a single key to the interpretation of Acts, and we should resist any effort to make judgments about which purposes are superior, inferior, original, or derivative. We should rather try to read the story taking it on its own stated terms, letting it have its way with us.

Dear Theophilus

In each of these theories of the purpose of Acts, Luke's decisive purpose is alleged to be some factor behind the text rather than within it. Might the place to begin a study of Acts be at the beginning, with the book's own statement of purpose to Theophilus (1:1–5)? Acts claims that it is *kerygma—a proclamation of what has happened.* This proclamation or witness is in direct continuity with the Gospel of Luke (1:1) The Acts prologue, of similar style and addressed to the same reader, Theophilus, makes explicit reference to the earlier volume. The familiar Lukan theme of promise/fulfillment is continued with the overlapping material at the end of Luke and the beginning of Acts. The Gospel closed with the promises of the Father to be realized in Jerusalem (Luke 24:49) and with the ascension. Acts extends the account of the ascension into the descent of the Spirit at Pentecost.

Acts is proclamation, not in the sense of evangelical preaching to convert unbelievers but catechetical proclamation to strengthen believers. Like us, Theophilus already knew about Christ. What else did Theophilus need to know that occasioned Luke's narrative? Unfortunately, Luke never turns aside from his story to mention some explicit crisis of his day. We are told that ". . . the word of the Lord grew and prevailed mightily" (19:20). Over what did it prevail? As we study Acts you may compile your own list of possible adversaries to the gospel.

11

Despite Gabriel's assurance to Mary that "with God nothing will be impossible" (Luke 1:37), when one encounters official opposition, violence, misunderstanding, demons, it is easy for believers like Theophilus to lose hope. Or was the problem tensions within the church itself? Right at the beginning of Acts Judas betrays his Lord, disciples lie to one another (5:1–11), and there is bitter controversy over the inclusion of gentiles. At times Luke's account of the early church borders on the romantic and the ideal, but he does not flinch from depicting perils within the community as well. Were these accounts meant to give a disillusioned Theophilus hope? Whatever the exact situations which occasioned this dialogue with Theophilus, whoever Theophilus was, he is all of us. For who in today's church has not at some time had his or her faith tested by external opposition or by internal squabbles of the church?

The prologue turns us to what must be a central concern for Acts; namely, the relationship of Jesus Christ to his church in the present crisis. The story that Luke told of the advent of the Messiah continues. But how? In the second prologue the author defends the continuity between past and present—the story continues. But Luke is well aware that the earthly ministry of Jesus is now history. The apostles are chosen by God for a task (1:2) undergirded (Luke 1:4) by the resurrection, which is confirmed "with many proofs" (1:3). For forty days the risen Christ instructed his disciples about the kingdom. Interestingly, this instruction is not mentioned in the Gospel of Luke, perhaps to signify that discussions about the kingdom have now, in the period between resurrection and ascension, been limited to the apostles to insure continuity. Apostles are identified as those who are witnesses to the resurrection (1:21–22), those who had participated in these events "accomplished among us" (Luke 1:1). Theophilus may trust the narratives of Luke-Acts because they were directly received from eyewitnesses. They insure that our faith continues to be apostolic, continues to be based upon the facts.

This stress upon eyewitnesses does not mean that the time of Jesus and the time of the church are bound by a simple historical link of memory or organizational continuity. The decisive factor is the Spirit for whom the apostles are to wait. The fulfillment of the promise of empowerment by the Spirit comes at Pentecost when power is received to witness "to the end of the earth." The Spirit enables the "facts" to have continuing

12

influence over the church. So in reading Acts we are not reading a mere history of early Christianity. The centrality of the Spirit in equipping the apostles to bear the "word of God" and to prevail over their tribulations tells us that here is an account of the power of the word of God as it leaps over every barrier and makes clear the amazing plans of God (12:24) so that, "The word of God increased and the number of disciples multiplied greatly . . ." (6:7).

The prologue tells us that the author desires to follow "all things from the beginning," "accurately," and in "an orderly account." We are therefore quite justified in interpreting Luke as an organizer and interpreter of actual history, but also as a preacher and artist who is both a careful collector and a critical arranger. Acts represents a creative organization of the tradition so that our faith might be strengthened.

The multiple concerns of Luke's attempt to strengthen the church's faith makes difficult later efforts by scholars to reduce the purpose of Acts to one single factor—but its richness, diversity, and scope make it all the more useful to Theophilus' church—as well as our own.

The Presence of Christ in Acts

Luke has his own way of affirming the promise that, "For where two or three are gathered in my name, there am I in the midst of them" (Matt. 18:20).

Always, the word of God is preached "in the name of Jesus Christ" (4:30). By the name of Christ sin is forgiven (10:43) and demons exorcised (16:18). The idiom "name of Jesus Christ" is Luke's expression of the presence of Christ, but not in any magical way. Rather, the preached word unleashes the power of the resurrected Christ so that the gap between the earthly Jesus and the resurrected Lord is bridged by the Spirit.

Many sermons in Acts show a consistent pattern: The sermon closes with the assertion that Christ lives and reigns with God. On the basis of the "mighty works of God," there is an appeal for repentance (2:38) and an offer of such benefits as forgiveness, blessing, the Spirit, peace, and salvation (4:12; 13:26). The good news which stays news is that the ancient promises to Israel have been fulfilled, all to show "what the prophets and Moses said would come to pass" (26:22).

Luke defines the content of the good news in terms of the Old Testament and defends it as such. The proof-from-

13

prophecy appeal of Luke's Gospel becomes even more frequent in Acts (cf. chaps. 3, 7, 13). While the church is no longer in a direct encounter with the presence of the ascended Lord, as it was during the forty days, the presence of Christ is accessible in the preached word of his apostles. The promise to Israel is now realized by means of the word.

There is a virtual *ordo salutis* in Acts in the repeated, consistent outlining of the means by which those who did not participate in the earthly ministry of Jesus are assured that "the promise is to you and to your children and to all that are far off, every one whom the Lord our God calls to him" (2:39). This reassurance indicates that those interpreters who have said, unlike Matthew 18:20; 28:20 or John 17, that Luke presents a theology of Christ's absence miss Luke's unique affirmation of the sustaining presence of the risen Lord. Since the ascension, Jesus is no longer present in bodily form but is now at the "right hand" of God. Yet it is the same exalted Christ who is now the one in whom we live and move and have our being (17:28), the same Christ who is so intimately involved with his church that he asked the church's chief persecutor, "why do you persecute *me?*" (9:4).

Through the power of the Spirit, Jesus' work continues in his servants. "He who hears you, hears *me,* and he who rejects you rejects *me*" (Luke 20:16, author's itals.). The promise of Luke 6:40 that "a disciple . . . will be like his teacher" is fulfilled in these witnesses in Acts who, like their teacher, both act and suffer for the truth of Christ in ways parallel to the action and suffering of Christ himself. Thus, rather than say that someone is healed "in the name of Jesus" (3:6, 16), Peter can say interchangeably, "Jesus Christ heals you" (9:34).

With the descent of the Spirit at Pentecost (Acts 2)—which Peter interprets in terms of Old Testament texts as the dawning of the day of the Lord—the last days are here. What first happened only to the apostles now occurs for every believer. The freedom of the Spirit and its gifts, the surprising way it touches people, are evidence that it is of God. The Spirit cannot be bought (8:14–24), although the apostles can bestow it by the laying on of hands (8:18). The gift of the Spirit to gentiles like Cornelius (11:15–18) proves that even gentiles shall be heirs to the beneficence of God. The presence of Christ knows no boundaries.

At Pentecost, the universal scope of God's salvation was

14

proclaimed as all heard in their own tongue "the mighty works of God" (2:11). The inclusion of gentiles is a major concern of Acts. But we must see this inclusion as Luke saw it—*as realization of the promises to Israel.* Contrary to traditional theories about the identity of Luke, I believe that Luke was more likely a Jew than a gentile, or at least a proselyte to Judaism. Throughout Acts, Luke is intent to show that the Christ event is solidly grounded in God's promises to Israel. Luke does not describe the rejection of Israel followed by God's selection of some new People of God. Faithful Israel responds as it always has throughout history. The disobedient portion of Israel does not negate the promise nor is it negated by the entrance of gentiles into the legacy of Israel. God continues to have only one "people for his name," and God continues to be with his faithful ones through the gift of the Spirit.

The Position of Acts

The location of Acts within the canon of New Testament writings influences interpretation. Some argue that Acts is positioned in its present location in order to provide a historical link between the Gospels and the Epistles. Recent study indicates that Acts did not figure prominently in the ordering of the New Testament.

We know that Luke-Acts is the work of one author, though Acts probably became part of the canon somewhat later than the Gospel. Whatever the original linkage between Luke-Acts, they were divided in the canon: Luke became part of the four-fold Gospel collection and was interpreted within that collection. Acts was assigned another location that linked it with the apostles' witness and set it apart from the evangelists. But not too much should be made of its present placement in the canon. What later interpreters should note about Acts as a canonical writing is that canonizers preserved both Paul's letters and Acts. In so doing they put Acts in a context which differed from that of the author of Acts who wrote without knowledge of Paul's letters. Because Acts offers a more-or-less-coherent, history-like narrative of Paul's ministry, it provides a geographical and historical framework Paul's letters lack. Historically, the church used Acts as an interpretive guide for the Epistles until later interpreters discovered tensions between Acts and the Epistles. Acts entered the canon, as did the rest of the New Testament writings, well after the time of Paul. In so doing, Acts

15

became part of the church's need to place Paul in the larger context of the church's theology. Acts helps to assure the place of Paul and his theology within the church.

Even though we now know some of the real tensions between the theologies of Luke and Paul which cannot be resolved without one destroying the witness of the other, Acts does provide later interpreters with a model of interpretation. Acts is an example of an early attempt to show the significance of Paul's life and witness for a new generation of believers who did not share Paul's actual ministry. While Paul and the Twelve together function as the church's leaders, Acts subordinates Paul to the Twelve—Acts' way of indicating that the authority for all religious experience, including that of Paul, is subject to the criteria imposed by the ministry of Jesus (of whom the Twelve were witnesses—1:21–22).

Preaching in Acts

Few preachers doubt the value of the Gospels or even Paul's epistles for preaching. But what is the preacher to do with Acts—an apparent narrative about the church rather than about Christ?

Early Christian missionary proclamation contained enthusiastic reports of the formation of churches (e.g., Rom. 1:8; II Cor. 3:1–3; I Thess. 1:8–10). Pride in one congregation's ability to withstand persecution was a source of comfort to others (I Thess. 1:6; II Thess. 1:4). The summary of the gospel in I Corinthians 15:3–11 contains a tradition of the apostles and their congregations.

Furthermore, Luke's Gospel makes a person's experience worthy material for proclamation as Jesus tells the cured demonic to go back home, "and declare how much God has done for you" (Luke 8:39). In Acts 26:16 the risen Christ tells Paul, "I have appeared to you for this purpose, to appoint you to serve and bear witness to the things in which you have seen me and to those in which I will appear to you." From the beginning, proclamation is not only about the meaning of Jesus or the facts of the Christ-event but also about what this meant to women and men who had their lives changed by the event.

A more basic difficulty for modern interpretation of Acts through preaching and teaching may lie in our contemporary confusion about and distrust of the church, both as the vehicle and as the result of God's salvation in Christ. There are many

16

people, many even in the church, who quite easily sever the church from its Christ, seeing the church as a dispensable, optional, even unnecessary aspect of the Christ-event.

Luke's preoccupation with the church led some earlier commentators to accuse him of "early Catholicism." Whatever the term may mean, it betrays the feeling that when one has become greatly concerned about the formation of the church one has become less concerned with the pure, original, unadulterated message of Jesus. Acts challenges such thinking with an eloquent rebuke to any attempt to disembody Christ by separating this Messiah from his Messianic community or to relieve the church of the burden of being tested and challenged by the apostolic witness. The risen Christ is so closely linked to his church that he can say to Saul, "Why do you persecute me?" when Saul persecuted the church (9:4–5; 22:7–8; 26:14–15). Those who accuse Luke of an "absentee Christology" (C.F.D. Moule) must account for the church (for better or worse!) as the very presence Christ has chosen to take in the world.

Acts claims that it was ecclesiology, as much as Christology, which ultimately separated Judaism and Christianity. Acts is part of the argument between the synagogue and the church about who constitutes the People of God and how the faith of Israel is to be embodied in human community into the future. Because the constitution and embodiment of faith is at the heart of all teaching and preaching called Christian, Acts places us within a debate which is as vital a concern for the church today as when Luke wrote for Theophilus.

17

Prologue
ACTS 1:1–26

Acts 1:1–14
Waiting and Praying for Restoration

"Lord, will you at this time restore the kingdom to Israel?" (Acts 1:6; Luke 9:11). That was the question on everyone's mind. The disciples were instructed by Christ for forty days (1:3), like Moses on the mountain (Exod. 24:12–18), but they still had questions. Now, they must wait in Jerusalem for the promised gift of the Holy Spirit (1:5). The risen Christ makes two responses to the disciples' question about the restoration of the kingdom: (1) "It is not for you to know the times or seasons . . ." (1:7), and (2) "But you shall receive power . . . [to be] my witnesses in Jerusalem and in all Judea and Samaria and to the end of the earth" (1:8).

A number of years ago the scholar Ernst Käsemann felt that passages like Acts 1:6 explained the purpose of Luke-Acts. One does not write church history if one expects the world to end tomorrow. The writing of Acts signals that the once taut expectation for the imminent return of Christ has now been relaxed. The eschatological hope no longer motivates the church of Theophilus. But this overlooks the complex nature of apocalyptic hope. For Luke, as for Paul, "the form of this world is passing away" (I Cor. 7:31). Since Christ, all previously existing relationships of power are being transformed. It is not simply that the world is expected to end soon but that the world view as it had been, the methods and values for determining worth and significance in the world, has ended. There is now a new reality.

For Luke, that new reality involved the vision of a Jesus who is raised to rule with the Creator of the universe. Death, the ultimate "ending"—the master fact which determines most of our horizons, our values, our projects—has been ended in the resurrection of Christ. Luke's "history" is the story of that new reality which has turned the world upside down, relativized all existing relationships, and enabled believers to live as people "between the times"—between the end of an old age held by the powers of death and evil and a new age where the future is still to be fully realized, still open-ended to the movements of the Spirit.

When the disciples gather after Easter, they do so as those who wait and question. What they know of what has happened in the resurrection is the source of their hope but also of their yearning. They want Christ to fulfill his promise of restoration, to finish the work begun. When? they ask. As the recipients of their Lord's instruction and as witnesses to his death and resurrection, they know that the decisive battle has been fought and won—but not yet. Now, in the meantime, they wait as those who are still dependent upon the Father's faithfulness, those who have no control over the timetable of a beneficent God who graciously allows enough time to accomplish the work begun in Jesus. This time between ascension and Pentecost was once designated by Karl Barth as a "significant pause" between the mighty acts of God, a pause in which the church's task is to wait and to pray, *Veni, Creator Spiritus.* This text therefore appears in the Common Lectionary on the Seventh Sunday of Easter, between Easter and Pentecost, in a time of expectant waiting for the Spirit.

But their waiting is not empty-handed. They wait in hope, as those who know that their Master has been "taken up" (1:2) where he is "exalted at the right hand of God" (2:33). After the ascension, when Christians speak of God they must also speak of Christ, for Christ now reigns with God. The followers of Christ know that the one who served, taught, and loved them now rules for them. But this knowledge is no smug *gnosis* of the privileged first few. It is a knowledge which demands a witness. Thus, in the meantime, they are given a job to do and will have power with which to do it. The time between Easter and the restoration of the kingdom is the gracious interim for witness. The opening episode ends with the angelic reproof, "Why do you stand looking into heaven?" There is work to be done; let the church be about that work in the meantime, secure in the promise that Jesus who was so dramatically taken from his disciples shall return to them in the same way.

In a few opening verses Luke manages to reprove both the

20

enthusiasm and speculation of uninformed apocalypticism, as well as the despair and stodginess of a church without apocalyptic hope. There is also reproof for any church which wistfully longs for some departed leader, as if the church were a mere memorial society for a dead Jesus. In the meantime there is the promise that the same force which empowered Jesus shall be present with the church.

The response of the disciples to the instruction, reproof, and the promise is exemplary. They gather to pray (1:12–14). In an activist age one might expect the disciples to undertake some more "useful" activity. They are told to be witnesses "to the end of the earth" (1:8), and their first response is prayer. The action demanded of the church is more than busyness and strenuous human effort. Disciples have been told that the promised kingdom is a gift to be given in God's own time and that the promised Spirit is also by God's grace. Their mission requires more than even their earnest striving.

They pray therefore for empowerment to be obedient, responding to Jesus' promise in Luke 11:9–13 to, "Ask, and it will be given you . . . the heavenly Father [will] give the Holy Spirit to those who ask him!" They pray for the promised kingdom, knowing that "they ought always to pray and not lose heart" (Luke 18:1). Gathering to wait and to pray are depicted as two primary activities of a faithful church (Isa. 40:31). Waiting, an onerous burden for us computerized and technically impatient moderns who live in an age of instant everything, is one of the tough tasks of the church. Our waiting implies that the things which need doing in the world are beyond our ability to accomplish solely by our own effort, our programs and crusades. Some other empowerment is needed, therefore the church waits and prays. Our waiting and praying also indicate that the gift of the Spirit is never an assured possession of the church. It is a gift, a gift which must be constantly sought anew in prayer.

Even to know all *about* Jesus, even to have received instruction from Jesus himself for forty days is not enough to accomplish the church's mission. The challenge is not the intellectual one of *knowing* enough to tell about Jesus but rather the challenge is to have the authorization and empowerment which enable succeeding witnesses to be *doing* the work of Jesus. Until those who know the facts also experience the power, they do well first to wait in Jerusalem and to pray.

21

Should we be disturbed that Luke appears to report the ascension in two different ways? Did the ascension occur on Easter evening (Luke 24:51) or forty days later (Acts 1:3)? Many reasons have been devised to explain the contradiction—from assertions of Lukan carelessness to speculations that Luke wrote Acts so much later than his Gospel that he forgot when the ascension occurred!

Luke was an artist, not a newspaper reporter. The contradiction in the accounts of the ascension are clues to the author's intentions. In Luke 24 the ascension is a conclusion, a dramatic finale to Jesus' earthly ministry. The one whom Pilate and Caiphas sought to entomb is taken up in glory. In Acts 1 the ascension is the beginning presupposition on which the church is based. The end becomes the beginning as the story continues. Luke is looking at the same ascension from different points of view, drawing from it different implications for the community.

In Acts two languages are used to describe what has happened in Christ—one, the language of *resurrection* victory over death; the other, the language of *ascension,* sitting at the right hand of God and empowerment. These two motifs shall meet in Acts 2 at Pentecost when the life and power of Christ shall be given to disciples through the Spirit. When things go poorly for Theophilus and his kin in the church, when the world falls apart, things come loose, and chaos threatens, it is good to know who is in charge, who rules. In the words of the ancient Ascension Day anthem, *Deus Ascendit,* "God Has Gone Up," not gone away from the church but gone up to be the empowerment for the church, as we shall learn vividly in the next chapter of Acts.

Acts 1:15–26
Leadership in the Community

Leadership in this post-Easter community is the concern of the rest of chapter one. The community which gathers to wait and to pray is an unusual one—a fact attested by Luke's parenthetical mention in 1:14 of women who had been with Jesus since Galilee (Luke 8:2; 23:49, 55; 24:10–11) and of Jesus' mother and brothers. The inclusion of women in the roster of the community would not have been missed by a second-century reader, as an indication that already we have a group which breaks barriers.

Furthermore, we have a thoroughly Jewish community which has a mission to the house of Israel. In Luke 9:1–6, the Twelve were sent to Israel. Jesus promised that these Twelve would sit upon thrones judging the twelve tribes (Luke 22:28–30). The twelve tribes must have twelve witnesses, thus the concern within this section to find a replacement for the traitor, Judas.

The number one hundred and twenty also figures prominently in the mission to Israel. According to Jewish law one hundred and twenty males were required to form a synagogue with its own council—already the disciples have enough people to form a legitimate community. All is done in faithfulness to Judiasm, says Luke.

When Peter stands to speak (vv. 16–22), his speech, like all of those in Acts, is designed for Luke's readers. We are not reading a verbatim eye-witness record of Peter's speech. Peter quotes from the Greek Septuagint, the Scripture of Greek-veaking Jews—even translating "Alkaldama" for them, as if his audience would not know Aramaic, the language of the original Jewish-Christian community in Jerusalem. So the interpretive issue cannot be the historical, Did Peter really say these words in this way? but the homiletical question, Through this speech, what is Luke trying to say to his readers in a community of a much later time than that of Peter? as well as the narrative question, How does this speech contribute to the plot or movement of the story of Acts?

The speech is comprised of two parts, each set off by forms of the Greek *dei,* "it is necessary" (vv. 16,21). Everything that happens does so as a necessary fulfillment of Scripture and the purposes of God (cf. 4:12; 5:29; Luke 2:49; 4:43; 12:12; 13:14). Even tragic events, such as the betrayal of Jesus by Judas, can be caught up in the movement of God's purposes. Judas betrayed Jesus by collaborating with those who put him to death. Now, whereas Christ has gone up to rule with God, Judas has gone "to his own place" (1:25). Judas, even though he "was numbered among us and was allotted his share in this ministry" (1:17), fell away and received his just fate (1:18–20).

The church then prays that new leadership may come forward from the community, a process characteristic of other

23

occasions when the church seeks divine guidance (e.g., 1:14; 4:31; 9:11; 10:2; 12:5; 13:3). The election of Matthias gives Luke the opportunity to define who an apostle is (1:21–22), a definition which Paul would not share. An apostle is someone who is among the Twelve, someone who had been with Jesus from the "baptism of John until the day he was taken up" into heaven.

The apostolic circle is drawn only from eyewitnesses who can give a reliable account of the Jesus-event (Luke 1:1–4). This concern for first-hand witness is Luke's way of guaranteeing the authenticity of his account. When Luke speaks of "disciples" he is speaking of all Christians, in distinction from the Twelve (cf. Luke 6:1; 9:1)—unlike the way Matthew and Mark use the term. The Twelve he calls "apostles." In a time when there is great skepticism about our ability to recover any reliable facts about "the historical Jesus" and diverse theologies of this or that attempt to enlist a fancifully reconstructed Jesus to back up their ideologies, we do well to consider the importance of Luke's stress upon eyewitnesses as reliable bearers of the "facts." The "facts" of the Jesus-event are not so amorphous as to enable us to make Jesus and his good news mean anything we please (the peril of all forms of Gnosticism). We must attend to the story. While the witnesses do not tell us everything that we might like to know about Jesus and his message, they do give an "accurate and orderly account" to judge contemporary interpretations.

Matthias becomes part of the Twelve and the number is once again complete. Leadership in this new community is based both on qualification (vv. 21–22), and on divine choice (v. 24). It is derived both from "the bottom up"—from the ranks of those persons whom the prayerful community chooses to lead—and from the "top down"—as a gift of a gracious God who does not leave his community bereft of the guidance it needs to fulfill its mission. Leadership is not an optional matter for the community nor is it some later invention foisted upon a once free and democratic church by authoritarians seeking power. Valid leaders link the church to the events which originated the church and become, by their own work and witness, the means by which the church fulfills its mission.

At this point leadership in the church seems to be defined in terms of witness—the apostle is someone who has seen and heard something, a witness to the resurrection who now witnesses to others. Like Peter, the apostle testifies to what has happened so that it may continue to happen within the church.

Yet, Peter's speech reminds us that what has happened up to this point in the story includes both apostleship and apostasy. Far from painting some idealized portrait of how wonderful everything was for the apostles, Luke places Peter's speech about Judas at the beginning as a somber reminder that traitors were among the ranks of the disciples from the first. In fact the first speech within the post-Easter community is made by the one who also fled in the darkness and loudly denied his Lord when confronted by the maid (Luke 22:56–62). Infidelity first occurs among those who presume to lead. There is no deceit or betrayal encountered among the church's pagan despisers or its unbelieving Jewish kin that has not been first experienced in its own ranks. Jesus had warned of the possibility of betrayal (Luke 12:8–12; 22:31–34). The church has no cause for conceit at this point, for Luke has reminded us, even before the story of empowerment begins, that a disciple, one privileged to witness the whole Christ-event from the first, can and had betrayed his Lord. No scorn for later despisers of the gospel, no judgment upon later infidels, can match the sober, gruesomely detailed picture of the end of Judas or the irony that the one who speaks of Judas did himself deny and curse his own Master.

The church meets no failure or deceit in the world that it has not first encountered in itself—even among those who founded and led the very first congregation.

PART ONE

Witness in Jerusalem, Judea, and Samaria

ACTS 2:1—9:43

The Community Is Born: What Happened at Pentecost

ACTS 2:1–47

"Unless the LORD builds the house, those who build it labor in vain" (Ps. 127:1). The community, rather than taking matters into its own hands, getting organized and venturing forth with banners unfurled, has withdrawn to wait and to pray. The next move is up to God. It is up to the risen Christ to make good on his promise to bestow the Spirit and to restore the kingdom to Israel. In a sense this is what prayer is—the bold, even arrogant effort on the part of the community to hold God to his promises. In praying, "Thy kingdom come, thy will be done," we pray that God will be true to himself and give us what has been promised. Prayer is thus boldness born out of confidence in the faithfulness of God to the promises he makes, confidence that God will be true to himself. What may appear as prayerful insolence by the church in praying that we shall receive the Spirit, the kingdom, power, and restoration is in fact the deepest humility, the church's humble realization that only God can give what the church most desperately needs.

In telling the story of Christ, Luke, more than any of the other Gospels, expends great detail upon Jesus' birth. In Luke's Gospel the birth stories become a kind of vignette of the rest of the story. "In my beginning is my end," says the poet T.S. Eliot. The start of a person's life indicates the direction his or her life will take. Much that will have significance later can be seen in our origins. Therefore it is with great interest that we

27

turn to the birth of the church at Pentecost. (In fact, a comparison of the birth of Jesus in Luke with the birth of the church in Acts yields fascinating parallels: both stories begin with the arrival of the Spirit. In both the period immediately before is not devoid of the Spirit's work. In both the promise is contrasted with John the Baptist.) Knowing the way Luke handles a story, we can expect to learn much from this infancy narrative of the first community.

It is popular to refer to Pentecost as the birthday of the church, and there is much truth in that. But it is more accurate to speak of Easter as the birthday even of Pentecost. The story of Pentecost must be read within the context of Luke 24: the risen Lord was made "known to them in the breaking of the bread" (Luke 24:35); he "opened their minds to understand the scriptures" (v. 32), and he promised to give them the same power which moved him, telling them to "stay in the city, until you are clothed with power from on high" (24:49). When Luke disjoined the resurrection from the ascension and Pentecost in his narrative, he could not have done so with the intention that we should read these as three separate, disparate events. At Pentecost the power of God, made manifest at the resurrection and ascension of Christ, is bestowed upon the People of God. Originally, in the church's celebration of the liturgical year, Easter, Ascension Day, and Pentecost were more closely linked. Today, the average congregation may experience these events as separate phenomena, thus missing the truth that both the ascension of Christ and the descent of the Spirit at Pentecost are further explications of the wonder of Easter. Fortunately, recent liturgical reforms seek to set the liturgy for Pentecost within the context of the great fifty-day celebration of Easter. The opening prayer for the Catholic Mass for Pentecost asserts, "Almighty and ever-living God, you fulfilled the Easter promise by sending us your Holy Spirit" (Adolf Adam, p. 90).

Acts 2:1–13
The Sound of a Mighty Wind: Pentecost

In listening to the story of the formation of the church at Pentecost, we are pursuing the truth about this peculiar new community. We are not inquiring into the truth as facticity—truth as to what happened. Rather, we are concerned about truth as to what is claimed—what is asserted in the story about the nature of this community. In reading the Pentecost account in the second chapter of Acts, we are part of an author's struggle to bring to reality something of the truth about the church, something which cannot be known except by this story. Therefore we shall pass over questions of probable historical context, possible psychological motives, or other questions that might interest us; we must let the story have its way with us. We shall let the narrative redescribe and create new reality for us, trying to uncover the answers to the questions the story would have us ask. In reading the stories of Acts, we may note that these Acts narratives seem to have little interest in the things that make for a "good story" today—relentless introspection, detailed individual character development, probing interiority. We may read a great deal about Peter or Paul in Acts but learn little about them as individual personalities. Acts cares little for the trials and psychic makeup of individual personalities, because this is literature in service to the community. The community is at the center of Acts, with the God of the community being the chief actor in the drama.

The story of Pentecost day in Jerusalem is, for the church, a kind of "classic" (David Tracy, pp. 99–299), a story to which the faith community assigns authority and to which it returns again and again as a guide for its life. Here is revealed what the community is by recounting its origin in a powerful work of the Spirit. Sometimes this story has given the church hope; sometimes this story has judged the church and found it wanting.

Luke seems to believe that the truth is available only as narrative, always hidden from direct explanation or easy accessibility. We can expect surprises because the truth here disclosed is not unambiguous. More than one interpretation can be offered for what happened in the upper room at Pentecost. No single formulation can do it justice. We are listening to the account of something strange, beyond the bounds of imagination, miraculous, inscrutable, an origin which, as far as Luke is concerned, was the only way one could "explain" the existence of the church. No flat, prosaic explanation can do justice to the truth of how the church came into being and how the once timid disciples found their tongues to proclaim the truth of Christ.

The ambiguity and mystery of the story are indicated by

the manner of narration. It is the dawn of the day of Pentecost and the followers of Jesus are gathered to wait and to pray. The new day begins with an eruption of sounds from heaven and of wind (2:2). Things are coming loose, breaking open. Can it be the same wind which on the very first morning of all mornings swept across dark waters, the wind of creation (Gen. 1)? The wind is once again bringing something to life.

What was first heard is then seen—tongues like fire (2:3). It is not until verse four that we learn that this strange irruption is none other than the promised Holy Spirit. John the Baptist had said that the Christ, "will baptize you with the Holy Spirit and with fire" (Luke 3:16). With playful ambiguity Luke expands these fiery "tongues" into the gift of "other tongues" that the Spirit miraculously enables the assembly to speak. The first gift of the Spirit is the gift of speech, the gift of speech in different languages. So we are hearing a story about the irruption of the Spirit into the community and the first fruit of the Spirit—the gift of proclamation.

The scene quickly shifts from inside the upper room, where the disciples are gathered, to the street outside, where the gospel is already drawing a crowd. In the beginning of his Gospel, Luke characterized John the Baptist as one who "will turn many of the sons of Israel to the Lord their God" (Luke 1:16). Out in the street, "Jews, devout men from every nation under heaven" (v. 5) for the first time confront the church, and their response is bewilderment. The irruption of the Spirit leads to proclamation by the community, which leads to the bewilderment of bystanders. These "tongues" are obviously various languages of "every nation under heaven," since each foreigner exclaims that "we hear, each of us in his own native language" (v. 8). No nationality of dispersed Jews is excluded from the proclamation, as Luke's rollcall of the peoples makes clear.

Yet nothing is clear to the bystanders, who are thoroughly "amazed and perplexed" by the whole episode, questioning, "What does this mean?" (v. 12). Some of the bystanders do not want to know. They have their own urbane, sophisticated yet mocking theory for such strange manifestations of religious enthusiasm: "They are filled with new wine" (v. 13). That power the church proclaims as gift of God the world explains as inebriation. The inbreaking of the Spirit is profoundly unsettling and deeply threatening to the crowd in the street, and so it must devise some explanation, some rationalization for such irrationality.

30

In so few verses Luke has given us a glimpse of much of the plot of Acts. His treatment of this inaugural episode reminds one of a similar opening scene, Jesus' visit to his hometown synagogue in Luke 4. There we see the congregation's pleasure with "Joseph's son" turn from admiration to wrath when Jesus reminded them of how the powerful love of God had irrupted into the lives of foreigners. The hometown first sermon becomes a foreshadowing of the rest of Luke's Gospel.

Acts 2 is a kind of precis of the rest of the story, functioning in much the same way as Luke 4. Once again, the power of God irrupts into a conventional assembly of the faithful in a most unconventional way ("Today this scripture has been fulfilled in your hearing" [Luke 4:21]).

Once again, everything hinges on the Spirit's ability to set proclamation in motion. Once again, the proclamation evokes questions, bewilderment, and scorn. Here, in the interchange between the faithful and those snide mocking ones and those earnestly inquiring ones in the street, we see a pattern which will be repeated again and again in Acts.

The crowd's questions become a cue for one of the disciples to stand and speak; and Luke expends about twice as many verses interpreting the meaning of the ecstatic events than he spent reporting the event itself. As in his Gospel, Luke uses miracle as an occasion for proclamation.

Who could have predicted the one who now speaks? We have heard him speak before in Acts 1:16–22. But then, because of our still lingering memory of how Peter himself had proved quite capable of repeated betrayal when the going got rough (Luke 22:31–34, 54–62), we could hardly hear Peter speak to the necessity of finding a replacement for the betrayer Judas. It was Peter who only "followed at a distance," Peter whom the maid drove to utter the terrible words, "Woman, I do not know him" (Luke 22:57). We left him weeping in the courtyard, a disciple tested and found wanting.

Therefore, we detected something a bit hollow in Peter's quick effort to condemn and then to replace Judas in Acts 1:16–22, reminding ourselves that Judas was not alone in his treason. Yet here, before the half inquiring, half mocking crowd, Peter is the first, the very first to lift up his voice and proclaim openly the word that only a few weeks before he could not speak, even to a serving woman at midnight.

In Genesis 2:7 the Spirit of God breathed life into dust and created a human being. In Acts 2:1–4 the Spirit has breathed

31

life into a once cowardly disciple and created a new man who now has the gift of bold speech.

The richness of Luke's account of Pentecost yields other layers of interpretation. We, in church listening to this story, resemble the crowd in our multiple interpretations of so strange and wonderful an event. For one thing, we recognize that Luke's story of the gift of the Spirit differs from the account in John 20:22. Luke seems to have separated into three events what had once been regarded as one event—the resurrection, exaltation, and bestowal of the Spirit. Perhaps Luke does this in order to give each aspect of the Easter triumph its own development in the story. Also, Luke reads the Spirit in a different light than that of the Fourth Gospel. There, the gift is related to the binding and loosing of the church, the forgiveness of sin. Here, even though forgiveness of sin is included (Acts 2:38), the Spirit is the power to witness, the engine that drives the church into all the world. By separating the resurrection from the ascension/exaltation by forty days, Luke created the sequence that is familiar to us in our celebration of the liturgical year, even though, as we noted above, resurrection, ascension, and Pentecost should be viewed as a unit, a threefold explication of the power of God to accomplish what he wants in spite of all obstacles. The wind blows where it wills.

One popular interpretation of Pentecost is that this story signifies that Babel has been reversed (Gen. 11:1–9). Human language, so confused at Babel, has been restored; and community, so scattered there, has here been restored. It is doubtful that Luke had this in mind. The "mighty works of God" are proclaimed only to Jews at this point. The time is not yet ripe in the story for the division between Jew and gentile to be healed. The story does not claim that there is only one language now—Luke reports that the disciples speak in a multitude of languages. Nor is there a claim that Pentecost is about the miracle of hearing instead of speaking, so that everyone receives instant translation. The miracle here is one of proclamation. Those who had no "tongue" to speak of the "mighty works of God" now preach.

It is doubtful that Luke is describing ecstatic speech here, the *glossolalia* of I Corinthians 14, because that sort of speech needed translation for anyone to understand. Judging from the discussion of *glossolalia* in I Corinthians 14, the Spirit manifested its presence in a variety of ways in Paul's churches. Luke's concern is with the description of a Spirit-empowered intelligible proclamation in foreign languages (2:6, 8).

Other interpreters have attempted to link the story of Pentecost to the giving of the law on Mount Sinai—the old law was given on Sinai, a new law was given at Pentecost. The thought might belong to Paul (II Cor. 3), but not to Luke. In Peter's following speech (2:14–40), there is no reference to Sinai or to the covenant. Linkage between Israel's beginning at Sinai and the church's beginning at Pentecost is tenuous and can only be accomplished by references to material outside of the story itself (Talbert, *Acts*, pp. 14–15).

To those in the church today who regard the Spirit as an exotic phenomenon of mainly interior and purely personal significance, the story of the Spirit's descent at Pentecost offers a rebuke. Luke goes to great pains to insist that this outpouring of the Spirit is anything but interior. Everything is by wind and fire, loud talk, buzzing confusion, and public debate. The Spirit is the power which enables the church to "go public" with its good news, to attract a crowd and, as we shall see in the next section, to have something to say worth hearing. A new wind is set loose upon the earth, provoking a storm of wrath and confusion for some, a fresh breath of hope and empowerment for others. Pentecost is a phenomenon of mainly evangelistic significance, as the central question of the crowd makes clear: *What must we do to be saved?* Whereas the crowd who heard Jesus' sermon in Nazareth sneered, "Is not this Joseph's son?" Luke is delighted to report that Peter's sermon inspired by the Spirit produced enthusiastic converts. Now "Jews from every nation under heaven" are coming to the good news. In these last days, as Luke 2:32 predicted, true Israel is being restored and, as we learn later (Acts 11:18), shall be a light to all the nations.

As the psalmist sang, "Our God comes, he does not keep silence, / before him is a devouring fire, / round about him a mighty tempest" (Ps. 50:3).

Acts 2:14–41
What Does This Mean?
A Pentecost Sermon

One reason why most of us enjoy reading the Gospels is that we all enjoy good stories. In this commentary we have stressed the power of narrative to unlock our imagination and

33

restructure our world view. But speeches, particularly sermons, are another matter. The conventional three-points-and-a-poem sermon is no one's definition of fun. Acts has some twenty-eight speeches, mostly by Peter and Paul, that account for nearly a third of the entire text. The interpreter of Acts must overcome a built-in bias against so much sermonizing. Why did Luke put so much of Acts in the form of speeches?

The crowd's accusation of drunkenness serves as a cue for Peter to make a speech. Here is a pattern we will see repeated in Acts. The church is confronted by a crowd, some of whom understand and some of whom do not. An apostle speaks, interpreting the gospel through a sermon. Luke's pattern was a favorite of classical historians. Through speeches, put upon the lips of distinguished historical figures, the ancient historian interpreted the meaning of events. At first this may seem a rather unimaginative, prosaic literary convention until we remember how, in our own day, Lincoln's Gettysburg Address did more than open a cemetery—it gave meaning and substance to a national cataclysm. Martin Luther King, Jr.'s "I Have a Dream" speech reinterpreted our history and constitution and mobilized a people into action for justice. A good speech can turn us inside out.

Furthermore, a good speech has an identifiable and memorable form. Good speakers develop a distinctive style and a particular way of dealing with their material. Even though not all speeches in Acts follow the same outline, C.H. Dodd identified a definite pattern in Acts for their presentation in apostolic *kerygma:*

1. The age of fulfillment, or the coming of the kingdom of God, is at hand (vv. 16–21).
2. This coming has taken place through the ministry, death, and resurrection of Jesus (vv. 22–23).
3. By virtue of the resurrection, Jesus is exalted at the right hand of God as the messianic head of the new Israel (vv. 24–36).
4. The Holy Spirit in the church is the sign of Christ's present power and glory (v. 33).
5. The messianic age will shortly reach its consummation in the second coming of Christ.
6. Forgiveness, the Holy Spirit, and salvation come with repentance (vv. 38–39 [p. 11]).

Dodd says, "We may take it that this is what the author of Acts meant by 'preaching the kingdom of God' " (p. 24). Here is the core of apostolic preaching as portrayed in Acts. But who is the audience for this preaching? Unbelievers in the street? In our earlier discussion of the purpose of Acts, we asserted that Acts was probably written for "insiders"—Christians who were struggling to retain the boldness, faith, and confidence in the face of new internal and/or external struggles. The Luke-Theophilus dialogue was part of a long conversation between God and the people of God. Luke is the moderator between Theophilus' church and the panel of eyewitnesses of the Christ-event. It is the church's own skepticism, doubt, and despair which is the audience for Peter's speech.

Any good speech is more than *what* was said, and *to whom* it was said; it is also a matter of *how* it is said. First, Peter bluntly counters the mockers' assertion of drunkenness (vv. 14–15). Crowds had earlier made the same charge of drunkenness against Jesus himself: "Behold, a glutton and a drunkard, a friend of tax collectors and sinners!" (Luke 7:34). The church sees plainly that these events, experienced by the crowd as only disruptive inebriation and scandalous irrationality, are fulfillment of prophecy (vv. 14–21). Joel said that in the terrible and wonderful last days there would be an outpouring of the Spirit on everyone (Joel 2:28–32). The Spirit, once the exotic possession of a prophetic few, is now offered to all. The crowd, which also knows the Scriptures, do not see what the Scriptures so clearly prove.

We shall see this technique of promise and fulfillment throughout Acts, just as it is seen in Luke's Gospel. Its goal is to closely link the history of Israel with the life of Jesus and to assert that the community the Spirit forms is in unbroken succession of Israel's own pattern of expectation and realization. Israel exists as the fulfillment of God's promise to Abraham, a promise Luke reiterates frequently (Acts 3:25; 7:2–8, 17; Luke 1:15, 72–73). When Jesus was born, it was foretold by the prophets. Jesus, filled with the Spirit, confirms the messianic hopes (Luke 4:16–19). Even Jesus' suffering and death, such scandals to the world, were part of prophecy (Luke 24:44). After his resurrection, it suddenly becomes clear to the disciples that the seemingly baffling events of Christ's life and ministry were part of God's plan (Luke 24) and are the basis for their mission to preach to all the nations (Luke 24:47–48).

In Peter's speech we are listening to a Jew speaking to fellow Jews, linking the story of Jesus with the Scriptures of the

35

Jews. For Luke the Scriptures of the Jews are the primary context within which Jesus' life is comprehended. The Old Testament is not "Christianized" in this process, rather it is allowed to speak its own word about the coming salvation. Nowhere does Luke speak of the "founding" of the church or of the formation of some "new Israel." There is only one Israel—the faithful people who respond faithfully to the promises of God. The story of Jesus both gathers and divides Israel. The disciples in Acts, who in Luke's view are the core of truly faithful Israel, preach the word by which Israel's mission to all the nations is at last brought to fulfillment: "For the promise is to you and to your children and to all that are far off, every one whom the Lord our God calls to him" (2:39).

The response to Peter's rehearsal of the story of Jesus is immediate and specific—the crowd wants to know what to do (2:37). The *kerygma* has the power to evoke that which it celebrates. People are moved to repent upon hearing the story. Fortunately for the crowd and all successive hearers of the story, the gift of the Spirit and the forgiveness of sins is not simply for eyewitnesses or those who were among the first to see and hear. No, "the promise is to you and to your children and to all that are far off, every one whom the Lord our God calls to him" (2:39).

The power being offered here is not that of Peter's homiletical ability to work the crowd up into an emotional frenzy or in the crowd's sincere inner determination to get themselves right with God. The story of Peter's Pentecost speech is told so that there is no doubt the power is that of the Spirit. The word which convicts the crowd is the *externum verbum*, the "external word," (Luther) that comes from without. True, the crowd responds, asking what they should now do. But their action is response, not initiative. The word Peter has spoken to them is neither something they have derived from within themselves nor is it part of their own experience or natural inclination. None of that can save them, for they are, as are we all, part of a "crooked generation" (2:40).

What saves them is the story of what has happened. What has happened is that in Jesus the Christ there is a power loose in the world which is power for them. They have not been looking for Jesus; rather, they are the ones "whom the Lord our God calls to him" (2:39). This externality of the Spirit and its work for them is signified by Luke's use of the passive imperative verb form in Acts 2:40, a use obscured by most of our English translations. It is not so much "Save yourselves . . ." but let yourself be saved! Here is salvation, not as earnest human striving but salvation beyond such striving, salvation which only comes as the call and work of the Spirit which both testifies to and enacts salvation among the crowd. The Spirit that inspired prophets like Joel now inspires Peter to tell what has happened for Israel. God's restoration of a prophetic people has begun.

A note of urgency is added by the way Luke reports the immediate reaction of the crowd and Peter's quick response to their question. Time is short. Luke adds to the Joel quotation, "in the last days" (2:17) and "above" and "signs beneath" (2:19), to create an eschatological, end-of-time mood in the scene. The images remind us of the discourse on the signs of the end in Luke 21:10–11, 25. Peter "testified with many other words and exhorted them" because of the urgency of the time.

The response demanded by Peter is straightforward: repent and be baptized in the name of Jesus Christ (v. 38). Interpreters of this response should take care (1) not to reduce this into a step-by-step pattern for a person's salvation: a person is "cut to the heart" (v. 37), repents, is baptized, receives forgiveness, then receives the Holy Spirit. This pattern of conversion appears nowhere else in Acts. Elsewhere when Luke recounts the conversion of a crowd he merely says that many believed (4:4; 5:14) or that they turned to the Lord (9:35). Here is no order-of-salvation, but rather a conclusion of Peter's speech. In his speech Peter has asserted the guilt of the Jerusalemites for the death of Jesus (2:22–23, 36). When they ask what they must do, the context makes clear that something must be done about their guilt. In other accounts of conversion in Acts repentance and forgiveness play a part, but here the theme of repentance and forgiveness are central aspects of conversion. For Luke the ability to repent and the possession of the Spirit are gifts of God (5:31–32; 11:18). Even as the Spirit is a gift, the repentance and forgiveness of Israel are also miraculous gifts. The story of Pentecost day began with the gift of the Spirit to the assembled apostles. Now the day concludes with the gift of reconciliation for those who heretofore stood on the outside. Taken in the context of Luke's narrative as a whole, this account of the conversions at Pentecost may be most significant as a piece of the larger story of the amazing growth of the Christian community. The rather surprising, overwhelming response of Peter's audi-

37

ence can only be described as a divine gift. The movement of the good news to "the end of the earth" has begun (see *Reflection: Conversion in Acts*).

Nor should we (2) attempt to make too much out of the report of baptism in the name of Christ followed by mention of the gift of the Holy Spirit (2:38). This is not some sequential pattern being reported here, as later references to baptism and the Holy Spirit in Acts will show (10:47; 19:1–7). Luke does not intend to suggest a sequence of first "water baptism" and then "spirit baptism." Water and Spirit are together. In fact, when the crowd wonders what they must do to be saved, that is, what they must do to receive forgiveness and the Spirit, Peter presents repentance and baptism.

On the other hand, (3) there is no mechanistic relationship between water and the Spirit, as other references in Luke-Acts to the reception of the Spirit show. Luke 3:16 records John the Baptist declaring, "I baptize you with water; but he who is mightier than I is coming, . . . he will baptize you with the Holy Spirit and with fire." Acts 1:5 (and 11:16) appears to contrast water baptism with Spirit baptism. But Acts 10:47 and 19:1–7 affirm the unity of water and Spirit. Luke does not contrast water and Spirit but rather wants to underscore the distinctive aspect Christian baptism brings to the older baptism of John— the Spirit. In a sense there are two kinds of baptism in Luke-Acts, but they are not Spirit versus water. Rather they are John's baptism of preparation for the Christ and Jesus' baptism by water and Spirit. Luke knows no clear-cut pattern of how and when the Spirit is given. Acts 10:44–48 shows Cornelius and his family receiving the Spirit *before* they were baptized. But in Acts 19:5–6 the Spirit comes on the disciples of John the Baptist when Paul lays his hands on them *after* their baptism. Surely this diversity within Luke-Acts is testimony to the diversity and freedom of the experience of the Spirit within the church of Luke's day.

Finally, (4) not too much should be made of the early baptismal formula, baptism "in the name of Jesus Christ" (v. 38), as if the Spirit is somehow disconnected from this formula. Acts 2:38 gives the formula of the name of Jesus with the promise that in submitting to baptism "you shall receive the gift of the Holy Spirit." The Spirit blows where it will in Acts, connected with the act of baptism and laying-on-of-hands but refusing to be bound by later ecclesiastical definitions and conventions. To be baptized in the name of Jesus Christ is to participate in his life-giving Spirit.

Thus, Peter's Pentecost speech ends with empowerment being offered to all. The crowd, formed from the ranks of a "crooked generation," is not to be left to its own devices. It is the recipient of Spirit-empowered preaching. While Sunday morning sermon recipients in the pew may consider their preacher's sermons a dubious gift, we should ponder again the significance of how, in Paul's words, "faith comes from what is heard, and what is heard comes by the preaching of Christ" (Rom. 10:17). What people say helps to determine the world in which they live. Luke constructs what Peter should have said at Pentecost and therefore what world he thinks the crowd should embrace. The speech points beyond Peter to the God who saves. It is the God who keeps promises that matters in this sermon, so that when the sermon ends no one is in doubt that there is a God who is busy in the world. The speech effects the condition it reports:

> Thou hast made known to me the ways of life;
> thou wilt make me full of gladness with thy presence (2:28).

Acts 2:42–47
The Gospel Embodied in Community

If Acts were written from a purely contemporary point of view, we might expect all of the uproar of Pentecost, Peter's moving sermon, and the crowd's eager response as reported in 2:1–41 to be the end of the story. Contemporary religious life is plagued by momentary enthusiasm, periodic outbursts, and superficiality. In fact in contemporary parlance, "enthusiastic" (literally: filled with God) is a virtual synonym for a short-term high that does not take root in long-term commitment. So we become suspicious of religious emotion, suspecting that all of this charismatic fuss and bother will amount to little. The claim that "there were added that day about three thousand souls" moves us little, even though Luke intends to impress. We have seen these revivals and outbursts of piety come and go.

But Luke will not leave us there. Instead, he shows an immediate embodiment of the Pentecost enthusiasm. Our gaze

39

is directed toward the church, where we see a fourfold embodiment of the gospel:

1. They devote "themselves to the *apostles' teaching.*" The once popular distinction between the apostolic *didache* (teaching) and *kerygma* (preaching) was overdrawn. Certainly, Luke makes a distinction between what is said to outsiders and what is proclaimed within the ongoing life of the church. Far from any modern mushy "inclusiveness," Luke is quite careful to separate those on the inside, who know, from those on the outside, who do not know. Yet teaching the ones who know about what is known continues to include the gospel. In fact Acts itself was part of the ongoing attempt of the church to reflect upon the implications and applications of the gospel within the church so that the church might continue to be faithful to its calling. The church is not to drift from one momentary emotional outburst to the next, to resuscitate Pentecost on a weekly basis; rather the church moves immediately to the task of teaching, keeping itself straight about what it is and what it is to be about.

2. The church is in *fellowship.* The Spirit has produced *koinonia.* Some have remarked that the real miracle of Pentecost is to be found here—that from so diverse assemblage of people "from every nation under heaven" (2:5) a unified body of believers is formed. What is more, this *koinonia* cannot be some merely warm-hearted *animorum concordia,* human-initiated brotherly and sisterly love. It is a fellowship which produces astounding "wonders and signs" (2:43), not the least of which was that "all who believed were together and had all things in common," selling their possessions and distributing them to all (2:44–45). Later commentators seem intent on showing such claims to be an idealized and romanticized creation of the later church. Their interpretations testify more to the loss of the church's confidence in the ability of the resurrection faith to overturn all material and social arrangements. That Luke later speaks of the generosity of Barnabas in 4:36–37 suggests that this early communal sharing was somewhat exceptional within the community. Yet the commonality of goods is set forth as concrete testimony that something unsettling, specific, and substantial has happened to these people. Deuteronomy 15:4–5 promised a land free of poverty. That land now takes visible shape within a fellowship that goes beyond the bounds of conventional friendship. In Luke 19:8 a little man is confronted by the gospel and responds by parting with material goods (cf. Luke

40

12:13–34). Now, a whole community does the same. Furthermore, the spirituality described here is considerably more than some ethereal outburst. Everything they once held has been set free so that the word *koinonia* means something.

3. The church engages in *"the breaking of bread."* The gathering of the fellowship at the table is another tangible, visible expression of the work of the Spirit among the new community. Go through the Gospel of Luke and note all occasions when "he was at table with them." Each dinner-time episode in Luke is a time of fellowship, revelation, and controversy. Jesus was criticized for the company he kept at the table: "This man receives sinners and eats with them" (Luke 15:2), they charged. He failed to make proper distinction between persons at his table. We know, from contemporary experience, that social boundaries between persons are often most rigidly enforced at the table. Eating together is a mark of unity, solidarity, and deep friendship, a visible sign that social barriers which once plagued these people have broken down. Whether this "breaking of bread" is a reference to our Eucharist or Lord's Supper is a matter of debate. Probably, Peter's church of Luke's day would not know our distinction between the church *merely* breaking bread and the church breaking bread as a sacramental religious activity. In good Jewish fashion, when the blessing is said at the table, the table becomes a holy place and eating together a sacred activity. We do know in verse 46 that their partaking of food with glad and generous hands suggests the exuberant joy at the advent of the Messiah (so Bultmann). Perhaps every meal for the church was experienced as an anticipation of the Messianic banquet, a foretaste of Jesus' promise that his followers would "eat and drink at my table in my kingdom (Luke 22:30)." In their eating and drinking the resurrection community is already a partial fulfillment of that promise, enjoying now what shall soon be consummated in the kingdom of God. The prophet's call is fulfilled,

> "Ho, every one who thirsts,
>   come to the waters;
> and he who has no money, . . .
> Come, buy wine and milk
>   without money and without price" (Isa. 55:1).

4. The church also has *prayers,* possibly at the Jewish hours of prayer for daily devotions. Furthermore, we are told that they continued to attend the temple (2:46). In the midst of all the

41

newness, the community does not neglect the traditions of the ancestors, does not cease being devoutly Jewish. In all these activities of teaching, fellowship and sharing, breaking of bread, and praying we see a well-rounded picture of the church, the marks of authentic embodiment of the Spirit in the community's life, a canon for the measurement of the church's activity today. As one views modern congregations, many with their hectic round of activities—yoga, ceramics, basketweaving, daycare—one suspects that socialization is being substituted for the gospel, warm-hearted busyness is being offered in lieu of Spirit-empowered community. One wonders if the church needs to reflect again that when all is said and done "one thing is needful" (Luke 10:42), namely to embody, in the church's unique way, the peculiarity of the call to devote ourselves "to the apostles' teaching and fellowship, to the breaking of bread and the prayers" (2:42).

The order of activity in 2:42–47 is not presented as a primitive order of worship from which we can construct an early Sunday service pattern (against Jeremias, pp. 118–22). Rather, Luke is fond of this type of summary (cf. 4:32–35; 5:12–16) as a means of tying together two literary units (in this case Peter's speech to the crowd and his speech before the temple). More importantly, 2:42–47 focuses our attention on the main concern of Acts—the community. In Acts individual personalities have their place in the story, particularly Peter and Paul, but are they the purpose of the story? Neither Peter nor Paul is developed with much depth of detail. Luke had little interest in apostolic biography or a primitive life of the saints. The protagonist of Acts is the Holy Spirit, enlivening and driving the young church. This summary of the activity of the church focuses our attention away from preoccupation with individual actors toward the true concern of the story—the community.

What Does the Gospel Do?

ACTS 3:1—4:31

42

Our story moves from the crowd and its response to the gospel to the temple, at the hour of prayer. The gospel has moved the community to the very heart of national religious life, to the temple itself, where the gospel will do its work and encounter opposition. We should remember that by the time Acts was written the mission to the Jews had ended for Luke's church. Luke is looking back and pondering the significance of the fact that "He came unto his own and his own knew him not." Of course, we are jumping ahead of ourselves. We do not know that yet. All we know at this point in the story is that the gospel is being preached as the fulfillment of the promises of God to those whom the promises were made—the people of Israel. Here, with the temple and all that it represents serving as a backdrop for the unfolding drama, we shall see in two events what the gospel does to people. The gospel is the power of God, a power which elicits healing for some, astonishment for others, and anger for those whose vested interests are threatened by this new power set loose in the world.

Acts 3:1–10
Healing and Witness at the Temple

The second chapter of Acts ended with a rather cozy picture of the church gathered for teaching, fellowship, the breaking of bread, and the prayers. We were told that those who believed were of one mind and heart and held all things in common. The history of the church has many examples of short-lived Christian communities that defined the church as a rather closed, cozy club of the elect. After all, our intra-church fellowship can be so warm and supportive, why venture outside into the cold, cruel world?

Perhaps, because such chummy inversion is tempting for the church, this is why Luke immediately follows his account of life within the new body of believers in Jerusalem with an account of the infant church's confrontation with the world around it. Yesterday's church was fond of singing the old hymn, "Sweet Hour of Prayer, Sweet Hour of Prayer, that draws me from a world of care." Luke goes to great pains to show that the church's gathering to break bread, teach, and pray joyfully was in no way a detour around the misery of the world. For no sooner had Peter and John gone up to the temple to pray (v. 1) —good, devout Jews that they were—than they are confronted

43

by a man who had been lame since birth. The path toward significant prayer is a way that goes straight through, not around, human misery.

The crippled man does what totally dependent and helpless people often do—he asks for a handout. He has no other hope than to live by the crumbs that are cast from the tables of those who have been born in a more fortunate condition than he. To the man's surprise, he receives much more than he asked for. He asked for alms; he received healing (3:6–8).

The lame man asks for money and is told by Peter, "I have no silver and gold, but I give you what I have; in the name of Jesus Christ of Nazareth, walk" (3:6). From time to time throughout Acts there will be confusion over this issue of money. In Ephesus Paul creates an uproar when he runs afoul of community financial interest (19:21–41). In Macedonia, Paul and Silas deprive some slave owners of their means of livelihood and are thrown into jail (16:16–34). Simon Magus makes a fatal mistake in assuming that the Holy Spirit is up for sale (8:9–24). Here, a crippled man asks for alms but the community which holds all goods in common has little silver or gold to offer him. Temporary modest financial gain and charitable handouts are not what this community is primarily about.

What does Peter have? Peter has the power of the name of Jesus. By telling us that this is a man who was "lame from birth," Luke underscores the drama of this event. The comparison of the man who lies helpless and dependent at the gate compared with the man who now is seen "walking and leaping and praising God" (3:8) makes the healing all the more impressive. As in Luke's Gospel, we see that the message of Jesus is inextricably related to its power to heal. The community has this same power to offer to the world. Here is a community which does not simply offer suffering people kind words of empathy. This community possesses the same power so manifest in the ministry of Jesus. When Jesus commissioned the Twelve, he "gave them power and authority over all demons and to cure diseases" (Luke 9:1–6).

When the seventy were sent out (Luke 10:1–16), they returned with joy because "even the demons are subject to us in your name!" (Luke 10:17). Although the followers of Jesus do not have silver and gold, they have something infinitely more valuable—the power to heal in the name of Jesus Christ. Evidence of this power draws "wonder and amazement" (3:10) from bystanders. Their amazement provides a cue for Peter to proclaim to the people who stand before the temple what the healing means. Presumably, healing power can come from many different sources. The good news is not simply about the possibility for healing, for while health and wholeness may be taken as evidence of the presence of the kingdom (Luke 10:9), salvation is much more even than health—a truth which can be known by the astonished crowd only because someone in the community like Peter is able to tell the story.

The significance of unleashed saving power continues to be an issue for faithful interpretation. There were plenty of people in Luke's day who were willing to blame the crippled man's condition on his sin or on the sin of his parents. In our own day the conventional explanation for such physical infirmity lies more along the lines of certain biological or physiological causes. In the eyes of the faithful community, both the heartache and the healing of the world's misery are read differently. Joel had promised "signs on the earth beneath" (Acts 2:19), and when asked about the authenticity of his own mission, Jesus responded by citing the evidence that "the blind receive their sight, the lame walk, lepers are cleansed, and the deaf hear, the dead are raised up, the poor have good news preached to them" (Luke 7:22). Either the community is able to point to signs of healing power at work in the world because of what has happened in Christ or the community is without evidence for its claims.

The healing power is unleashed "in the name of Jesus Christ of Nazareth" (3:6), as the name of Jesus is the direct link between the living and active Lord in heaven and his community on earth. It is under this name that the sick are healed (3:6, 16; 4:7, 10), miracles take place (4:30), and sins are forgiven (10:43). At baptism this is the name laid upon each Christian (2:38; 8:16; 10:48; 19:5). This name is invoked as the authority for the disciples' teaching and preaching (4:17-18; 5:28, 40). This is the name for which believers are ready to die (5:41; 9:16; 15:26). In this name Jesus is present, along with his saving power, to the degree that Peter can say simply, "Jesus Christ heals you" (9:34).

Peter goes to great pains to stress in his interpretation of the healing miracle that it is not by the disciples' power or piety that the man is healed (3:12) but rather it is by the name of Jesus (3:16). The grammatically difficult sentence of 3:16 seems to be

Peter's attempt to clarify that this healing power has come as a *gift*. Neither the piety of the church nor of the healed man has effected this miracle. *Nothing magical has happened here* (human attempts to control divine powers in our behalf), for Acts takes care to distance the work of the Christian community from magic (8:9–11, 19–24; 13:12; 19:18–19). Power, even power which appears to effect good work, can be misinterpreted or misused; therefore all manifestations of power must be interpreted and put in their place. The community cares deeply about the exercise of healing power, not simply because there is much misery in the world that ought to be set right but because this healing is experienced as visible evidence of the presence of the community's Lord and Savior.

This healing motif appears later in Acts as a summary of Jesus' ministry:

> You know . . . how God anointed Jesus of Nazareth with the Holy Spirit and with power; how he went about doing good and healing all that were oppressed by the devil, for God was with him (10:36–38).

Acts 3:11–26
Testimony Before the People

The portico of the great temple in Jerusalem provides the setting for the second of Peter's major speeches in Acts. With the healed man still clinging to him, Peter accounts for what has happened. Whatever has happened, it is not "by our own power or piety" (3:12). The healing has occurred by the name of Jesus (3:16), the same Jesus who was handed over to the Roman authorities and killed in place of a murderer. We find no substitutional atonement in Luke, no notion that Jesus Christ had to die to satisfy some divine requirement of justice. No, the explanation for Jesus' death in Acts is simply human perversity. The formula *"You . . . killed . . . God* raised from the dead" (3:14–15, author's itals.) is typical of Luke. There is little *theology of the cross* in Luke of the kind we find in the writings of Paul, no assertion here of the Pauline theology that somehow the cross is a manifestation of the powerlessness of God so that humanity might be saved. The cross for Luke is a scandalous sign of the

46

rejection of God's anointed one by those he came to save, a tragic human "no" that God has overcome in the powerful "yes" of the resurrection. When confronted by God's Messiah, humanity got together and did what it often does in the face of truth—violence and crucifixion. Fortunately God has responded to humanity's action with action of his own—the resurrection. To be a follower of Jesus is to be a witness to God's powerful action in response to human rejection (3:15). In verse 17 Peter addresses his audience as "brethren," assuring them that any actions they committed "in ignorance" can be set right by receiving the Savior whom they rejected. This Christ was "appointed for you" (3:20). There is only one thing to do now—repent. A decisive turning around is required.

The penalty for not repenting is terrible. Before, the people acted in ignorance. But now it should be clear from Peter's speech that the lordship of Christ was foretold by "holy prophets from of old" (3:21) as well as by Moses (3:22). All the prophets from Samuel on proclaimed the truth embodied in Christ. The covenantal promise to Abraham that "in your posterity shall all the families of the earth be blessed" (3:25) is fulfilled. Those who do not acknowledge the truth the prophets foretold about Jesus shall suffer the terrible fate of being "destroyed from the people" (3:23). In other words, the Jew who does not turn to Christ is no longer a member of God's people.

Peter can make this claim only on the basis of the Lukan assertion that *true* Israel consists of those who are faithful to the patriarchs and the prophets of Israel. In every age in Israel some have obeyed and some have not. Those who are faithful to the promises of God deserve the designation of being the true Israel and those who do not obey are outsiders.

It is a severe, harsh argument. But we should remember that you and I are listening in on a debate, a debate long since ended as far as the church was concerned by the time Luke wrote Acts, between Jew and Jew over who was the true Israel. It is a debate we will continue in succeeding chapters of Acts, but for now, let us note that by the stark either/or manner in which Peter poses the issue it is a life-and-death argument over who is the true heir to the promises of God (see *Reflection: Luke and His Fellow Jews*).

At this point in Acts, it is clear that Jesus Christ has come only for the Jews, a fulfillment of the promises God made to Israel at the very dawn of its history. God "sent him to you first"

47

(3:26). But here is a gift that is not simply a matter of biological inheritance. Even the chosen of Israel must repent and turn from their ways to be a part of the good news. There will be no second generation Israel, no grandchildren for God, only those who have repented and turned toward God are of God. Even the chosen ones, the insiders, must now repent and turn aside from their false securities toward the new order. Peter's call to repentance reminds one of the sermon by John the baptizer early in the Gospel of Luke: "Bear fruits that befit repentance, and do not begin to say to yourselves, 'We have Abraham as our father'; for I tell you, God is able from these stones to raise up children to Abraham . . . every tree therefore that does not bear good fruit is cut down and thrown into the fire" (Luke 3:8–9). The contemporary church which today may be tempted to rest upon the smug self-assurance of salvation by biological birthright ought to listen to Peter's depiction of God's determination to have a people who will be faithful to the promises. Whether the people are composed of those from the wondering crowd who hear and repent or people created from the stones in the River Jordan, God will have a people. Which shall it be for us?

Acts 4:1–22
Testimony Before the Authorities

With the people stirred up by the apostle's testimony of the resurrection, it does not take long for the authorities to swing into action to protect the interests of the establishment. The establishment responds to troublesome stirrings among the people and disturbing new ideas in the conventional establishment manner—the authorities arrest Peter and John. They had better act quickly, for the last time Peter spoke at Pentecost three thousand people were converted! Now, before the temple, before the very seat of the religious establishment, five thousand repent. The Jesus disturbance is in danger of becoming a mass movement. Luke paints the scene in beautifully dramatic tones. On one side are the rulers, elders, and scribes of the capital city—those who were "of high-priestly family" (4:6). On the other side stand Peter and John, "uneducated, common men" (4:13). The rulers' question is one that rulers usually ask to common disturbers of the peace—who gave you the authority to be doing all of this? Rulers generally assume that they control the instruments and symbols of authority and power, so they are shocked when power appears to be emanating from ones so lowly as Peter and John.

It is only by the Holy Spirit that a man like Peter is able to speak before such an assemblage of the powerful, and when he speaks we wonder if there is a touch of irony in his opening remark. Peter and John have been dragged before the authorities like common criminals, but what is their crime? They are guilty of "a good deed done to a cripple" (4:9)!

The stone the builders of the nation rejected as an unworthy foundation for national aspirations has become the cornerstone of hope in the future (4:11). Now the authorities have a real problem on their hands. They are backed into a corner by two uneducated men. A miraculous work of healing has occurred. If they clamp down upon these two troublesome commoners, there could be trouble among the people. After all, the establishment must *appear* to exist for the benefit of the people.

So the authorities take what is always the first step by any authoritarian leadership—they order Peter and John to keep quiet. Suppression of the press, control of the media, banning of books—the rulers always hope that there is some way to keep this sort of thing quite, some way to control the people's access to information. Unfortunately for the rulers, trying to keep spirit-filled apostles quiet is like trying to hold back a breaking wave. These witnesses are not primarily trying to stir up trouble, they simply want the freedom to "speak of what we have seen and heard" (4:21).

For the moment, all the authorities are able to do is threaten and then release them. In the hearing of the story we pick up some familiar parallels from Luke's account of Jesus. Even as Jesus moved toward a collision with the powers that be, so do Jesus' followers. Even as the authorities were initially thwarted in their attempts to keep Jesus quiet, so these authorities are unable initially to silence Peter and John. And even as, in Luke's Gospel, the opposition and determination of the authorities gradually builds, we feel that we are witnessing the beginning of opposition which will one day gain enough strength to damage the young church. In other words, everything that happened to Jesus seems to be happening to those who follow him.

49

As Peter and John return to their friends, we cannot help

but note in passing that when Peter spoke before the people five thousand repented and became part of the movement. But when much the same testimony was given before the authorities, Peter and John were sent packing and no one was saved. A man whom the world regards as unlearned and ignorant has made a group of powerful men look impotent and confused.

Acts 4:23–31
A Prayer for Boldness

If I, like Peter and John, had had a close and potentially disastrous brush with the authorities, my prayer would be for divine protection rather than boldness! Yet, the only thing the community asked of God is the power "to speak thy word with all boldness" (4:29). It is God's business to heal and to work signs and wonders in the name of Jesus (4:30). It is the community's business to speak the word with boldness in the midst of the mighty acts of God. The trembling and shaking of the place signify that the apostles' prayer has been answered, and once again they are given a bold tongue to utter the word of God. Boldness is a highly favored Lukan virtue (2:29; 4:13, 29, 31; 9:27, 28). Was Theophilus facing trials and tribulations that required boldness? We suspect this was the case; for there are too many instances in Luke-Acts where disciples are called upon not to shrink in the face of persecution. Luke's typical accents are found later in the risen Lord's message to Paul: Do not be afraid; do not be silent; I am with you; no one will harm you; I have many of my own people here (18:9–10).

What do Christians do when persecution threatens to undo the community? They turn to God, the same God who created the world and all of its inhabitants, the God who holds all things within his power. Even persecution, even persecution by powerful people, does not take us out of God's hand. The same power which brought the world into being, which enables the community to worship will also be with the community in its times of persecution.

50

Throughout this section we have seen a relationship between *divine deeds* and *human words.* Here is a God who comes to us not simply with words but also with mighty acts of healing. But the mighty acts of healing must be interpreted and proclaimed, witnessed and defended through words. There is also an interplay of *witness* and *worship.* The community moved from its time of prayer to a time of confrontation with the misery of the world in the form of a crippled man. Then, after arousing the ire of the authorities and testifying to the world and its rulers concerning the power of Christ, the community once again withdraws for prayer, seeking to be given in worship the power it needs to witness boldly to what is happening in the world. In this rhythm of action and speech, witness and worship, the church discovers the source of its life.

Challenges Within and Without

ACTS 4:32—6:7

Sections of this portion of Acts appear as the first reading for the Sunday after Easter (traditionally called, "Low Sunday") within the Common Lectionary. At first glance, we may wonder what these rather newsy accounts of everyday life in the early church have to do with Easter, particularly because they deal in great part with the problem of money. After a congregation's exuberant celebration of the resurrection on Easter, it may seem a bit crude to revert to such mundane concerns as possessions, money, the sale of property, and how to get things done within the church on the Low Sunday after Easter. But in Luke's mind everything that follows is integrally connected to "their testimony to the resurrection of the Lord Jesus" (4:33). The resurrection makes possible true generosity and bold living.

When you think about it, the quality of the church's life together is evidence for the truthfulness of the resurrection. The most eloquent testimony to the reality of the resurrection is not an empty tomb or a well-orchestrated pageant on Easter Sunday but rather a group of people whose life together is so radically different, so completely changed from the way the world builds a community, that there can be no explanation other than that something decisive has happened in history. The tough task of interpreting the reality of a truth like the

51

resurrection is not so much the scientific or historical, "How could a thing like that happen?" but the ecclesiastical and communal, "Why don't you people look more resurrected?"

Acts 4:32—5:11
The Challenge of Possessions

We are not surprised to hear Luke claim that "the company of those who believed were of one heart and soul" (4:32) because we are accustomed to hearing such pious, often unrealistic claims made about Christian congregations, even within our own day. Preachers sometimes tend toward rosey exaggeration. But when Luke claims that "no one said that any of the things which he possessed was his own, but that they had everything in common" (4:32), our ears perk up. How can this be? Karl Marx claimed that nearly every human attitude and action could be traced to economic sources. Luke was not a Marxist, but he was enough of a realist to know that there is a good chance that where our possessions are our hearts will be also. A surprisingly large amount of the Book of Acts deals with economic issues within the community. Much of Luke's Gospel also deals with matters of money. Consider the parables of the Debtors (Luke 7:41–43), the Good Samaritan (10:29–37), the Rich Fool (12:16–21), the Unjust Steward (16:1–8), the Rich Man and Lazarus (16:19–31), and the parable of the Pounds (19:11–27)—all but one of these parables are unique to Luke. Wealth is not, for Luke, a sign of divine approval. It is a danger. The rich young man could not part with his money (Luke 18: 18–23), and another rich man was declared "thou fool" because of his silly reliance on well-filled barns (Luke 12:15–21).

"Why are we always talking about money in the church?" one of my church's officers asked complainingly. "All we do is talk about money, giving, and the budget. I wish we could get beyond this and talk about the spiritual things that are really important for a church."

His was an understandable but misguided wish for the church. In responding to him I noted that we had discussed all sorts of issues in church board meetings, but none of the issues under discussion were as volatile and potentially divisive as our congregational arguments about money. At least in this sense Marx was right: There is a kind of economic determinism at work in our lives. Money makes the world go around.

Ernest Becker noted that as belief in God and other traditional sources of immortality eroded in Western culture, money assumed a god-like quality in our lives, our ticket to enduring significance in the face of death. We sometimes say, in the face of materialism, "You can't take it with you." But that observation does not defeat our materialism; it reveals its source. We cannot take things with us as we go into the oblivion of death; but we can pass financial power on to our offspring. We endow a chair at the university or have a pew named for us at church. Money is thus, in Becker's words, our "immortality ideology," our modern means of insuring that even if I must die my name, my family, my achievements, my power will continue after I am gone. Only Luke tells the story of the rich fool (12:13–21), the one who assumed that his possessions gave him god-like security against the invasions of mortality. The first banks were temples and the earliest coins were stamped with the images of gods.

"How hard it is for those who have riches to enter the kingdom of God!" said Jesus (Luke 18:24). The disciples spoke for us all in asking "Then who can be saved?" (Luke 18:26).

But the same wonder-working power of the Spirit which made a lame man walk in the preceding section has enabled a man named Barnabas to sell his field and to give the proceeds to the apostles, who made distribution of such gifts to those in need (cf. Deut. 15:4–5). The church takes care of its own, thus creating in its life together a kind of vignette, a paradigm of the sort of world God intends for all. Justin Martyr marveled of his own church, not far removed in time from Luke's church, "We who once coveted most greedily the wealth and fortune of others, now place in common the goods we possess, dividing them with all the needy" (I *Apology* 14:2–3). The power which broke the bonds of death on Easter, shattered the divisions of speech at Pentecost, and empowered one who was lame now releases the tight grip of private property.

Lest any should think that the material question is a small issue, Luke moves from the positive account of the generosity of Barnabas to the chilling tale of Ananias and Sapphira. There, possessions and what they do to us is a matter of life and death, the very first crisis to hit the young community. Unfaithfulness and deception are as close at hand as the community's own life.

53

In lying to the community and its leaders about the disposition of his property, Ananias has lied to God (5:3–4). In pitiless, dispassionate, and clinical detail, Luke describes the death of the two deceivers. Those who like the rich fool (Luke 12:16–21) attempt to secure life through material things receive not life but death. One of Jesus' disciples was the first to abandon Jesus for money (Luke 22:1–5).

If money is somehow linked with our idolatrous attempts to secure immortality for ourselves, it is also the occasion for much self-deceit. There is something quite natural about the lies of Ananias and Sapphira, for we all know the way we rationalize and excuse our own covetousness, acquisitiveness, and greed. "I'm not really all that well off," we say. "I have all I can do just to make ends meet." "I worked hard for this and deserve it." Our lies are a correlate of our materialism, for both our materialism and our self-deceit are our attempts to deal with our human insecurity, our human finitude, by taking matters into our own hands. Luther once called security the ultimate idol. And we have shown time and again that we are willing to exchange anything—our family, our health, our church, the truth—for a taste of security. We are vulnerable animals who seek to secure and establish our lives in improper ways, living by our wits rather than by faith. This "self-securing mentality" (E. Farley, p. 141) is at the heart of all failures to live by faith in God.

The church in the person of Peter confronts the lies of Ananias and Sapphira, because deceit of ones self or ones brothers and sisters in the church is a way that leads to death. The story is harsh, severe, uncompromising in the telling; but how is falsehood ever confronted except in a manner which always seems severe to the one tangled in deceit? The cost of not confronting our deceit over possessions is high—nothing less than the very death of our life together. The ancient *Didache* opens with, "Two ways there are, one of Life and one of Death, and there is a great difference between the two ways" (VI, 15). The ethical stance of these early Christians, their beliefs about matters like money, were concrete applications of their theological assertions. The church was called to be an alternative community, a sign, a signal to the world that Christ had made possible a way of life together unlike anything the world had seen. *Not* to confront lies and deceit, greed and self-service among people like Ananias and Sapphira would be the death of

54

the church. The Epistle of James (1:9–11; 2:1–7) indicates that more than one early congregation was destroyed by the failure of Christians to keep riches in their place. Could that be why in ending the stark account of Ananias and Sapphira Luke uses the word "church" for the very first time in Acts (5:11)? Here in struggling with money the community first experienced itself as the disciplined community of truthfulness.

In his attempt to encourage Theophilus, Luke paints a positive picture of the early community. But it is not a romanticized, idealized portrait. These are real people who are pulled in different directions by the same real tendencies which tug at us. These are real congregations where, on any Sunday, one is apt to meet both faithfulness and foolishness seated beside one another on the third pew from the left. It is important that we follow Luke's realism in our contemporary evaluations of the church. These are real people struggling to be faithful in a world which makes faithfulness problematic. There will be disappointments, unpleasantness, disputes, and some who put their hand to the plow will look back. Sometimes, those who are looking back, the Ananiases and Sapphiras of the church, are us.

Acts 5:12–42
Again Healing and, Again, Official Opposition

After the rather grim story of the death of two deceivers (5:1–11), the lights are turned up again at center stage and Luke shows us the life-giving power of the gospel at work. The growing swell of signs and wonders, of new converts becomes a cresting wave sweeping aside every impediment. People kept their distance from the apostles, not out of fear of them but from great awe and wonder. But the masses of miserable, helpless, sick, and afflicted people press upon them. Even Peter's shadow is able to heal! Paul may have difficulties with magician-like super apostles (II Cor. 12:11) but not Luke, who unlike Paul has a good deal more interest in the power of the apostle than in the apostle's humble witness to the cross, where "power is made perfect in weakness" (II Cor. 12:9). As Luke sees it, good

news which is powerless to change some of the world's misery
is hardly good news.

When John the Baptist sent messengers to inquire whether
Jesus was indeed the one whose advent was promised (Luke
7:20), Jesus responded:

> "Go and tell John what you have seen and heard: the blind
> receive their sight, the lame walk, lepers are cleansed, and the
> deaf hear, the dead are raised up, and the poor have good news
> preached to them. And blessed is he who takes no offense at
> me" (Luke 7:22–23).

We are justified if in reading this account of healing we
think of the earlier story of the healing of the crippled man in
3:1–10 and the official response in 3:11–26. That controversy-
provoking act of compassion and proclamation has now been
repeated ten, a hundred times over; so we should not be surprised that the religious establishment, represented by the Sadducees, reappears, this time with renewed determination to put
an end to this Jesus commotion. The last time, the council let
the apostles have their say and then, after being dumbfounded
by Peter, released them. This time they take no chances and
arrest them outright.

Yet something about the gospel renders prisons ineffective.
With the comic speed of an old "Keystone Cops" movie, an
angel sets the apostles free, and by daybreak they are back
making trouble at the temple. Then follows an even more
comic shuttling back and forth from council to jail, back to
council, with the discovery of the apostles busy at the temple,
teaching (5:21–25). Luke, who may not have been clear about
the exact structure of the temple hierarchy, calls Israel's council
of elders the "senate of Israel" (5:21). Not to worry. There is a
sense in which when one has observed the behavior of one
threatened politician—gentile or Jew—one has seen them all.

Once again, Luke makes clear that at this point any problems of the apostles are with the authorities, not with the people
as a whole. The same fearful, inept, conniving officialdom who
conspired with the Romans to send Jesus to the cross is up to its
old tricks again. Once again, it must take account of the success
of this new movement among the common people who hear
gladly that which the authorities have tried vainly to keep
quiet.

Peter again counters the authorities' charges with, "We

must obey God rather than men" (5:29). How does it sound in the ears of these religious officials to be reminded by this commoner that *they* are supposed to be obeying God also, rather than collaborating to keep a lid on the status quo in Jerusalem? These religious leaders whose lives are supposed to epitomize complete obedience to the will of God have exchanged that sacred duty for the role of official power brokers and Roman quislings, whose job it is to keep their own people from causing too much trouble for the Roman occupation forces. Peter's speech has touched a nerve in their compromised hearts, for "When they heard this they were enraged and wanted to kill them" (5:33).

Lest we think that membership in the academic and religious establishment automatically disqualifies one from any shred of righteousness, we note that Luke has the apostles saved from almost certain death by the intervention of rabbi Gamaliel, one of the most widely known and revered rabbis of his day. Gamaliel's speech uses much the same scriptural argument we have encountered elsewhere in Acts—if this movement is a human, sociological phenomenon alone, it will collapse in its own time and amount to nothing. But who is foolish enough to try to stop the movements of God? The other members of the council do not bother with Scripture or reason. Their anger and official indignation are their only sources of thought. At the crucifixion Luke described Joseph of Arimathea as "a member of the council, a good and righteous man, who had not consented to their purpose and deed; and he was looking for the kingdom of God" (Luke 23:50–51). Simply by being a member of the establishment an official is not thereby made deaf to the gospel. The key qualification is that one be "looking for the kingdom of God."

By having Gamaliel present a reasoned, intelligent argument, Luke implies that others who made the effort to think through the case of the church would come to a similarly favorable conclusion. Faced with innovation and possible new revelation, the traditional faith community should not resort to force against innovators (5:33) but should wait and see (5:34–39) and let truth make its own way. The noble Gamaliel's advice to leave the Christians alone in order that the world might see what will become of all this represents Luke's own appeal to the foes of the church, an appeal summed up in the very last word of Acts: *unhindered.*

57

The apostles leave with their lives but not without suffering—thirty-nine lashes killed many a prisoner. Yet, in the topsy-turvy value system of the apostles even terrible torture elicits "rejoicing that they were counted worthy to suffer dishonor for the name" (5:41) in emulation of their Leader (5:31)—an unusual christological title found only in Acts, which possibly signifies the close relationship between Christ and his band of followers. The ones who continued with Jesus through his trials (Luke 22:28) are now led through their trials by their now-exalted Leader.

Jesus' promise is fulfilled: ". . . When they bring you before the synagogues and the rulers and the authorities, do not be anxious how or what you are to answer or what you are to say; for the Holy Spirit will teach you in that very hour what you ought to say" (Luke 12:11–12).

Acts 6:1–7
Leadership in the Community

Something there is about religious communities that makes them among the most conserving and traditionalist groups within a society. Today's clerical vestments were the clothing of everyday Romans of the fourth century. Contemporary ecclesiastical terminology is replete with strange words from dead languages. The church's traditionalism may be partly ascribed to the church's need to conserve what is true, to remain faithful to the truth once received. We have seen in the speeches in Acts the gospel proclaimed through remembrance of past promises to Israel. The Pharisees and Sadducees on the council are only doing their duty in protecting the faith of the ancestors from destructive innovation. But in their effort to conserve what is true, they, like Jesus' critics before them, have missed the truth.

In contrast to the council, the Spirit-led community is ready to move in order to remain obedient to the Spirit. A new challenge has arisen within the community. The community is multiplying and new organization and leadership are needed. The "Hellenists" (probably, Greek-speaking Jews of the diaspora) feel that their widows are being neglected in the daily

58

distribution of goods. There was a long tradition of care of the poor within the synagogue, and Christians continued this practice. But distribution has become unmanageable.

In saying "It is not right that we should give up preaching the word of God to serve tables" (6:2), the apostles are not disparaging such work; they are taking decisive action so that this necessary social (and liturgical?) administration might be assured—even though their words imply that the task of preaching is a primary apostolic duty. Although Luke does not use the term "deacon" for those who are selected to serve in the table fellowship, it may be that Luke is accounting for the origins of a diaconate. Hands are laid upon these new leaders—a gesture of the bestowal of authority and power taken from Judaism.

Although the interpreter of this passage should take care not to read too much into this account concerning the origins of our later ordained ministry, it is fair to draw a few conclusions about leadership within the community of the Spirit: (1) *Leadership within the church arises from the community's quite mundane but utterly necessary functional needs.* In Luke, Jesus is called by God in baptism and Jesus called the Twelve. Now the Twelve call others to ministry within the congregation. One need not search for some mystical basis for the origins of the ordained ministry other than the need within the church for certain jobs to be done so that the whole community might be about its ministry. Luther was correct in denying that the essence of the ordained ministry resides in some indelible character detached from the congregation and conferred in ordination. The essence of the ordained ministry is derivative of and accountable to the ministry of the church as a whole.

(2) *Leadership arises from "below" not from "above"*—by dribbling down from God to Jesus, to the Bishop through the hierarchy, to the clergy, at last to the lowly laity. The process of ordination moves in the other direction—leaders arise from the needs of God's people for guidance and service. At the same time leadership is from above, a gift of the Lord (Eph. 4:8–11; I Tim. 4:14), therefore the church prays as it lays on hands (Acts 3:6). God does not leave the community bereft of leadership but gives worthy servants beyond the bounds of the first apostles.

(3) *The ordained ministry in its present form is an adaptation of the church to its leadership needs.* The Twelve evolve into other forms of leadership. The present orders of clergy

59

were not fixed in stone from the beginning of the church, were not established by divine decree. The church creates certain types of leadership for the community to function. What the church has established, the church may change. From the first, so 6:1–6 implies, the church demonstrated an admirable ability to attend to the essential and to follow the leading of the Spirit and to respond creatively to new challenges. The community needed something done and devised a means of doing it. Also, judging from the Greek names of the seven who were chosen, these men may have come from the Hellenists themselves, the segment of the church which felt discrimination. If so, the church also showed an awareness that leadership drawn from the oppressed may do the best job of representing the interests of the oppressed. In the church's current debates over who should be ordained and how, does the church continue to display this missional vitality?

With all the dramatic episodes of witnessing and persecution, testimony and martyrdom which bracket 6:1–6, this brief account of administrative problems at First Church Jerusalem and their solution may seem a bit pedestrian. But through this vignette Luke reminds us that administration of and daily care for the internal needs of the congregation is also vital ministry, not something to be disparaged or devalued in the midst of other more exciting and outward acts of witness. Operating the copy machine, planning next Sunday's worship, ministering to divisions between oldtimers (Jewish Christians) and new arrivals (Hellenists), caring for elderly widows, and faithfully administering church funds are also aspects of service to the Spirit.

The Story of Stephen

ACTS 6:8—8:3

In recording the appointment of the seven (6:1–7), Luke is able to focus upon two men who will move center stage for awhile—Philip and Stephen. In Stephen we encounter the trial and suffering of one who is neither the Christ nor an apostle. Persecution, we find, is not to be reserved for the "stars" of the story—anyone who is faithful may suffer for the faith. And suffer they will, for the stakes are being raised as persecution moves from warning (4:21) to flogging (5:40) to death (7:58). Moreover, while earlier chapters portrayed the people in the crowd as ignorant but still capable of receptivity, this once-wondering crowd turns into a vicious mob (6:12) stepping into line behind their leaders in persecuting the church. In other words, the story of Stephen is a pivot point, a watershed in Acts.

Acts 6:8—7:53
Arrest and Witness

Stephen is obviously engaged in forms of ministry other than waiting on tables within the community (6:1–5). This "second-generation" leader is doing what heretofore only the apostles did—"great wonders and signs among the people" (6:8). When his actions lead Stephen's fellow Hellenistic Jews to make charges against him, Stephen's combined "wisdom and the Spirit" easily scatter his accusers. The defeated Hellenists now launch a smear campaign against Stephen, charging that he has slandered "Moses" (the law, the Torah) and "God" (the temple, the cult), that Jesus will destroy the temple and modify the customs instituted by Moses (6:11–14), charges which will later be leveled against Paul (21:20–21, 28; 24:7; 25:8). Religious innovation is the charge, a charge which Stephen shortly will attempt to refute by showing that he and his fellow Christians are the ones who are faithful to the tradition whereas his accusers are not. With face shining "like the face of an angel" (Luke's way of setting the stage for a major pronouncement by indicating that the Holy Spirit is upon the one who speaks), Stephen replies to the high priest's "Is this so?" with the longest speech in Acts—an indication of its importance within the total narrative.

Stephen's speech says, in so many words, "You have your nerve to charge that I have violated Moses and his law—look at you!" Beginning with Abraham, Stephen recounts for his audience the long journey of faith which began with God's promise to bring Abraham's people to a place where they may worship (7:2–7). Joseph is then mentioned, Joseph whom his own brothers sold into slavery (7:9–16). Even as far back as Joseph, there

61

was conflict within the family of Abraham. Yet God was with Joseph. The efforts of his brothers only served to further God's plans. Next the story of Moses is recalled in loving detail and awe—showing that Stephen cannot be justly accused of blaspheming against Moses. Stephen reminds his audience that Moses in his day got little affection from his own people, who "refused to obey him" (7:39). Here was their savior, their liberator, and they failed to recognize him, asking, "Who made you a ruler and a judge over us?" (7:27), an insolent retort which Stephen says caused Moses to flee to Midian—even though Exodus 2:15 says that Moses fled from the wrath of Pharaoh, not that of his own people.

The speech lurches from selective reminiscence to passionate indictment at verse 35. With relentless jabs Stephen tells his hearers that it was *this* Moses, *this* deliverer "whom they refused." From rebellion against Moses the people degenerated to heathenish idolatry (7:39–43). Old Simeon had foretold that Jesus would occasion the "fall and rising of many in Israel" (Luke 2:34). Even as Jesus in his first sermon at the synagogue in Nazareth reminded the congregation of the unpleasant testimony of history that "no prophet is acceptable in his own country" (Luke 4:24), so Stephen, by turning the community's own Scripture back upon the community, has reminded his audience that the community once rebellious and idolatrous can easily be so again. And we all know from history what happened to Jesus that day in Nazareth after his sermon!

Yet even in the midst of rebellion and idolatry Stephen admits, there was a "tent of witness" (7:44). Things went well until Solomon took it upon himself to build the temple. In a curious revision of history, Stephen sees Solomon's act as apostasy, using a portion of Solomon's own temple dedicatory address (I Kings 8:20–27) to assert that "the Most High does not dwell in houses made with hands" (7:48). Thus, the devotion to the temple is depicted as disobedience (cf. Heb. 8—9 where the tabernacle is regarded as the true place of worship). After quoting Isaiah 66:1–2, Stephen begins to sound a bit like Amos or Jeremiah, concluding his speech with a torrent of accusations against "You stiff-necked people" (7:51), whom he accuses of the murder of God's righteous One.

62

In this polemical summary of Israel's history, everything hinges on the fact that they did not understand (v. 25), they always resisted the Holy Spirit (v. 51). Any softening of Luke's depiction of the opposition by the insertion of a few earnest inquiries in the crowd, a wise rabbi like Gamaliel (6:34–39), or a few priests converted (6:7) has hardened into a grim portrayal of rejection by all the Jewish people. It is the speech of one Jew (Stephen) in bitter life-and-death conflict with fellow Jews (the high council). It is the speech of a bitter family feud over who is *really* heir to the family fortune. We know from everyday experience of such familial infightings that these fights can be bitter indeed.

Perhaps we are witnessing in Stephen's speech the bitterness of one brother who has been disinherited by another. By the time this speech was composed by Luke, the conversion of Israel was now only a wistful and increasingly unrealistic hope. Jewish Christians had failed to convince their own brothers and sisters that this Jesus was their long-awaited Messiah. The continued existence of the Jews, moving self-assuredly on their journey begun in Abraham, must have been a bitter reality for the church to swallow, a baffling and pervasive retort to the church's enthusiasm for its message and mission.

Luke, writing sometime after the year 70, was confronted by the now-ruined temple of Jerusalem from which Jewish Christians had long before been expelled. Now he was attempting in Stephen's speech to speak to his own church's disappointment and bitterness over the rejection by the Jews of the gospel that was supposed to be their good news (see *Reflection: Luke and His Fellow Jews*). However, when contemporary Christian interpreters utilize Stephen's speech, we must remember that *we are reading the speech of the persecuted church, of which Stephen was a martyr and Luke was a defender.* The church has now in many parts of the world changed places with the council members who bore the brunt of Stephen's charges. To appropriate Stephen's defense against persecution as our excuse to persecute the Jews would be a blasphemous misuse of the text.

What would be Stephen's account of the faithfulness of a church whose history began with stories of bold and compassionate martyrs but which now contains stories of the church's silence and complicity in Auschwitz and Buchenwald?

Stephen's speech reminds the church that one of the most significant aspects of our legacy from Israel is Israel's ability to use its own Scripture as a means of self-criticism. Ezra (Neh. 9) recounts Israel's history of disobedience and the devastation it

63

brought upon the people as a means of calling the people back to ritual purity. Jesus' sermon in Nazareth (Luke 4) uses stories of prophets to rebuke Israel's inability to be a light to the nations. Judgment begins with God's own house, judgment delivered through the courageous determination to tell our own history honestly.

In the history of the church's dealings with God's Chosen People, in the church's complicity in the martyrdom of Jews in all too numerous pogroms and resettlements culminating in the Holocaust, how does our history judge our fidelity to the teachings of the righteous One (v. 52)?

Acts 7:54—8:3
Martyrdom of Stephen and the Persecution of the Church

Stephen's speech seals his doom. Through a recollection of Israel's history, Stephen has unfolded a drama of a people's infidelity to the purposes of God. Now, heaven opens and Stephen exclaims, "I see . . . the Son of man standing at the right hand of God" (7:56). The speech began in answer to the high priest's question, "Is this so?" Does Stephen speak "blasphemous words against Moses and God" (6:11)? No. But Stephen does utter the "blasphemous" assertion that Jesus is now at the right hand of God, ascended to rule. Throughout Acts, visions are a primary means of God's making clear to earthly disciples the reality of heavenly facts. The ending of Stephen's speech is, like most good speeches, a climax, the point Luke wants to stress. In one of the few cases in the New Testament where the title "Son of man" is used by someone other than Jesus (7:56; cf. John 12:34; Rev. 1:13; 14:14), Luke has Stephen assert that Jesus is now the exalted Lord. This is who Jesus really is—the long-awaited and exalted Messiah who now rules over all, who must be acknowledged and obeyed or rejected at the peril of rejecting God himself. They plug their ears in hopes of silencing such words, for if Stephen's vision is true, then those who dare to oppose this Jesus are indeed enemies of God. The accusers now stand accused. Here is the vision Luke wanted to show us all along, the climax of the Stephen episode—the exaltation of Christ.

The storm which has been steadily gathering force throughout Acts breaks with all fury. The vision of glory sets the demons loose. Any semblance of a proper judicial proceeding degenerates into an angry mob as Stephen is dragged outside the gates of the Holy City and stoned to death. As he dies, he utters a prayer (7:59) modeled after a short Jewish bedtime prayer (Ps. 31:5), except for one crucial modification—Stephen's prayer is addressed to "Lord Jesus" rather than God. Seated at God's right hand, Jesus is invoked at the hour of death, the same Jesus whose attitude at death (Luke 23:34) is emulated by Stephen. The martyr's last prayer is that his enemies also be forgiven. Jesus' followers die like Jesus.

Although Luke has a theological quarrel with the council and its priests, he cannot directly associate them with the death of the church's first martyr. The murder of Stephen is depicted as the action of a lynch mob, since under the heel of Rome the Jewish council were probably powerless to sentence one to execution. The crowd which had once been attracted to and amazed by these followers of Christ has now spoken its democratic verdict. And as the stones fly they lay their garments at the feet of a man named Saul.

The persecution of Stephen is not an isolated act of violence. The community (except for the Twelve) is now hunted down and scattered into Judea and Samaria. Earlier, it had been predicted that the gospel would be taken by witnesses into "all Judea and Samaria" (1:8). Little did the followers know then that the impetus for this far-flung evangelism would be persecution! These refugees, scattered like seed, take root elsewhere and bear fruit. God is able to use even persecution of his own people to work his purposes. Not even this new demonic force named Saul will quench the spread of the gospel.

Upon entering the cafeteria at Princeton Theological Seminary, one sees three bronze plaques inscribed with the names of Princeton graduates who, like Stephen, paid for their vision in blood:

Walter Macon Lawrie—Thrown overboard by pirates in the China Sea, 1847.

John Rogers Peal—Killed with his wife by a mob at Lien Chou, China, 1905.

65

> James Joseph Reed—Fatally beaten at Selma, Alabama,
> March 11, 1965.

These names remind us of some later-day witnesses who went before us, some of whom paid dearly for their witness to the truth.

Stanley Hauerwas has written about the mass suicide at "Jonestown" when hundreds of followers of Jim Jones and his "People's Temple" took their lives and the lives of their children (p. 106). He notes that in contemporary media accounts of the event two dominant theories were put forth to explain Jonestown: (1) The followers of Jim Jones were under the hypnotic spell of a maniac. They were insane victims of an insane leader who led them to suicide. (2) The followers of Jim Jones were mostly poor, ignorant, oppressed people whose suffering made them easy prey for the alluring promises of a crazed messiah like Jones. In other words both theories assumed that in the modern world only insane people would die for what they believed.

In the United States we have "freedom of religion," which means that we are free to exercise our faith—as long as we do so within certain limits, as long as I do not become a fanatic—like the poor, deranged folk at Jonestown who committed suicides rather than forsake their belief in Jim Jones. Although we have freedom to be religious, that does not seem to involve freedom to die for what we believe, because only a crazed fanatic would do that.

Yet the story of Stephen reminds us practitioners of polite, civil, mentally balanced religion that once there were Christians who quite joyfully parted with possessions, family, friends, even life itself in order to remain faithful. Luke does not demean the sacrifice of Stephen by reducing his death to psychological or sociological factors, the way our media explained Jonestown. Rather, Luke sees Stephen as a hero of the faith, a quite rational person who died for the same faith by which he lived. Indeed not to die for what you hold most dear would seem, to the church of Acts, to be the essence of irrationality, even insanity. So many Christians (and Jesus) died at the hands of the Empire because it was impossible to reconcile the Christian claim—that is, that God, not nations, rules the world—with those of a progressive world empire. Martyrs continued to follow the path of Stephen until such time as the church's political threat to the empire was obscured by a new theology in which

66

Christians relinquished their own politically imperialistic claims to "obey God rather than men" (5:29; cf. W. H. Frend).

Luke has no quarrel with people who are willing to die for their faith—to die for a faith that, unlike that of Jim Jones, is *true.* Stephen was not a suicide, for as a Jew he knew that his life belonged to God, his life was (as his dying prayer indicated) held in the hands of God. Prohibited from taking our lives yet ready to give our lives if our continued existence means forsaking our faith, this is how we must live and die as Christians. What is worth living and dying for? That is a question behind Acts 7:54—8:3.

Witness Beyond Jerusalem

ACTS 8:4—9:43

"Now those who were scattered abroad went about preaching the word" (8:4). With that ironic remark, we begin a new step in evangelization. It is ironic that the violent pogrom which was supposed to put the troublesome Christians in their place has only served to put them out in Samaria. Now a new personality steps to the fore—Philip, whose ministry among the Samaritans serves to move the gospel one step beyond its originally intended recipients. The rather abrupt introduction of the stories about Philip's confrontation with Simon and his baptism of the Ethiopian suggest that Luke has drawn on older material about Philip—first as a wonder-worker who boldly challenges a magician and second as an instrument under divine direction who masterfully interprets Scripture so that a court official is converted. Luke retells the stories about Philip in the service of his account of the amazing spread of the gospel into unlikely places. Even though the insertion of the Philip material seems rather abrupt and discontinuous, placed here between the death of Stephen and the conversion of Saul it allows Luke to step back from the unfolding narrative and assume the role of teacher to instruct us in the nature of the gospel. The truth of the gospel is more than success in winning converts and martyrs. The gospel is a truth so demanding, so strange, that it is possible to get it

67

wrong. Therefore we step back a moment from the drama of the spread of the good news to ponder the tragedy of the misunderstanding of it. This gospel that is worth dying for (Stephen) is surely more than some sort of magic or some powerful commodity to be bought and sold.

Acts 8:4–25
The Gospel Is not Magic nor Is It for Sale

A long history of enmity between Jews and Samaritans lies behind this account of the mission into Samaria. While the Samaritans were considered by many Jews to be racially impure and religiously inferior, they did worship Israel's God, observed Moses' laws, and looked forward to the arrival of a messianic figure. But that accounted for little in the conventional Jewish evaluation of Samaritans. When Jesus' critics curse him, they call him "a Samaritan" (John 8:48). "Jews have no dealings with Samaritans," notes John 4:9. Neither Jew nor gentile, the Samaritans were charged with working both sides to their own advantage. Josephus said the Samaritans "alter their attitude according to their circumstances, and when they see Jews prospering, call them kinsmen, . . . but when they see Jews in trouble, they say they have nothing whatsoever in common, . . . but they declare themselves to be aliens of another race" (*Antiquities,* IX, 291). Samaritans appeared elsewhere in Luke's story (Luke 9:51–56; 10:29–37; 17:11).

Matthew's Jesus tells his disciples, "Go nowhere among the Gentiles, and enter no town of Samaritans" (Matt. 10:5). Yet here is Philip out among the Samaritans. In Philip's conversion in Samaria yet another miracle is being worked: Nationalistic recrimination is being overcome through the Spirit; Jew and Samaritan are being joined.

Yet it is out in the wilds of Samaria that the missionaries encounter a recurring adversary—magic. It is fine to take the gospel beyond the bounds of the rejecting orthodox believers, those who know the traditions of the elders, even if they reject the gospel. But in so doing, out in Samaria, misunderstandings and misapprehension of the gospel are more likely. Missionaries

68

must also be theologians because everyone's idea of good news is not necessarily *the* good news of Christ.

Enter the popular magician, Simon. We are told that Simon's great work evokes amazement from the people of Samaria. The apostles have also received marvel and amazement from the multitudes. Yet Luke's report of Simon's "saying that he was somebody great" (8:9) suggests that we are encountering someone other than Jesus' wonder-workers who attribute their power to the Spirit and not to themselves. Simon knows power when he sees it and is baptized by the one who performs such "signs and great miracles" (8:13).

One feels a certain sympathy for Simon. He is a man who is no stranger to the use of power to effect healing—a man whose "profession" makes him somewhat akin in prestige and power to the medical profession in our own society. He sees a power at work for good in the Holy Spirit and wants to purchase some of it to use himself—whether for the good of others or his own advancement, Luke does not say. What Luke does say is that the Spirit is a divine *gift*. It is not some power at the beck and call of wizards like Simon. The power to heal and exorcise, as noble and impressive as that work may be, is subordinate in Luke's mind to the apostles' power to mediate the Spirit, the power which poor Simon was deluded into thinking could be bought with silver. Luke wants no mistake that the attempt to buy God's gracious gift is a serious matter. Commercial interests and worldly entrepreneurship do not mix well with the Spirit. Peter's rebuke is fierce—"You and your money can go to hell!"

Magic may be defined as the attempt to control divine powers through the application of certain techniques or esoteric formulae. Acts has a uniformly low opinion of such practices (13:4–12; 19:19). The church has a never-ending struggle to define its faith in distinction from magic. Mark Twain's Huckleberry Finn says that he tried prayer and found that it did not work. He put a shoe box under his bed and prayed that it be filled with gold. He awoke in the morning and the box was still empty. Whatever Christians mean by the effectiveness of prayer, the power of the Spirit, the grace of God, we do not mean magic. The essential distinction seems to lie in Peter's recognition that all such manifestations are *gifts* of God—surprising, undeserved, unmanipulated, uncontrollable (8:20).

What do we make of an evangelism which, while including even the Samaritans, does not hesitate to exclude those like

69

Simon who do not fit the lifestyle or the theology of the community of the Spirit? In a time when the community was fighting for its very life, it fought not by reducing its witness to the lowest common denominator, a catchy slogan fit for a billboard or a bumper sticker, but rather by building walls about itself, by carefully defining itself, and by rebuking and excluding those like Simon who did not change their heathenish lifestyle and attitudes. Rather than baptizing the status quo or resorting to mushy affirmations of popular practices ("Even though I disagree with some of Simon's techniques, he does draw a lot of people and he does do a lot of good."), the church demanded repentance (8:22).

We will leave the interpreter to find his or her own examples of "simony" in the church today. It should not be difficult—in a world of television evangelists, "super churches," and politically powerful preachers—to think of someone who like Simon projects himself as "somebody great" and equates the gift of the Spirit with worldly standards of power and success.

In passing, a word should be said about a problem within this section that is less easily interpreted than the magic of Simon. Why did the baptism of Philip lack the gift of the Spirit? Perhaps Luke has taken an earlier story about a magician to make a definitive statement about the Spirit. That earlier tradition made a distinction between Philip's authority and that of the apostles. Luke wants to assert once again the primacy of the Jerusalem church in any new mission thrust. Or is Luke attempting to explain the contemptible behavior of a man who, although he was baptized, did not appear to be motivated or enlightened by the Spirit. We may be reading a segment of the tradition which predates the eventually standardized and unified pattern of baptism and laying-on-of hands. We do not know. What we can be reasonably confident about is that baptism, the laying-on-of-hands, and the reception of the Spirit constituted a unified action by the church (2:38; 19:5–6). We should not attempt to infer a disjuncture between the Spirit and baptism here as if the Spirit is optional equipment for Christians, an exotic "second blessing" for some but not for all in the church. Nor does this text offer any rationale or explanation for the institution of the later practice of Confirmation, a practice which was sometimes (disastrously) explained as the bestowal of the gift of the Spirit well after baptism. In fact, Luke has Peter and John come out to Samaria from Jerusalem to lay-on-hands, to complete the baptismal action, for it would be incomprehensible that someone could be "in the name of the Lord Jesus" (8:16) yet without his Spirit, that one could be part of the community without having the Spirit which made community possible.

Acts 8:26–40
The Unhindered Gospel

Peter and John return to Jerusalem, but the restless Spirit has other things in mind for Philip. In verse 26 the narrative continues, not with Philip but with "an angel of the Lord." Philip is the protagonist of this section, or is he? It is the angel whom we meet first, ordering Philip around, ordering him to do an absurd thing—travel down a deserted road at noon! This is not the first nor will it be the last time in Acts that someone will hear a seemingly absurd order from the Lord (e.g., 5:20; 9:11–12; 10:9–16).

Only the angel talks. Philip says nothing: "And he rose and went" (v. 27). Philip is compliant, obedient, taking no initiative on his own. Out on this deserted road Philip meets, of all people, an Ethiopian. Philip responds to the Ethiopian's questions about what he is reading, then the Spirit seizes him and takes him to Azotus. So who is the real protagonist of this story?

The eunuch Philip encounters on the desert road from Jerusalem to Gaza is described in considerable detail. Contrary to popular interpretation, he need not be a castrated male who was excluded from the temple (Deut. 23:1). Rather, we are reading a story about an important man, a foreigner, though possibly a Jew, a powerful person who has much power and authority as the queen's minister—except the power to understand the word of God. Yet he is willing to be instructed by Philip in "the good news of Jesus" (8:35).

Luke's audience would be fascinated with this Ethiopian. In the Greco-Roman world the term "Ethiopian" was often applied to black people. The Odyssey speaks of "far-off Ethiopians . . . the furthermost of men" (1:22–23). In other words, here is a person from an exotic land, the edge of the world, timbuktu, someone whose dark skin made him an object of wonder and

71

admiration among Jews and Romans (cf. F. M. Snowden). This warns us not to consider the Ethiopian as a despised or deprived person—quite the opposite. He is a powerful, though exotic, court official, a well-placed and significant person who is receptive to the truth. He beseeches Philip to interpret for him and then to baptize him. Here is an earnest inquirer who reaches out and is graciously included into the actions of God.

He is converted and asks what hinders him from baptism. Perhaps we have here in the word "hindered" a fragment of the early baptismal liturgy which asks of a candidate, "What hinders this person from being baptized?" an affirmation of the inclusiveness and graciousness of baptism (cf. Cullman, pp. 71–78). Whether or not this is the case, Luke certainly places this baptism at a strategic position in his narrative. The baptism of the Ethiopian official is situated between the baptism of Samaritans and, in chapter 10, the baptism of a gentile. The Ethiopian's religious status before baptism is left in doubt—we do not know for sure that he is a Jew, possibly he is a "God fearer" or proselyte, but we do not believe he could be a gentile. Luke leaves us with the impression that in the unhindered baptism of this man the evangelistic thrust has moved from Jew, to Samaritan, out to the boundaries of the world, at last to the threshold of the gentiles. Psalm 68:31 is fulfilled, ". . . Let Ethiopia hasten to stretch out her hands to God."

Furthermore, Luke's excessive use of divine prodding and interventions in this story—an angel giving directions, the Spirit commanding the presence of water, the Spirit carrying Philip away—are paralleled in only one other story: the story of Cornelius (Haenchen, p. 315). The mission to the gentiles depicted in the baptism of Cornelius, the presence of the gospel out here in the desert of Gaza with this Ethiopian of somewhat murky physical, religious, and ethnic status can only be attributed to the constant prodding of the Spirit. If the good news is being preached out there, it is the work of God, not of people. No triumphal, crusading enthusiasm has motivated the church up to this point, no mushy all embracing desire to be inclusive of everyone and everything. Rather, in being obedient to the Spirit, preachers like Philip find themselves in the oddest of situations with the most surprising sorts of people.

72

Eusebius says that the Ethiopian whom Philip baptized returned home and became an evangelist (*Historia Ecclesiastica*, 2.2. 13–14). While our text says nothing of this, we can understand how this lively story of an Ethiopian who appears from nowhere, responds to the gospel, and joyfully goes his way elicited an imaginative response from the church, for in his story we see what the good news can do.

Acts 9:1–19*a*
An Enemy Becomes a Brother:
The Conversion of Saul

Flannery O'Connor once said of Paul, "I reckon the Lord knew that the only way to make a Christian out of that one was to knock him off his horse" (p. 355). No passage in Acts is more familiar than the account of the conversion of Saul, yet few passages are more subject to misinterpretation (for one thing, the New Testament never says that Paul was on a horse!). Our familiarity with Acts 9:1–9 is part of the problem. The story of the Damascus road experience has passed into the lore of evangelical Christianity to be lovingly retold and reiterated as the paradigmatic instance of conversion to Christianity. When we speak of Paul's Damascus road experience, Luke's account is what we are talking about, not Paul's own sparse comments on the subject. Paul never describes a Damascus road experience. Even limiting ourselves to Luke's account, we may find that the story makes different claims for itself than later-day interpreters have made for it. If we attend to Acts 9:1–9 with care, we may be rewarded with new insights for today's church.

The first thing we should note is Luke's rather curious placement of this story. Why does Luke introduce it here? We must wait until 11:25–26 before Paul's mission begins in earnest. No sooner is Paul introduced here in chapter 9 than Luke drops Paul and takes up a long and equally engaging story of the conversion of a Roman centurion. We may miss Luke's point if we focus too exclusively upon Saul himself, as if this is an ill-placed first chapter in Paul's biography. The story of Saul's conversion fits within a larger context of concern over dramatic conversions. Beginning with Acts 8:4 we have read about the conversion of Samaritans, then an Ethiopian, now the conversion of Saul. With each story the conversions become more dramatic, taking us further from the nucleus of the original community in Jerusalem. Acts 9 constitutes an abrupt insertion into the flow of the narrative about the activities of Philip, but its insertion makes more sense if we see this story as another account of conversion that continues the movement of the gospel unto the ends of the earth.

We met this Saul back in 7:58. Luke calls him "a young man" who watched over the garments of those who stoned Stephen. But he is not just any young man, not just an innocent bystander. He not only approved of Stephen's death (8:1) but also led a violent persecution of the community. "But Saul was ravaging the church, and entering house after house, he dragged off men and women and committed them to prison" (8:2–3). Saul is introduced as a violent, active, resourceful persecutor of the young community. Luke then leaves Saul and his persecution of the church to tell a couple of conversion stories. By doing that, Luke has set the stage for the most dramatic conversion of all—the conversion of the most notorious enemy of the church, a man named Saul.

Acts 9:1–19 is but one of *three* accounts of the conversion of Saul. Only an event of the greatest importance would merit such repetition by an author whose hallmark is brevity and concision. Scholars have wondered about the relationship of the three conversion accounts. Some have speculated that Luke is drawing upon three different earlier sources. Others believe that Acts 9 is the core of the tradition about Paul's conversion while Acts 22 and Acts 26 are later Lukan constructions, which tell us more about Luke's theology than about Paul's conversion. Following our effort to take the text on its own terms, let us lay aside such issues and stick with the story, asking how the three accounts demonstrate Luke's theological development of various aspects within the original account of the conversion, paying particular attention to where this first conversion account is located within Luke's unfolding narrative (cf. B. Gaventa, pp. 52–95).

In sticking with the story, we may find it to be a bit disappointing from a modern point of view. An important story it may be, but we are told so little about the protagonist. Luke tells us nothing of Saul's background, education, or inner motives. Considering subsequent interpretation of this story in which great imagination is expended describing Saul's alleged inner turmoil, doubts about his faith, his experience of a dark

74

night of the soul, and so forth Luke's account is stark. About all Luke has told us is that Saul is "enemy number one" for the church.

Interpreters should resist efforts to read feelings and motives into Saul that Luke does not mention and should instead focus upon what Luke tells us. Saul was hard at work "ravaging the church" (8:3). Stephen reminded the mob that their forebears persecuted the prophets (7:51–53) and Saul's encounter with Jesus puts Saul in that company of persecutors. Stephen calls his enemies murderers; Saul breathes "threats and murder" (9:1). Saul's murderous activity is in sharp contrast to Stephen's final words, "Do not hold this sin against them" (7:60). Here is a faith strong enough to forgive even murderous enemies. Just how far this forgiveness extends will be shown in these verses. The joy of the Ethiopian which concluded the previous story stands in sharp narrative contrast to the portrait of a ravenous man "still breathing threats and murder against the disciples" (9:1). While there is much that Luke does not tell us, Luke leaves no doubt that we are reading *the story of an enemy.*

What happens to the enemies of the church? In answer Luke tells a story in four scenes:

Scene one (9:1–2): Saul takes the initiative in a search and destroy operation against the church. Saul, rather than the high priest, is the persecutor (v. 1). The persecution is not confined to Jerusalem but is taken out toward Damascus. There is no discussion of Saul's motives or goals. All that we can say about him for sure is that he is an enemy (reiterated in 26:11).

Scene two (9:3–9): Enroute to Damascus there is an abrupt interruption in Saul's journey. Thrust into Saul's program to save Judaism is the question, "Saul, Saul, why do you persecute me?" The light, Saul's falling to the earth, tell us that something quite extraordinary, abrupt, divine is happening here. Compare the double vocative, "Saul, Saul," with other stories of divine calling and interruption: "Abraham! Abraham!" (Gen. 22:11), "Jacob, Jacob." (Gen. 46:2), "Moses, Moses!" (Exod. 3:4). The question, "Why do you persecute *me?*" accentuates the close relationship between the risen Christ and his disciples. To persecute a follower of the Master is to persecute the Master. ". . . he who rejects you, rejects me" (Luke 10:16). Gaventa (p. 58) notes that nearly every other use in Luke-Acts of the verb "to persecute" occurs with reference to Paul (7:52; 22:4,7,8; 26:11,14,15). For Luke, Paul is *the* persecutor.

75

Saul's response is interesting. He wants to know who the "me" is whom he is persecuting. He fully intends to persecute those whom he regards as enemies of God. Can it be that the faithful persecutor of God's enemies has become God's enemy? Saul's address to the voice contains irony since he calls him "lord" or "sir." The one whom Saul now calls "my lord" will be his Lord, as the crucial turning point in verse six indicates. The voice moves from accusation to commission, indicating that this story is not simply about conversion but also about vocation, a call. Saul will not only become a believer but also a person with a role to play for God. With verse 6, Luke's portrayal of Saul as the bitter, active enemy of the church comes to a close. A voice, a presence, has encountered this Saul and now nothing about him will be quite the same. As for Saul's companions, they "stood speechless, hearing the voice but seeing no one" (v. 7). Is it not interesting that these others can be present and yet not see what Saul sees? They are unmoved by the event which is already changing Saul's life. Conversion, it would seem, while a result of the objective act of God in a person's life is also intensely personal, often confusing family, friends, and bystanders, who find it difficult to comprehend what has happened to the recipient of conversion.

The nature of the change is striking: Saul is helpless. He opens his eyes but cannot see. He is led to Damascus by the hand and is unable to eat or drink for three days. The one who was so active going to and fro, seeking letters of introduction, pursuing believers all the way to Damascus has now become passive, helpless, like a little child. Thus will Saul, the enemy, enter the kingdom.

Scene three (9:10–16): The one who once persecuted the disciples is now helped along by one of those disciples, one named Ananias. As is customary in Acts, Ananias learns what he is to do through a vision. Hearing his name called, he responds with the biblical, "Here I am" (cf. Gen. 22:1; I Sam. 3:6, 8). Ananias raises reasonable objections to the instructions of the vision. He has already heard all that he needs to know about this Saul "from many" concerning the terrible things that he tried to do to "your saints." Can it really be that you want me to go to this enemy?

The voice does not argue with Ananias. It simply repeats, "Go." Then comes the bombshell. This Saul is not simply an enemy or persecutor but a "chosen instrument," more, he is "*my* chosen instrument." The noun "instrument" is used elsewhere in Luke-Acts with the literal meaning of a container or vessel (10:11, 16; 27:17; Luke 8:16; 17:31). The calling of Saul is not simply to believe in Christ but to be a particularly chosen instrument of Christ who shall "carry my name before the Gentiles and kings and sons of Israel." The one who was out to persecute those who "call on the name" (v. 14) is the one who now goes forth to bear the name (vv. 15, 16). The call gives us a foreshadowing (although not in the exact order of occurrence) of Paul's future work. Haenchen notes that verse 16 exactly reverses Ananias's words in verses 13 and 14 (p. 325). The one who did much evil to the those who call on the name will now suffer "for the sake of my name."

Scene four (9:17–19a): Ananias does as he is told. He lays on hands and Saul is both healed and receives the Holy Spirit. No longer does Ananias speak about "this man" but to "Brother Saul." The despised enemy, the alien, has become a brother. Does Luke intend the phrase "on the road by which you came" (more literally, since the verb is imperfect, "on the road by which you were coming") to remind us of verse 2 where the "way" refers to the believers? On the way to do in the followers of *"the Way,"* Saul was turned around and set on the way. "The Way" is probably the earliest self-designation of the followers of Jesus, the earliest term for the church. Nearly every religion sees its converts as pilgrims, wayfarers embarked on a journey toward some new plane of existence. The Chinese *tao,* the Hebrew *halakhah* (rule, regulation, literally: the going) depict the religious life as an eventful path toward truth. Luke is fond of using the image of a journey as a metaphor for what it feels like to be a follower of Christ—a Lord who takes us from where we were to a new place we could not have gone without his call and his leading.

Saul's transformation is complete as he is baptized and receives food (the Eucharist?). We need not speculate on some sort of detachment of the Spirit by the laying-on-of-hands from baptism. The two are mentioned here together to stress their unity rather than their separation, although the initiatory pattern with which we are more accustomed is baptism followed by laying-on-of-hands. Verses 17–19a are a miracle story, sharing much in common with other miraculous healings in Acts. But unlike those healings, the focus is upon the subject of the healing rather than the healer. Ananias functions in the story as a model for discipleship. Lacking the official status of Peter or Philip, he is enlisted as a messenger of God and a mouthpiece for Saul. He addresses the feared Saul as "Brother," offering fellowship to Saul in much the same way as the apostles laid hands upon the once-despised Samaritans (8:14–17). The Lord's disciples are not only the prominent "heroes" of the faith like Peter or Philip but also ordinary folk like Ananias, who walk on stage for a particular mission and then exit as the story moves on. Ministry is a function (a job to do for the Lord) more than a status or a privilege. By the end of this scene faithful Ananias disappears.

Note the condition of Saul at this point. Once helpless and inactive, he now rises, is baptized, and takes food, once again responding to God but this time, according to Luke, responding to the Lord Jesus.

Having witnessed this drama in four scenes, we are ready to draw some interpretive conclusions. First, when we consider all modern attempts to psychologize the story, to reduce it to an account of Paul's inner turmoil, or the tortured, interior struggle of an individual before salvation, we find little support within verses 1–19. *It is the objectivity of the story rather than its subjectivity which strikes us.* It is not an account of what was going on within this man, Saul, but rather a story about a man who was encountered, quite objectively and externally, by something or someone from without. Something has happened to him; a voice has spoken to him, quite apart from whatever his own inner struggles may or may not have been. Conversion, according to verses 1–19, has to do with someone being approached by God (and God's representatives—Ananias and friends) and being changed in the process of that encounter.

Related to the first conclusion is a second: *Conversion, change of the radical kind worked in Saul is something Christ does, not something we do.* All of this has come to Saul as a gift. In his rather sparse comments about his conversion, Paul could speak of this as the period when he chose "to reveal his Son to me" (Gal. 1:16). Admittedly, it is a peculiar gift, since it is a gift which will involve suffering. We might wonder why Christ has picked this zealot as a "chosen instrument." But such questions, and attendant fanciful speculation, are irrelevant. The choices of God are usually inscrutable, particularly when those choices involve persons who are chosen to do the work of God. Saul joins a long list of reprobates (Jacob), murderers (Moses), and odd characters whom God has chosen as vessels for God's work. "You did not choose me, but I chose you" (John 15:16).

Which leads to a third, and related, conclusion: *This sort of conversion involves a journey from self-confident indepen-*

78

dence toward child-like dependence. The one who knows so much must become as one who knows nothing, one who must be led by the hand, healed, and instructed by the very ones he once despised. In this painful, baffling interim we turn and become as a little child. We progress by regression and go forward by falling backward. Such turning and helpless regression, accompanied by blindness, confusion, speechlessness, hunger, and childishness is, for this peculiar faith, the very beginning of wisdom.

The church hears such a story and marvels at the power of God to *transform the enemy into the brother.* Sandwiched between the episodes of the Ethiopian eunuch (8:26–40) and the conversion of Cornelius (10:1—11:18) is a story about how God chose to move toward the gentiles through the one whom the church feared and hated (cf. the interesting parallel in II Macc. 3 where God turns around an enemy who set out to persecute God's people). Saul is also called Paul (13:9). In his name Saul-Paul, one a Hebrew name, the other Latin, this former enemy will be a bridge between Jew and gentile.

Like Ananias, contemporary disciples must be ready to be surprised by God's transformation of our enemies into our brothers and sisters, for the church knows not who may be the recipient of the inscrutable choices of God (see *Reflection: Conversion in Luke-Acts*).

Acts is strewn with these accounts of conversion that demonstrate the cultural and social transformation which is worked when the gospel is heard and believed. Hans Mol (pp. 45–53) has delineated steps within the conversion process which illuminate Luke's accounts of conversion. The first stage he calls *"detachment from former patterns of identity."* Luke 3:8 has John the baptist urging the people of Israel to abandon their false securities and adopt a new pattern of life in expectation of coming judgment. In Acts 9:19*b*–31 we shall see Saul coming into the new community and beginning the process of developing a new pattern of identity. Next, Mol notes *a time of meaninglessness and anomie.* While Paul himself may not have described personal doubt and misery as a prelude to his conversion, Luke definitely describes conversion as involving a period of rootlessness and confusion. Paul wanders about blind; the Ethiopian is confused about what he reads in the Scriptures; Peter has a puzzling vision of a heavenly handkerchief (Acts 10—11). *A dramatic transition from darkness to light, from chaos to meaning,* is Mol's third stage of conversion. Acts 9

79

depicts a light from heaven and a voice which brought Saul to faith. He is blind and then he sees. Finally, *the faith community supports and accepts the initiate into their life together.* The newly converted Saul is welcomed, baptized, and shares in the table fellowship of the church. Paul says that he was given "the right hand of fellowship" (Gal. 2:9). The enemy is addressed as "Brother Saul." Conversion is not an individualistic attainment or personal possession; conversion moves one into the care and nurture of the body of believers. As we shall see in Acts 10—11 and its account of Peter's vision (and "conversion"), one never becomes so wise or adept at faith that conversion stops or one is immune from divine surprises. Conversion keeps on happening, the turning continues within the community (see *Reflection: Conversion in Luke-Acts*).

Yet none of this should lead us to conclude that every conversion is basically the same. Paul's conversion is a story about a call, a specific call to someone who is chosen for specific divine mission. *There is no indication that Luke attempted to make Paul's conversion normative for every Christian.* Acts 9:1–19a is a paradigm for the call of an *apostle,* a concern which will be made more explicit in our examination of Acts 9:19b–31. Different people come to Jesus along different routes, a truth which is self-evident when we note that this conversion is set within the larger context of a number of other conversions, none of which is the norm for every Christian except as every conversion is the result of an encounter with a gracious and loving God who does not leave us to our own devices, "For it is the God who said, 'Let light shine out of darkness,' who has shone in our hearts to give the light of the knowledge of the glory of God in the face of Christ" (II Cor. 4:6).

Acts 9:19b–31
The Persecutor Becomes the Persecuted

It does not take long for Saul's conversion to bear fruit: "... immediately he proclaimed Jesus, saying, 'He is the Son of God' " (9:20). His actions demonstrate that Saul has been converted for a mission. Behind the account of Saul's conversion in Acts 9:1–19a and this account of its immediate consequences is Luke's larger concern to lay the theological groundwork that will justify the gentile mission. The bringing of the gospel to the gentiles was not something which came about through human initiative, Luke argues, but through divine leading. Each step is validated through divinely given signs and visions, including the visions which were given to Saul.

In Acts 9:19b–31 Luke struggles with a more immediate problem. He has argued throughout for the preeminence of the disciples as those who have been witnesses to the resurrection. At the very beginning of Acts, Matthias was chosen to complete the apostolic circle that was broken by the death of Judas (1:15–26). Where does Saul fit into all this?

Luke depicts two types of disciples (Talbert, *Acts,* pp. 41–43), those Twelve who were with Jesus throughout his earthly ministry and those who are called later, like Saul. The Twelve represent the tradition of the community, the stories of origins which were lovingly retold and zealously guarded as time went on for the church. Those like Saul, who were not with Jesus from the first, witness on the basis of their present experience of Christ. As we saw in Acts 2, tradition alone was not enough for the first disciples. They had to wait for the gift of the Spirit, for experience of the presence of the risen Christ, before they could move out in power. Paul, who experienced the presence of the risen Christ, must wait until his experience is validated by the Jerusalem apostles before he can move out with the assurance that his good news is apostolic. He was warned that he must suffer for the name of Christ (9:16) and that promise is quickly fulfilled as Saul escapes by night from Damascus in a basket (v. 25; cf. II Cor. 11:32–33). But even suffering is not validation enough. Barnabas must take Saul before the apostles who listen to his story (after first overcoming their fear of the dreaded enemy) and are informed that Saul, the one who was once busy persecuting the church, is now being persecuted as one who is busy "going in and out in Jerusalem, preaching boldly in the name of the Lord" (9:28).

In his commentary on this passage, Munck (p. 86) is contemptuous of Luke's contention that Saul must appear before the apostles to have his conversion validated. "If it was Christ who had called Paul, the verdict of mankind could not have been relevant." His comment is typical of contemporary arrogance which elevates individualistic, personal, subjective experience over communal, ecclesial, corporate judgments. Luke-Acts knows no split between tradition or experience. Both are necessary for a full and faithful witness to the risen Christ. The

81

Twelve knew the facts of Jesus' career, yet still needed to experience his present power. Paul had a dramatic experience of Christ's power, and Paul himself stresses that he is on par with the rest of the disciples and that he came to an independent realization of the truth of Christ (Gal. 1). Yet Luke insists that Paul had to set his experience within the facts of the tradition. Both sets of disciples suffer for the truth, both serve the same Lord; though they come to him by different routes, both need one another to insure both power and fidelity in the contemporary community. Without the experience, the "facts" can be cold and dead. Without the test of tradition, our spiritual experiences can become radically subjective, severed from the community, and flights of mere fancy. Not every good news is *the* good news.

John Wesley advocated the fourfold test of Scripture, reason, tradition, and experience. Calvin emphasized the twofold call to ministry—God calls but the church must also call. These were later attempts to embody the wisdom portrayed in Luke-Acts of tradition and experience. Paul becomes the preeminent apostle to the gentiles in Acts, but Luke cannot make him the same as the Twelve. The two paths of discipleship belong together. Here is a warning against our contemporary tendency to devalue tradition and thus make truth the sole possession of "the arrogant oligarchy of those who happen to be walking about" (G. K. Chesterton's words). Someone's experience, even someone as invigorated as Paul and even an experience as dramatic as his, is subject to the examination and validation of the experience of the community.

The church is not only the validator of personal religious experience but a necessary component for its continuation and growth. In speaking of conversion two sociologists note: "To have a conversion experience is nothing much. The real thing is to be able to keep on taking it seriously; to retain a sense of its plausibility. This is where the religious community comes in. It provides the indispensable plausibility structure of the new reality. In other words, Saul may have become Paul in the aloneness of religious ecstasy, but he could *remain* Paul only in the context of the Christian community . . . This relationship of conversion and community is not a peculiarly Christian phenomenon" (P. Berger and T. Luckmann, p. 158). No matter how wonderful our experience, the experience can continue in us and can transform us only when it is embodied in community.

82

Finally, Acts 9:19*b*–31 suggests that conversion and subsequent discipleship often involve suffering. Up front Saul is warned that he must suffer much for the sake of the Christ who calls him (9:16). Saul's career soon fulfills the prediction. Not only is he the immediate victim of an attempted murder but he also encounters hostility and threat everywhere he attempts to tell what has happened in Christ. In Lystra, Paul is stoned and left for dead (14:19). He is beaten and imprisoned in Philippi (16:19–24) and forced to flee in Thessalonica (17:5–10). Today, when the good news of Christ is often presented as the best deal a person ever had, the solution to all personal and economic problems, and a good way for self-satisfied people to become even more satisfied, we do well to ponder the rough beginning of Paul's attempt to live out the good news. Discipleship, it would seem, is not necessarily the end of our problems but is more likely the beginning of problems which we would gladly have avoided if God had left us to our own devices. Before his conversion, Saul had the upper hand in life. He was in control, a persecutor of others. Now, after his encounter by Christ, he is a vessel, an instrument in someone else's project, one persecuted rather than persecuting. Luke's Paul may not be too concerned with the historical Paul's "theology of the cross," but the Paul in Acts will have ample opportunity to feel solidarity with the crucified One whom he now serves. Once again the community learns in the conversion of Saul that God can use even suffering and persecution as a means of spreading the gospel and building the kingdom. Spreading the gospel by word and deed is, after all, what discipleship is about, rather than self-satisfaction, happiness, and pleasure (see *Reflection: Conversion in Acts*).

For now, the church is able to live at peace, knowing that whether it be at peace or at war God is committed to the use of the church for the accomplishment of the kingdom.

Acts 9:32–43
Peter Heals Aeneas and Raises Tabitha

Older historical criticism of these stories about Peter yielded little fruit for the interpreter. The abrupt and discontinuous way they are inserted into the narrative, immediately after a rather coherent account of Paul's conversion, suggested only that they came from an older, more primitive legend about Peter.

Our approach is to inquire not into questions of how, when, and where but to seek what Luke was trying to proclaim by his literary presentation of these stories. What was Luke trying to claim about the gospel? The first story, the healing of Aeneas (9:32–35) is sparse, without detail or much development. Narratively and theologically it breaks into the expected flow of things. Peter goes "here and there" among them, rather prosaically going about his duties. Then, confronted with the paralyzed Aeneas, Peter proclaims "Jesus Christ heals you." Where there was helplessness, caughtness, and bondage, the word, the name, has created fresh possibility. Aeneas rises. What is more, Aeneas becomes a witness in his new vitality to what Jesus Christ can do, because many of his neighbors "turned to the Lord."

This vignette of the word creating new life where there was once only bondage prepares us for an even more discontinuous, abrupt insertion into the flow of things. At Joppa there was a woman named Tabitha. She merits the only use of the feminine form of the Greek word for "disciple" in the New Testament, a rather abrupt insertion in itself (considering the conventional scheme of relations between men and women). This feminine disciple exemplifies further discontinuity within the accustomed pattern of things. Here in this new community no one stays in his or her place. Common fishermen are preaching to the temple authorities, paralyzed old men are up and walking about and changing lives, and a woman called Gazelle heads a welfare program among the poor at Joppa. In her work Tabitha is busy making a new configuration of power in which God uses what is lowly and despised in the world to bring to nought the things that are (I Cor. 1:26–31).

Widows, by definition, are poor, on the bottom rung of society, without anyone to represent them or to protect them. These are the ones to whom Tabitha, the Gazelle, has given life. She dies and her life-giving work dies with her. The community sends for Peter, not telling him why he must come with haste. Her death has caused a crisis in the community. Now the most vulnerable ones have no one. Their coats and garments are tangible evidence of the life of Tabitha and what her death means for them. These widows do not concern themselves with questions of theology, are not interested in the consolations of the possibility of a better world someday. They are too poor, too consumed with the need to get by one day at a time for such speculation. Tabitha is gone; how will they survive? As Elisabeth Schuessler Fiorenza has noted, "in the first century—as today—the majority of the poor and starving were women, especially those women who had no male agencies that might have enabled them to share in the wealth of the patriarchal system" (p. 140). We are reading a discontinuous story of the marginalized, a story lovingly recounted by widows and people like them, a story which echoes II Kings 4:32–35 suggesting that like the prophets of old apostles bring power to bear on behalf of the poor.

Surprise! Death will not have the final say. There is a power loose which is able to break the last recalcitrant region (I Cor. 15:26). In this new community widows will not be left to perish. Tabitha is restored to them by Peter's bold word and act of solidarity. The name of Jesus Christ bears the same life-and-death-giving power as the creator of the whole universe. All the boundaries of life, the highest heavens, the breath of life obey his command. Yet the story says that this name belongs to widows and others who have no hope nor power except this name.

This new, discontinuous community, abruptly pushed into the flow of history, stands beside those who have no one, even as its Lord stands beside them. Lacking the power of the world, silver and gold, it has only one resource—the word, the name which transforms all structures and arrangements, changing them from structures of death into structures of life.

Luke explains nothing in these stories, nor can you or I as interpreters. How God's agents wrench life from death is not something so trivial as to be explained. The stories can only be told and heard, asserted, inserted into life as they are thrust into the flow of Acts. It is not Peter who turns our history inside out but the story, the story which proclaims that our history is not closed and that there is someone, some subversive reality, there for the widows of this world.

Every community, every family, every congregation exists within certain settled, fixed arrangements of power and weakness, life and death. People are told that there is a divinely established chain of being, a fixed order in which we are to find our place and stay there. Tabitha is to stay home and let the

85

men devise an affordable welfare system. Peter is to stay with his fishing nets and leave theology to the scholars, and Aeneas should obey doctor's orders and stay in bed. But the Word comes to these people in the presence of these who, like Peter, come out among them and stand beside them. These miraculous events are subversive of the present order, for they announce a new age, an age where reality is not based upon rigid logic or cause-effect circumstances but upon God's promise. Each miraculous intrusion is a sign that "If it is by the finger of God that I cast out demons, then the kingdom of God has come upon you" (Luke 11:20). Every time a couple of little stories like these are faithfully told by the church, the social system of paralysis and death is rendered null and void. The church comes out and speaks the evangelical and prophetic "Rise!" and nothing is ever quite the same.

REFLECTION:
Luke and His Fellow Jews

Any law enforcement officer will tell you that he or she would rather try to stop a bank robbery than to intervene in a domestic argument. In the kitchen or the bedroom, in an enraged altercation between husband and wife or brother and brother, someone is likely to be hurt. More people are murdered by relatives than by strangers. Family feuds are the worst fights.

Stephen's speech (Acts 7) is a recollection of troubles within a family. Stephen begins with the promises to Abraham "our father." The subsequent history of Abraham's family is the history of the unfolding of God's promise to bless. But it is, in Luke's hands, also a story of conflict within the family, of Joseph's jealous brothers who sold him into slavery, of Moses' rejection by his own brothers and sisters (Acts 7:23–29). There has always been trouble within God's family, says Stephen.

As we read Acts, we read of continued conflict within the family of God. The modern interpreter of Acts walks through a mine field in his or her attempts rightly to read the place of these "Jews" in Acts. This commentary has been guided by the assumptions that (1) Luke-Acts is the product of a long and

86

painful family feud within Israel and the church since the advent of Jesus. Luke was (2) probably a Jewish-Christian himself; by the time Acts was written, (3) any real hope of the church for the evangelization of Israel was over, and (4) Luke still felt it essential to base his proclamation of the gospel upon the gracious fulfillment of God's promises to Israel. Thus the title of this reflection: *Luke and His Fellow Jews.* So far as is possible, we must read Acts not from the spurious vantage point of gentiles standing next to Jesus, giving it to the Jews in Nazareth (Luke 4), but rather as members of the household of God with the Jews, for whom the presence of Christ is both blessing and judgment.

Luke's severe depiction of those Jews who reject the gospel may sound harsh, spiteful, and downright anti-Semitic to our ears because we later-day Christians have, in effect, traded places with that unbelieving segment of Israel who responded with violence to early Christian truth claims. Acts reminds us that in any age there are believers who would rather kill those who do not share their faith than to trust their truth claims to stand or fall on their own. Alas, this has been the sad story of the church's dealings with the Jews.

Even a superficial knowledge of the history of the church's relationship with the Jews should send a shudder down our gentile spines. The "sword" brought by Jesus first severed Jew from Jew and then in a singular perversion of the gospel severed Jew from gentile. Whether by the crusader's sword, Hitler's ovens, or Christian evangelism, the once persecuted church became the persecutor of Jesus' own people.

Of course, none of our later-day anti-Semitism explains Luke's account of troubles between synagogue and church in Acts. Luke never urges Theophilus to raise a sword against God's own Chosen People—to do so would negate the claims of the very gospel Luke is attempting to preach. Both Jews and Christians had been the victims of Rome's cruel response to religious disputes. The gospel was about another way.

David Tiede has argued that we must not view Acts as establishment literature, as an attempt on the part of the dominant to justify their newly-won dominance. Rather, Acts is an inner-Jewish attempt to come to terms with the devastation resulting from the abortive Jewish wars against Rome and the terrible destruction of Jerusalem in A.D. 70. This devastation affected Christians no less than Jews. Where was God during the devastation of God's temple and the bloody persecution of God's people? Was anyone among the faithful to be blamed for this tragedy? What is the hope for the future? Now that the temple is gone (Acts 7:49–50), how shall we be faithful? These are questions of the oppressed, arguments among those who have nothing left but the promises of God. The stakes are high and when much is at stake we can expect the arguments to be fierce. A family under great stress, under constant assault from without, dispenses with the pleasantries.

Yet we cannot read Acts without feeling uneasy about Luke's repeated instances of Jewish obduracy and persecution of the Way. Do stories like Luke's account of the stoning of Stephen contribute, if even subtly, to modern gentile antagonism toward the Jews? Yes, they certainly do, and may continue to do so unless care is exercised in the interpretation of these texts.

These are stories of Jew versus Jew, not Jew versus Christian. The church was the misunderstood, persecuted, minority movement fighting for its life. Every instance of rejection, every failure to convert—especially in the context of God's Chosen People—was a life-and-death issue for the young church. Acts is the world of faith viewed, in a sense, "from the bottom up," from the standpoint of a ridiculed, persecuted, ignored, religious minority hanging between life and death on the fringes of the dominant culture.

Interpretive perversion occurs when we thoughtlessly apply the witness of Acts to our very different situation. Where the church is a predominant culturally established majority religion, we dare not read ourselves back into the role of Stephen nor contemporary Jews into the roles of those who threw the stones. The reverse is true: We are the ones who have stoned God's prophets and made countless martyrs of God's Chosen. If there is a rebuke in Acts to those in Israel who resort to coercion, collaboration with Caesar, and violence to settle their theological differences, it is a rebuke to us. How sad that the heirs of Stephen and Paul, witnesses who knew what it means to suffer for the truth, eventually resorted to the tactics some of the church's critics once used against us. In this sense the presence of Jews continues to be a kind of scandal to Christians. We look back upon the centuries of Christian cruelty to the Jews and wonder why our gospel failed to give more of us the resources rightly to live with,

88

defend, and even to die for the brothers and sisters whom our Lord died to save. The church's relationship to the Jews, a central concern of Acts, continues to be a key question for Christians.

With so great a potential for misinterpretation of Luke's struggle with his fellow Jews, we can understand why some have sought to clean up texts like the stoning of Stephen and to expurgate these hostile "Jews," or transform them into nondescript "critics," rather than risk fueling further animosity between Christians and Jews. Others accuse Luke of being "anti-Jewish" and question the advisability of the use of these questionable texts by the contemporary church. These proposals are misguided. As teachers and preachers in today's church we cannot sidestep the challenge of history. These texts require us to deal with the possible historical context, Luke's motivations and our own. Rather than change the text, let us change ourselves, clean up our perception rather than history. How could a person like Luke who goes to such pains to ground his entire theology in the Scripture and the hopes of Israel, who feels such pain, resentment, sorrow, and anger for the rejection of the gospel by his brothers and sisters in Israel be anti-Jewish?

There is no way around the obligation to preach and teach Acts in such a way as to make clear that this book is the means whereby the contemporary church is inextricably wedded to Israel rather than a pretext for our severance from the people who first taught us gentiles to look for the Messiah. We Christians really do have differences with the Jews. Their story is not merely subsumed by our story. The church is not the replacement for Israel. Even though Acts 2 (and, indeed, the whole of Acts) reminds us that the message of Jesus was first believed within Israel, Acts also tells how the church eventually found its most fertile soil among these who had no claim upon the promises God made to Israel. Acts bristles with the astounding insight that "Then to the Gentiles also God has granted repentance unto life" (Acts 11:18). As Luke sees it, Israel became a light to the nations with an intensity that blinded many, even within Israel. Conflict between Jew and Jew over Jesus, so central to the purpose of Acts, continues to be an issue for Israel and the church.

The Jews really have failed to see Jesus as their long-awaited anointed One. In an attempt to overcome our anti-Semitism, we must not buy the fallacious argument (so dear to

89

the heart of all anti-Semites) that Judaism is no longer a theological problem for Christians because the Jews have ceased to be God's elected people. As Paul says, "the gifts and the call of God are irrevocable" (Rom. 11:29). We gentile latecomers will not get out of our dilemma with the Jews through some sort of liberal intellectual imperialism that first demands that both Christians and Jews be converted into bland, universalized Western American pagans before we can live together. The best way back to our brothers and sisters, the Jews, lies through places like Acts. The more clearly we come to see the blasphemy of our dealings with Jesus' kinfolk, the better we understand Christ as the fulfillment of the prophetic promises to Israel; the more keenly we feel the unmerited quality of our inclusion into those promises, the more quickly will be healed the tragic separation within the family of God. To the extent that we believers—Christian and Jew—allow our faith in God to be diluted through nationalistic loyalties, pagan philosophies, or other alien truth claims we forfeit the theological resources whereby we are enabled to live together as family.

Christ's lordship, the message proclaimed by the witnesses of Acts, cannot be surrendered as guilt payment for the sins of Christians against those who do not believe that the gospel is true. The story of Christ is not made credible by using the sword to compel belief or to suppress the story until it is so watered down that the Jews will not recognize its offense. The only way this story of Jesus is made credible is the way of Acts—by our willingness to live and die by the gospel, not to resort to the means of Caesar, to live lives which do not blatantly contradict the love of which we speak.

Luke told a story about a troubled family (Luke 15:11–32) in which a younger son after a lurid sojourn returned home in rags and smelling of the cheap perfume of harlots. The waiting father received him with joy. A party began. But the older brother—the one who never left home, who remained in the field, faithfully working for the father—refused to go in to the party. The father came out into the darkness and pled with the brother to come in, but to no avail.

In our day the story has taken a sad and unexpected turn, one Luke could not have imagined. The younger brother soon lost his repentant, contrite spirit. The shock of his father's gracious reception wore off. He came to resent his older brother's failure to party at his homecoming. He began to scheme against his brother, to take on airs, to forget how fortunate he was to be in the Father's home. At last he even resorted to locking his brother out of the house. He bolted the door and the party which had been a celebration for the reception of a penitent became the victory bash of the triumphant usurper.

The music and dancing continued. The smug younger brother had it all to himself. But outside in the dark still stood the Father where Luke left him, out in the darkness, standing where he had always been, beside the older brother. The younger brother had succeeded in locking out his brother, but alas, he had locked out his loving Father as well.

PART TWO

Witness to the Gentiles
ACTS 10:1—19:20

The Gentile Mission Begins
ACTS 10:1—14:28

In the church today sometimes the question is asked, "Will the Jews be saved, even when they do not believe in Jesus?" The question is raised by one who perceives him or herself to be an insider concerned about the fate of the outsider. From the standpoint of Acts, it is a curious question. In Acts the issue is not, "Will the Jews be saved?" That issue had already been decided at the dawn of history by the promises of God to Abraham and the rest—God will have this people as his own. Every act of God since then, *including the gift of Jesus and the Holy Spirit*, demonstrates God's fidelity to that promise. "For the promise is to you and to your children and to all that are far off, every one whom the Lord our God calls to him" (2:39). The fidelity of God to his promise to Israel is the very foundation of the good news in Acts. It was a fact that required little demonstration.

The question requiring massive argument and all of the theological and literary skills at Luke's disposal for an answer was, "Will the *gentiles* be saved?" The question had, for all intents and purposes, been answered by the time Luke wrote Acts. But its answer was not self-evident and the case could not be closed. Luke's church based its preaching on the truth and fulfillment of God's promises to *Israel.* But here was the church at the turn of the first century facing Jewish rejection of the gospel, which should have been theirs, and gentile acceptance of a good news that was not addressed to them. Luke wrote in that rather confusing if not embarrassing period when the church had to explain to itself how such a state of affairs came

93

to be and why. Like the rest of Scripture, Acts is the church's attempt to understand its experience of God, an experience which can be quite confusing when it leads us toward people whom we had not expected to meet.

Yet the contemporary interpreter of Acts knows that the church still exists in a confusing if not embarrassing relationship to the Jews. In what way is the good news of our brother, the Jew, addressed to us? How do we stand in relation to the people who first taught us to look for a Messiah? Few mysteries of faith are deeper than the mystery of why others are unable to see what we see, unable to have faith in the One who gives our lives their ultimate significance. One explanation is that we are religiously perceptive whereas they are religiously perverse, and Luke is not above hinting at such an explanation. Yet to say that demeans the very ones who are the source of our expectation and through whom our Savior came. Alternatively one might say that now, after millennia of loving actions, God has at last rejected his own people. As Paul so eloquently testifies in Romans, this cannot be the same God whom Christians worship if God is unfaithful to his Chosen Ones. Yet again, we might surmise that the Jews have stopped believing in God because they do not believe as we believe—and Luke sometimes implies this in his more polemical moments. But to accuse of unbelief and atheism those who suffered a thousand pogroms and watched their children die in the Holocaust and yet still believed is a disgusting smugness in which we gentile Johnny-come-latelys should not indulge (see *Reflection: Luke and His Fellow Jews*).

As interesting as such questions may be for us, they are not Luke's questions. By Luke's day, Israel's verdict on Jesus had for the most part been delivered. A group which first thought of itself as a sect within Judaism was out of the synagogues and on its own. The church was rapidly becoming a gentile phenomenon, a fact Luke, to his credit, could still ponder with amazement and gratitude for the graciousness of God toward the gentiles, rather than with our contemporary gentile smugness. While Jewish rejection of Jesus troubled Luke, amazement at the inclusion of the gentiles, as well as the lingering questions such inclusion raised, were Luke's main concern in Acts. The fate of the Jews rested as it always had in the hands of a faithful and just God, the same God who now, wonder of wonders, had made a place within his chosen family even for gentiles.

The significance of how that came to be is the concern of

94

the next chapters in Acts. The story of Cornelius, which ends with Peter's speech to the assembly at Jerusalem, is the longest narrative in Acts, a seven-act drama of sixty-six verses. Judged solely on the basis of the amount of space Luke gives to the story, we know that we are dealing with a crucial concern of Acts, a pivot for the entire book, a turning point in the long drama of redemption.

Acts 10:1—11:18
To the Gentiles Also

How did the church arrive at a turning point where insiders were willing to include outsiders? Beginning in Jerusalem the good news has been taken out into Samaria, then, with the conversion of the Ethiopian, to the very "ends of the earth" (1:8). What is more, Saul, a vile persecutor of the community, has now become Paul, God's chosen instrument. Where will the gospel go next? A marvelously constructed seven-act drama tells the tale (Haenchen).

Scene one (10:1–8): Enter Cornelius: A gentile, a Roman, a gentile Roman army officer. Luke says he was "a devout man who feared God . . ., gave alms . . ., and prayed constantly to God" (10:2). Yet does that blunt the impact of a story about one who made his living in the military occupation of someone else's country? Cornelius reminds us of that pious centurion in Luke 7:2–10 who received Jesus' compassion. So he is a gentile yes, and a Roman soldier yes, but also one who is devout, as Luke's tireless reiteration of the centurion's piety in verses 2, 4, 22 and 30 are meant to show. He is an outsider, but one who is at least on the fringe of the community. Furthermore, he is a gentile willing to be instructed and guided. Cornelius' movement toward the faithful community now called church is not a matter of his choice or his heroic decision. A vision begins the narrative. In the story Cornelius (like Peter) is an almost passive actor in a drama being directed at every turn in the plot by someone greater than Cornelius or Peter.

Scene two (10:9–16): Cornelius has had a strange vision. Now it is Peter's turn to be confused.

Peter is praying at noon on the flat roof of a home. A large sheet is lowered containing all animals (except for fish—how could fish be kept in a sheet? [cf. Gen. 1:24]). Peter is told to slaughter and eat. The voice says, in effect, "Come on, then! Eat!" Three times the voice commands, but Peter shows his loyalty to the sacred dietary laws and refuses. Only these laws stood in the way of the assimilation (and thus, destruction) of Jesus as Jews. They identified, demarcated faithfulness in the midst of incredible pressure to forsake the faith, drop one's particularities and become a good citizen of the Empire. A little pork here, a pinch of incense to Caesar there, and it will not be long before the faith community will be politely obliterated. We must not read this story from the safe vantage point of a majority religion where broad-mindedness and toleration cost the majority nothing, but rather, read the story as it was first heard—from the minority point of view, people for whom a bit of pork or a pinch of incense or a little intermarriage was a matter of life and death for the community. The dietary laws are not a matter of etiquette or peculiar culinary habits. They are a matter of survival and identity for Jews. And yet, can it be that these laws are being supplanted by some other basis for survival and identity?

No wonder Peter is left baffled.

Scene three (10:17–23a): Cornelius' messengers arrive at Joppa seeking Peter. Once more Luke reiterates the story of the angel's visit to Cornelius (as he will again in 10:30 and again in 11:13), for there must be no forgetting among the audience that the script for this drama is being written by *God.* Peter does not know where he is going or why. Rather, he trusts the story to work its way out. Baffled he is, but still willing to be led. Like Mary at the beginning of Luke's Gospel, Peter could say, "I am the handmaid of the Lord." Disciples are those who at times say, "Lord, I do not know where you are leading me, but here I am."

Scene four (10:23b–33): The gathering of friends and relatives encountered at Cornelius' home will form an audience when the time comes, as we suspect it will, for Peter to make one of his famous speeches. As the narrative unfolds note that it shuttles back and forth from Peter to Cornelius, back to Peter, then to Cornelius. Both men have visions, both make speeches. Thus Luke highlights the dual nature of what is happening. Is this a story about the conversion of a gentile or the conversion of an apostle? *Both* Cornelius and Peter need changing if God's mission is to go forward. What the gathering first sees is the

96

mighty Cornelius at the feet of Peter, worshiping him. Perhaps we are to read this action as typical gentile naïveté about religious matters—a gentile will worship anyone (or anything) if given half a chance to do so. Perhaps. Powerful militarist Cornelius does not look too powerful down on his knees, clutching the knees of Peter. Yet already Peter graciously instructs Cornelius' misguided devotion, "Stand up; I too am a man" (10:26). Whatever Peter has to offer this man, it is something more than the power of his own personality. Then Peter speaks to the gathering, confessing that he has breached Jewish law only because God has rearranged his notions of clean and unclean. The bafflement of the vision (10:9–16) is resolved. Notice how frequently houses and hospitality are mentioned in the story. Contacts between Jew and gentile create domestic, household, table-time problems. Conversion to Christ becomes a mundane matter of "Who shall eat at our table?" The great amount of space Luke expends on this scene is an indication of its importance. Through the dialogue of Peter and Cornelius Luke creates a scene in which old divisions are broken down and these who once were at odds—Jew and gentile—chat amiably within the home that had been off limits to Peter. Placed here, and treated in this fashion, the scene serves as a warm, touching hint of the joyous new possibilities for community toward which God is leading both Jew and gentile. As with Jesus, who was criticized for the company he kept at the table, so Peter could claim that "there will be more joy in heaven over one sinner who repents than over ninety-nine righteous persons who need no repentance" (Luke 15:7).

Scene five (10:34–43): Now for the sermon, a sermon which opens with a stunning confession by Peter: "I now know that God shows no partiality." The speech then follows the outline to which we have become accustomed in Acts—proclamation, scriptural proof, summons to repentance. God is not a looker upon the face, does not play favorites, shows no partiality. Can we hear what an upsetting, exciting, world-reversing word this must have been to those whose faith was based upon assumptions of partiality, who had suffered in spite of and because of this partiality, and yet still believed? It was not an easy word to hear. Throughout Acts, step by step, laying scriptural proof on proof, gradually edging us out of Jerusalem and into Samaria, now into Joppa, past the converted Samaritans and then the Ethiopian, Luke has brought us face to face with this Roman soldier so that we may feel the full blast of the gospel, may know the reluctance of the disciples to be here, may know how long and painful was their journey to realize the full and frightening implications of the gospel—God shows no partiality! The subject matter of the vision was somewhat ambiguous—does the "common" and "unclean" refer to food or to people? That has now been made clear. The issue, as it turns out, is not simply about "unclean" food but also about "unclean" people, about who shall sit at our table. More specifically, the vision is about our own inability to know what or who is clean and unclean.

Now it remains for Peter to justify his position by Scripture—no easy task. First he asserts that "in every nation any one who fears him [God] and does what is right is acceptable to him [God]" (10:35). A good thought, but one not supported by reference to any biblical text. Certainly, God sent Jesus Christ to Israel (10:36), but that statement will not help him with Cornelius. The aside, "he is Lord of all," becomes the basis for a consideration of gentiles within the scheme of salvation. Peter is not reading some new idea into the story; rather, he is further penetrating the meaning of the affirmation that Jesus Christ is Lord. Because Jesus has ascended to reign with the Creator of all people, in the resurrection-ascension both redemption and creation are linked in Jesus Christ. A vision of the Lordship of Christ, ruling with the Creator of heaven and of earth, is the basis for Christian efforts at inclusiveness. One cannot have a Lord who is Lord of only part of creation. So in any nation any one who fears him and does what is right "is acceptable to him."

Peter then recounts, citing the same events and material of previous speeches in Acts, the Christian proclamation. But a careful look at the sermon indicates that Peter has not simply found some good Hebrew text to justify why he is here with Cornelius and his kin. His speech is more than "proof texting." The affirmation of Christ's Lordship is a theological statement gleaned from the experience and faith of the apostles, not something to be proved from the Torah or prophets. Peter's sermon is an attempt to struggle with his recently received new perception of the movement of the gospel. He has no proof text to justify himself. He is out on risky terrain without tradition or Scripture to back him up.

This is the way it sometimes is in the church. If Jesus Christ is Lord, then the church has the adventurous task of penetrating new areas of his Lordship, expecting surprises and new implications of the gospel which cannot be explained on any basis other than our Lord has shown us something we could not

98

have seen on our own, even if we were looking only at Scripture. This does not mean an undisciplined flight of fancy into our own bold new ideas or the pitiful effort to catch the wind of the latest trend in the culture under the guise of seeking new revelation. Rather, it means that we are continuing to penetrate the significance of the scriptural witness that Jesus Christ is Lord and to be faithful to divine prodding. Faith, when it comes down to it, is our often breathless attempt to keep up with the redemptive activity of God, to keep asking ourselves, "What is God doing, where on earth is God going now?"

Scene six (10:44–48): Any doubts about the validity of Peter's new insight into the impartiality of the gospel are assuaged by the irruption of the Spirit, which descends on Cornelius and his kin as confirmation of Peter's claims that the author of this plot is God. Any potential dilemma concerning the baptism of gentiles is thereby settled, for who could forbid baptism after the Holy Spirit is already with these people (10:47)? The wind has again blown where it wills (John 3:8), and now the church must account for its movements.

Scene seven (11:1–18): The gospel is not about the solo efforts of one enlightened and progressive leader who takes it upon himself to baptize gentiles. When Peter returns to Jerusalem, he has some explaining to do to the church. The story of the vision is retold for emphasis. Luke softens the resistance of the church by saying that it was table fellowship with gentiles which angered the saints at Jerusalem, when actually baptism (or the problem of circumcision—see Acts 15) was the probable root of their anger, although the two go together since baptism would initiate someone into the table fellowship of the church. Is the "table fellowship" issue a matter of who shall eat at the Lord's Supper? Luke leaves it ambiguous, probably because Luke's church would know no distinction between "religious" meals and "nonreligious meals." Who shall be admitted to the church's table is a thoroughly religious question. Peter now says that "the Spirit told me to go with them, making no distinction" (11:12). The church's silence and then response shows that it realizes a bold (and perhaps frightening) chapter has opened in the saga of the People of God. To gentiles also has God granted the ability to turn toward life. The real "hero" of the story, the "star" of the drama is not Peter nor Cornelius but the gracious and prodding One who makes bold promises and keeps them, who finds a way even in the midst of human distinctions and partiality between persons.

Gentiles like Cornelius are included, not as those who are basically nice people after all but as those who, like Israel, are able to repent (11:18). Repentance, contrary to popular misconception, is not a heroic first step I make toward Christ nor is it a feeling-sorry-for my sins. It is the divine gift of being able to be turned toward truth. Turning toward the truth about myself and my situation is quite beyond my power to accomplish. Like Cornelius, I cannot repent—turn around—on my own. So God does it for me. In Christ, God has turned toward us and "granted," given, us repentance (5:31; 11:18). Cornelius is surprisingly passive in this story, as if he is someone who is being swept along, carried by events and reacting to actions quite beyond his power to initiate or to control. This is the way it is with repentance. It is more than a decision we make ("since *I* gave *my* life to Christ"; "since *I* took Jesus as *my* personal Savior") or some good deed we offer to God; repentance is the joyful human response to God's offer of himself to us, the necessary, quite appropriate turn of a life which is the recipient of God's gracious turning toward us. Repentance is an act of God's grace. Everyone, says Peter (10:43), Jew or gentile, virtuous pagans like Cornelius or zealous persecutors like Saul, may now turn, return, to God.

Later, Ephesians would remind gentile Christians like Cornelius that they were "separated from Christ, alienated from the commonwealth of Israel, and strangers to the covenants of promise, having no hope and without God in the world. But now in Christ Jesus you who once were far off have been brought near in the blood of Christ. For he is our peace, who has made us both one, and has broken down the dividing wall of hostility, . . ." (Eph. 2:12–14).

REFLECTION:
Conversion in Acts

Thus far in Acts we have observed a crowd transformed from scoffers into repentant believers (2:14–41), a person from the exotic ends of the earth enlightened and baptized (8:26–40), a raging enemy made into a courageous brother (9:1–31), and a gentile soldier adopted by the church (10:1—11:18). Luke-

Acts is rich in these dramatic accounts of change worked by the power of the Spirit. Whatever the Gospel is about, it is about change of mind and life. It is well for us to pause and attempt to draw together some of Luke's images of conversion.

A logical place to begin might be with Peter's statement that the crowd is to "Repent, and be baptized every one of you in the name of the Lord Jesus for the forgiveness of your sins; and you shall receive the gift of the Holy Spirit (Acts 2:38)." Is this Acts' scheme for conversion?

As we noted in our more extended interpretation of this passage, we should not lift out this passage and make it the one model for conversion. Nowhere else in Acts is this pattern mentioned. The account of the conversion of the Ethiopian shows the dramatic way in which the Spirit directs the community out beyond the boundaries to all sorts of people (8:26–40). This account sets the stage for perhaps the most dramatic conversion of all, the conversion of Saul the enemy into Saul the brother (9:1–19*a*), which in turn moves into the conversion of Cornelius (and Peter!) as the community is converted into welcoming even gentiles into table fellowship (10:1—11:18). This survey suggests that Luke's accounts of conversion are far too rich to be reduced to one factor or one scheme.

By placing the stories of conversion in succession, a circumstance that knowing Luke's way of organizing material could not have been by chance, Luke portrays the dramatic fulfillment of Acts 1:8: "See, in these persons, the gospel has indeed gone to the end of the earth." The crowd in the street in Acts 2, the Ethiopian, and Cornelius were all willing, inquiring converts. Saul, on the other hand, was a fierce enemy. But Acts 9 shows that the gospel has power even over its enemies. Even healing can become an occasion for turning, as the stories of the healing of Aeneas (9:32–35) and the raising of Dorcas (9:36–43) conclude with comment that many "believed in the Lord" or "turned to the Lord" after these acts of compassion.

Taken within the context of the unfolding narrative, we can surmise what these stories of conversion meant to the community. After Acts 7 the church is left devastated by the murder of Stephen. Will the mob and the principalities and powers have the final say over the future of the gospel? Does the scattering of the believers in the ensuing persecution signal the end of the Way? No! The story is beginning rather than ending—as the conversion accounts in Acts 8—10 clearly demonstrate

101

(Gaventa, pp. 124–125). Accounts of conversion are lovingly retold by the church as confirmation of the continuing power of God to create the Christian community *ex nihilo,* fresh in each generation by the power of the Spirit. The church, even in its most trying times, may take heart, knowing that all is not left up to us nor is the community of faith of our sole creation.

One could argue that Luke is uninterested in individual conversion stories per se. The individuals who are converted are, except perhaps for Paul, left with their personality and individual background undeveloped. They are not so much individuals or typical examples of conversion as they are symbols for groups of converts, pieces in the larger narrative of the miraculous expansion of the church. No conversion, not even of the crowd at Pentecost, not even that of Paul, established a repeated pattern which is appealed to in the preaching of Acts. Unlike some evangelical interpretations, never is a conversion story an end in itself. Conversions are a part of the larger story of some issue within the life of the community. The gospel, at least in Luke-Acts, is not simply about getting people converted for the sake of conversion. Although we have focused upon individual accounts of change and turning, these conversions, even the mass conversion of Acts 2, result in adoption into the community, baptism, and the breaking of bread and prayers (2:42–47). The community must confirm and interpret Paul's Damascus road experience through Ananias and Barnabas. The community must ratify Peter's actions and Cornelius' conversion.

In our radically individualized mileau and our attendant radically subjectivized approach to conversion, we do well to note the communal, corporate quality of conversion in Acts. Conversion is adoption into a family, immigration into a new kingdom: a social, corporate, political phenomenon.

Luke's rich collection of conversion accounts warns the church against making any one pattern or scheme *the* standard steps for conversion. The turning wrought by the Spirit takes a variety of forms, leads to a variety of responses, and is context-specific. Each person is called by his or her own name, so to speak, and dealt with as the Spirit sees fit. When was Peter converted? When Jesus called him to follow or when Peter confessed that Jesus was "The Christ of God" (Luke 9:20) or when Peter discovered that he did not, after all, know who was clean and unclean (Acts 10:1—11:18)? Luke will not let us settle down with one account or one moment. Peter was literally "on the way" as a member of "the Way." He resolved to follow Jesus, wherever that might take him. Surprises greeted him at each significant turn in the road.

David Steinmetz notes that the Protestant Reformers were so convinced that sin is so deep-rooted in human thinking and willing, that the gospel is so demanding and different, that only a lifetime of conversion can change us into the new creations God has in mind for us. The modern evangelical notion that conversion is an instantaneous, momentary phenomenon is not rooted in the thought of the Reformers nor, we might add, in the thought of Luke. Even Paul's dramatic encounter upon the Damascus road (reported three times in Acts—with significant differences in each account), required interpretation, reflection, and the confirmation of the community. Presumably, we never become too old, too adept at living the Christian life to be exempt from the need for more conversion, additional turning. The Christian life is akin to the way in which Luke organizes the life of Paul—a series of journeys, pilgrimages, excursions out into some unexplored territory where all that is known is the faithfulness of God. Conversion is a process more than a moment.

Conversions in Luke-Acts are *stories about beginnings*— the beginning of a new chapter in the life of the church, the initiation of a new mission, as well as the beginning of a new life for the individual person. Conversion is the beginning of the Christian journey, not its final destination. Moreover, conversions in Acts are *stories about vocation*—someone is being called for some godly work. Conversion is not for the smug individual possession of the convert, but rather for the ongoing thrust of the gospel. Finally, conversions in Acts are *stories about the gifts of God*—God is the chief actor in all Lukan accounts of conversion. Even the smallest details are attributed to the working of God. Conversion is not the result of skillful leadership by the community or even of persuasive preaching or biblical interpretation. In many accounts, such as those of Philip's work with the Ethiopian, the mysterious hand of God directs everything. In other stories, such as the story of Peter and Cornelius, the church must be dragged kicking and screaming into the movements of God. Manipulation, strategic planning, calculating efforts by the community aimed at church growth are utterly absent. Even our much beloved modern

103

notions of "free will" and personal choice and decision appear to play little role in conversion in Acts. Conversion is a surprising, unexpected act of divine grace. *"By his great mercy we have been born anew to a living hope . . ."* (1 Peter 1:3*b*; author's itals.)

Today, many associate conversion with the excesses of revivalism or razzle-dazzle electronic evangelism, where any means becomes legitimate and conversion is the beginning and end of Christianity. Even the use of the term is rejected by some "liberal" Christians. As we have seen in Luke-Acts, conversion is not a peripheral event. Acts was written, we believe, not to convert unbelievers but to confirm converted believers. Working on a number of levels, dealing with a number of issues, Acts seeks to help the church identify itself to itself, to confirm it in its struggles, and to help adjudicate its internal disputes. Conversion as evidence of the miraculous power of God to make the church the church and to overcome every enemy and boundary is at the very center of the church's life. We ignore the phenomenon of conversion at the peril of losing the church. Here is a God who takes me, "Just as I am without one plea," as we are fond of singing in the old hymn, but encounters with this God do not leave us just as we are. Too much of mainline Protestantism is focused not upon conversion but upon accommodation, adjustment, and the gospel reduced to the status quo. Acts reminds us that change, turning are part of the Christian lifestyle.

A church which has no quarrel with Caesar's definitions of peace and justice, a church enabled by its culturally accommodated preachers to lessen the gap between the gospel and the status quo has no need to preach conversion. In such a church Theophilus will be told stories of people who overcame personal anxiety, who found security in conventional truth, who kept with their own kind and stayed safely home. No one needs religious conversion or cultural detoxification to bed down in this church. But if the church hopes for more, for a new heaven and a new earth, for people who know the cost of discipleship and are willing to pay, then, as Hans Kung says:

> We are to preach *metanoia.* We must entice people from the world to God. We are not to shut ourselves off from the world in a spirit of asceticism, but to live in the everyday world inspired by the radical obedience that is demanded by the love of God. The church must be reformed again and again, converted again and again each day, in order that it may fulfil its task (p.438).

In a time when there is much talk of the need for more organized and scientifically managed methods of church growth, our study of the conversions in Acts raises some tough questions for proponents of many of these methods. If the church is only about the wholesale "winning of souls" by whatever method is deemed most effective, then conversion has become the end of faith rather than its beginning. In Luke-Acts conversion is a by-product of the gospel, the result of one's encounter with the power of the Spirit, not the gospel. Luke has no interest in the utilitarian question of *how* people become converted or *how* the church ought to evangelize, what technique is most effective or what method yields the most certain results (Gaventa, pp. 150–151). These are stories about *God's* actions, not the church's programs.

Acts 11:19–30
Two Congregations: Antioch and Jerusalem

The winds of persecution which were stirred at the death of Stephen bore the followers of the Way all the way to Cyprus and Antioch (cf. 8:1). Again Luke reiterates that persecution spreads the gospel both to Jew and to gentile (11:20). The gospel is like a wildfire—stamp upon it in one place, it will ignite in another. Now it burns brightly with nothing to hold it back, for even the barrier between gentile and Jew has been surmounted. As elsewhere, the evangelistic success of the apostolic preaching is not of solely human creation. "The hand of the Lord was with them, . . ." (v. 21).

We note that the missionary thrust into new regions is still being orchestrated by the Jerusalem community (v. 22). Recall that after Philip reached the Samaritans Peter and John were sent from Jerusalem to ratify the process (8:14–17). Paul's dramatic conversion was confirmed by an examination in Jerusalem (9:26–30). Peter's movement toward Cornelius must be affirmed by the saints at First Church Jerusalem (11:1–18). In 15:1–35 Jerusalem will debate the missionary strategies of Paul. Lest we miss the significance of all this direction from Jerusalem, let us remember that Jerusalem is where the Twelve are in residence. Back in 8:1, we were surprised to learn that everyone fled Jerusalem except for the Twelve. The Twelve form the

105

historical base for the Jesus movement. Acts begins by identifying the Twelve as those who were with Jesus from his baptism until his ascension (1:21–22). They are the apostolic link with the historic ministry of Jesus, the bearers of the tradition, the source from which the mission of the church flows, the court of last appeal in the midst of controversy. Jerusalem and the Twelve who reside there are Luke's way of indicating the tradition, the norm for what is truly Christian about the mission of the church (Talbert, *Acts* p. 48).

In a missionary situation, when evangelists are out on the boundaries, opportunities for compromise or corruption of the gospel abound. Some evangelist may become confused into thinking that the church exists for growth alone or success in conversions or the inclusion of all people at any price. It is not enough for the saints in Jerusalem to know that "a large company was added to the Lord" (v. 24). People may be attracted to this new movement for all sorts of reasons—none of which may be Christian! So Jerusalem dispatches Barnabas to Antioch to examine this new practice of gentile conversion to make sure that it conforms to the apostolic norm. Fortunately, "When he came and saw the grace of God, he was glad; and he exhorted them all to remain faithful to the Lord with steadfast purpose" (v. 23). In 11:18 the Jerusalem church had given its blessing to the gentile mission. Now that permission is confirmed, extended, implemented by scores of nameless preachers who scatter and preach the Lord Jesus. We are not surprised that Barnabas was able to bless the work among gentiles at Antioch; after all, we are told that he was "full of the Holy Spirit" (v. 24)—the driving force behind the gentile mission in the first place (1:8).

Was Theophilus' church embroiled in some later-day heresy that made it necessary for Luke to appeal to the power of tradition as a way of resolving the dispute? We do not know. But we do know that time and again the church has attempted to keep itself on track by looking back and letting itself be judged by tradition. Today's church may not be so convinced of the necessity for contemporary practice conforming to traditional norms. Why should we submit to the judgment of the Creed, the scrutiny of Scripture, the opinions of dead people? Many are suspicious of the past, seeing it as a repository of misunderstanding, injustice, and benighted ideas. The Bible is an ancient book, full of old, culturally determined values. Therefore we must make our own way, using our own experience as our only guide. We thus ignore our own culturally determined biases (for the bias of the past is usually easier to see than our own) and cut the church loose from its moorings. Jerusalem and the Twelve who reside there stand as a warning to the church that we ignore our past, we jettison the apostolic "facts" of our faith, at the greatest of peril.

We should also note what Barnabas does for Antioch. While he blesses the mission to the gentiles there, "Barnabas went to Tarsus to look for Saul" (v. 25). For what purpose has he gone looking for Paul? He has searched for Paul so that he and Paul might return to Antioch and spend a whole year *teaching* these multitudes of new converts (v. 26). Barnabas has graciously opened the circle of leaders to include Paul. Paul has been given the imprimature of the Twelve as a legitimate teacher of the church.

The dramatic evangelistic thrust of the church *must be judged by the tradition of the Twelve* and these *new Christians must be nurtured.* Whatever the mission to the gentiles means, it does not mean getting names on a membership roll. It means winning disciples for the apostolic faith in Jesus. In Acts being a Christian is clearly a matter of having experienced the presence of the risen Christ by the power of the Holy Spirit. But it is also a matter of having the facts, understanding. Like the Judaism which gave it birth, Christianity (for now Luke means for us to understand that we are dealing with a distinct and recognizable movement of faith—still within Judaism to be sure, but moving along a new path as well) is a religion to be discussed, learned, debated, and taught. It was "in Antioch that the disciples were for the first time called Christians" (v. 26). Here is a faith so strange, so against the grain of our natural inclinations, that only by careful instruction and long-term nurture can it be apprehended in the lives of those who would believe.

In Acts 2:42 we learned that the dramatic experience of Pentecost culminated with the church devoting itself "to the apostles' teaching and fellowship, to the breaking of bread and the prayers."

If it is really true that the church is a counter-cultural phenomenon, that the truth of Christ comes to us from without, that being a Christian is against our natural inclination, then the church ignores the teaching office on peril of losing its soul.

107

Nurture is not the opposite of conversion but part of conversion, and nurture will characterize a church determined to equip its members to withstand the corrosive acids of a culture that does not know Christ. The church is not only about *conversion* but about *nurture* as well.

Acts 11:27–30 at first reading may seem an abrupt insertion into the preceding accounts of evangelization and nurture among the new Christians at Antioch. Closer examination, however, suggests that it is a fitting culmination of this section. Agabus has foretold that there will be a famine during the reign of Claudius, possibly the Judean famine of A.D. 46–47. The new congregation in Antioch—composed of gentiles who a short time before were considered questionable subjects for the gospel—responds generously to the appeal for help in Judea. The story reminds us of the reports in 2:44–45 and 4:32–37 that the followers of Christ shared their material possessions and had all things in common. Admittedly, this sharing in Antioch is less dramatic than the earlier report of a commonality of goods and property, but it does indicate that the sharing of material goods continues to be a hallmark of the authentic Christian community. It is also a tangible sign that gentiles and Jews really are one within the church. These gentiles really have been converted, for they evidence the time-honored Jewish practice of philanthropy. As the Jews in Jerusalem generously reached out to include even the gentiles in the gospel, so these gentiles reach out to share what they have with their less fortunate brothers and sisters in Jerusalem. The church is not isolated congregations, each going its own way, looking after its own household. The church consists of congregations yoked to one another—older congregations like Jerusalem giving birth to new ones and guiding and nurturing them in the true faith; younger congregations like Antioch responding to fellow congregations in need.

In a few verses Luke has again given us a vivid picture of the true church. A church empowered by the Spirit is one energized to reach out to the furthermost bounds, to proclaim the good news of what has happened for all people in Christ. The response to this proclamation is followed by extensive teaching and careful nurture. Effective evangelization and nurture are confirmed by material responsibility and sharing. *Outreach, nurture, mission*—testimony that a new congregation like Antioch conforms to the apostolic pattern of older congregations like Jerusalem.

The interpreter of this passage would do well to avoid the restorationist tendency to read Acts' accounts of the early church as simple models for later church life. The history of the church is replete with attempts to "restore" the church of the apostles—attempts which ultimately failed. They fail because they idealize church life and try to organize the present church on the basis of the all-too-brief organizational comments within the New Testament. Idealization and romanticization lead to rejection when we find that there is no perfect community of faith, because there is no church without error-prone people.

Moralistic calls for the church to restore the primitive harmony of the church in Acts deny the whole story of the church in Acts. Of course, Luke is attempting to encourage Theophilus' church (11:23), and one does not tell stories of failure and defeat to those who need encouragement. Yet this makes all the more amazing Acts' rich portrait of the early church. Early congregations had successes, settled tough disputes, and cared for one another; but they were also beset by many of the same inner difficulties which plague contemporary congregations. Some members fall away, some lie, others split up the church into feuding factions, and not all are pleased with the leadership. Theophilus and his church may therefore take heart—few dilemmas of his church have not been encountered *and overcome* in the very first congregations.

The church's Lord has given the church the resources it needs to overcome its problems. Every time the contemporary church tackles a problem and works it through it is making a statement of faith that "the hand of the Lord was with them" (11:21). This is not some impossible ideal but the real possibility for ordinary people who find their lives caught up in the workings of God, who trust the Spirit to enable the contemporary church to find its own creative solutions to contemporary challenges to the church.

We do well to ponder the way Luke ends these accounts of congregational life at Antioch and Jerusalem with mention of *money.* Not content to let us bask in the bright glow of successful evangelization of pagans or new church development, Acts insists that we attend to the significance of what the church does with its gold. Judas betrayed his Lord for cash (1:18). Ananias and Sapphira deceived the Holy Spirit and died because of money (5:1–11). Simon appeared a fool in trying to purchase the Holy Spirit (8:18). Later, we shall see Paul and Silas jailed when they disrupt the business practices of some Philippians (16:16–

109

24). The silversmiths of Ephesus rioted when the gospel disrupted their source of income (19:23–41). Love of money is one of the most insidious forces with which the gospel must contend. The battle between the truth of Christ and our homage to cash is relentless.

Yet the Lukan picture of money is not without its positive features. Even though the first Christians shared what they had, Luke assumes that they did own property (2:45; 4:37; 5:4). To be with others in the church is to commit oneself and ones goods to the needs of others in the church. "Private" property becomes a misnomer within the fellowship. When gentile converts in Antioch share their wealth with their sisters and brothers in Jerusalem, they are keeping wealth in its proper place. Donald Juel notes that centuries later Emperor Julian the Apostate complained that, "It is disgraceful that when no Jew ever has to beg, and the impious Galileans [Christians] support not only their own poor but ours as well, all men see that our people [Roman pagans] lack aid from us" (p. 93).

Jesus excoriated the Pharisees, telling them that ritual purity was not as important for their spiritual well-being as almsgiving (Luke 11:40–41). When Jesus lectured on the duty of charity (Luke 16:9–13), Luke observes, "The Pharisees, who were lovers of money, heard all this, and they scoffed at him" (Luke 16:14). In Acts the Christian community is shown to be adhering to the best traditions of Israel in its almsgiving. It is not a matter of reaching out to the "deserving poor" or "helping the poor to help themselves"—the puny justifications for charity one often hears today. Almsgiving is obedience to God's will.

Conversion is proved by charity. If the rich ruler desires to follow Jesus, he must go sell all and distribute to the poor (Luke 8:18–30). Zacchaeus must give half of all of his goods to the poor (Luke 19:1–10). Genuine repentance is accompanied by a change in one's relationship to one's own goods as well as generosity to the poor.

One senses a declining emphasis upon philanthropy within today's church. An older generation of Christians, nurtured in concepts of tithing of income and generosity toward the mission of the church, appears to be passing. Today we look to the government or to private philanthropic agencies to spread the wealth and to care for the unfortunate. We denigrate yesterday's "charity" as ineffective, paternalistic, and self-serving. Yet how much material responsibility do we feel for the less fortunate—even those within the church? My money is my business. What I give is a purely private affair. Pass more social legislation and spend someone else's tax money rather than call upon me for charity. We are more adept than Ananias and Sapphira (5:1–11) in deceiving ourselves about our selfishness and our acquisitiveness.

Acts 12:1–25
Persecution and Deliverance: Beware of Kings

"Herod the king laid violent hands upon some who belonged to the church" (12:1)—literally: stretched out his hand to do evil—a favorite expression within the Septuagint translation of the Hebrew Scriptures. That is what kings can do. They can merely stretch out their hands or say a few words or with the stroke of a pen send thousands of innocents into oblivion. In Mark 6:17–28 Herod beheads John the Baptist, because the king was pleased over a particular dance at his banquet. And in Matthew 2:16–17 Herod kills all male children in the region of Bethlehem rather than risk future competition for his throne. Luke may not know these stories of Herod's evil, but still depicts him as a vile enemy of the church. First, Herod kills James, the son of Zebedee (12:2); then he arrests Peter (12:3–5a). Back in Acts 4:25–26, Peter explained Pilate's actions by quoting the first verses of Psalm 2:

> "Why did the gentiles rage,
> and the peoples imagine vain things?
> The kings of the earth set themselves in array,
> and the rulers were gathered together,
> against the Lord and against his Anointed."

Even as Herod and Pilate conspired against Jesus, so they now rage against his followers.

Ironically, Peter's imprisonment comes during Passover, the feast of unleavened bread, the great and festive day of deliverance from Egyptian slavery. This day finds Peter languishing in bondage, not celebrating liberation. The people who once saw God deliver them from slavery now make prison-

111

ers of their own kin during the feast of liberation—a bitter irony Luke does not want us to miss.

But the church swings into action, using its power against the power of Herod. Will the church at last get the point, take up the sword as Peter tried to do after the Last Supper (Luke 22:47–51), and this time do more than take off a bit of ear? No. That sort of political expediency has ended for the disciples. "No more of this" (Luke 22:51)! The power of the church is the power of prayer—a seemingly impotent force in the face of Herod's legions. We might have hoped for some more effective political action against this injustice and oppression by the state!

The very night when Herod planned to bring Peter out (to kill him as he killed James?), a miraculous visitation by an angel delivers him from prison. The light, the angelic command, the chains falling away are all meant to be dramatic evidence that nothing can prevent the movement of God—even the chains and the prisons of Herod. What happens to Peter is too good to be true and Peter is incredulous (12:9). The delightful, almost comic aftermath at the home of the mother of John Mark shows that the whole church shared Peter's incredulity. The slave-girl who claimed to have seen Peter free and liberated was judged to be insane by those who were supposed even then to be celebrating the power of God to liberate. She must have felt like her sisters—Mary Magdalene, Joanna, Mary the Mother of James, and the other women—who tried to convince the incredulous men of the liberation worked in Jesus' resurrection (Luke 24:10–11). Such evangelistic testimony of liberation by those who are themselves in bondage is bound to seem "an idle tale" (Luke 24:11).

We who live in a time of almost religious reverence for the power of the state should sympathize with the amazement of these Christians. We look to the almighty state for our security, our well-being, our protection, and care of all the vulnerable and the needy within our society. The state gives us our identity, our ultimate loyalties as we step into line behind the flag, the fatherland, and national self-determination. The state has become our most commonly accepted means of self-transcendence, our means of insuring ourselves against all the vicissitudes of life. We complain about the nuclear armament of the modern state but have little way to extricate ourselves from our nuclear weapons, since our state needs much power in order to protect us. Like a god, our state promises us either ultimate security behind the balance of terror of the nuclear shield or else ultimate annihilation after the mutual destruction of nuclear war. The state holds for us the powers of life and death. Who can fight city hall? Can we understand that little band of Christians who huddled behind closed doors, fearful of the evil hand of Herod and his soldiers, incredulous that any power, even the power of God, could prevail against such a hand?

> "The Spirit of the Lord is upon me. . . .
> He has sent me to proclaim release to the captives, . . .
> to set at liberty those who are oppressed, . . ." (Luke 4:18).

Jesus' inaugural sermon in Nazareth receives its fulfillment in the free man who, even now, bangs at the door of the church to tell the assembled disciples that powerful Herod is impotent to stop the gospel (12:24). Will the church open the door to receive the one who has been freed by the opening of Herod's door?

From the horrible murder of James, to the frightening imprisonment of Peter, to his liberation, to the comic scene at Mary's house, to the murderous rage of Herod, Luke takes us to a concluding episode which marks the demise of Herod. The story in 12:20–23 is Luke's variant of a tradition found in Josephus (*Antiquities,* 19:8:2). Luke reworks the story in some significant ways. In Josephus' account the sun's reflection from Herod's silver armor elicits the crowd's acclamation. His bright armor makes him *look* like a god. In Acts, Herod makes a speech that makes him *sound* like a god. Luke, who has already demonstrated his great love for speeches, gives us not a word of Herod's great oration. Who cares what Herod says? The effect of the speech is what concerns Luke. The poor, starving people of Tyre and Sidon, under the assumption that flattery will get you anywhere, acclaim Herod as the best speaker they have ever heard—even better than God. Acts suggests two possible responses for subjugated, desperate people—submissive, blind adulation of the tyrant (the people of Tyre and Sidon) or subversive refusal to bow down before any other gods save the true God (Peter and the church). If people bow and scrape before the tyrant and flatter his speeches, it is not long before the tyrant starts to believe his own publicity releases. A king who takes upon himself airs of divinity—with his bright robes, pomp, and orations—begins believing that he is God. Oppressed, hungry people take note: Liberation comes in many

113

different forms, among them forms of liberation which are but other forms of oppression. There is liberation (Herod's brand) and then there is salvation.

The response of God to such silly presumption on the part of kings is swift, ruthless, pitiless, ugly desecration. Herod becomes food for worms. God is not nice to those who try to be God. Hitler perishes huddled in a bunker in Berlin. Mussolini is hung upside down. Thus ever to tyrants. Next to this ugly scene of Herod being devoured by worms, Luke laconically remarks, "But the word of God grew and multiplied" (v. 24). Herod has made his speech to the rapt approval of the starving people of Tyre and Sidon and is now silent. But the Lord's speech continues to explode into the world, multiplying, spreading, overtaking the world once held within the tight fist of the tyrant. As Mary warned in her *Magnificat*, the proud shall be humbled (cf. Luke 1:52–53; 14:11) in this new kingdom which is breaking other kingdoms. God, not kings, will have the last word.

Even though Luke-Acts has some rather positive things to say about rulers and the state (cf. Luke 7:1–10; Acts 13:4–12; 18:12–17; 19:23–41), rulers can overstep their proper functions and fail to "render to Caesar the things that are Caesar's, and to God the things that are God's" (Luke 20:25). When they do, God will deal with them in the harshest way, the way God has always dealt with tyrants and demigogues. Nothing, not even the power of Ceasar, must hinder the movement of the gospel (see *Reflection: The Politics of Luke*).

This story of deliverance is one of many in Acts. There will be others (cf. 16:11–40; 19:23–41). We expect that their cumulative desired effect was to fill Theophilus with hope. There is a possibility that Theophilus himself, or the church for which he stands as a representative, was in prison. But would Luke's gallery of pictures of miraculous deliverance have the opposite effect? Accounts of a dozen stupendous cures and miraculous answers to prayer might boomerang against the claimant. Tales of divine deliverance through prayer might fuel Theophilus' despair as easily as they would strengthen his faith. A person told by a television evangelist that "If you *really* have faith, you will be healed" is vulnerable to despair if healing does not come. The interpreter of these miraculous stories should consider the need to present them in such a way that confidence in God is tempered with realism and humility. Peter escaped

114

the long arm of Herod and was spared for yet another day of preaching the good news—but for a time only. The gospel continues unhindered, even though the bearers of the gospel may not.

The Politics of Luke

The conversion of Cornelius (10:1—11:18) affords an opportunity to reflect upon a central motif of Acts—the relationship of the developing church to the Roman Empire. Haenchen sees as a key to understanding Acts the fact that by "cutting adrift from Judaism Christianity also loses the toleration which the Jewish religion enjoys" (p.100). Haenchen felt that Luke wrote Acts to defend Christianity against the (Jewish?) charge that Christians are subversive to the state. Here are the basics of Haenchen's argument: As a tolerated religion, Judaism enjoyed a degree of Roman toleration; but the Romans could have had little understanding or sympathy for an upstart Jewish sect like the church. So Luke argues before Theophilus (a Greek name; was he also a Roman official?) that Christians are the true Israel—devout temple-goers, keepers of the law who refuse unclean food and fraternization with gentiles. Because of steadfast Jewish resistance and rejection to the gospel, the gospel went elsewhere—to the gentiles—but gentile converts were still required to keep the Jewish law insofar as they were bidden by the Hebrew Scriptures (15:21; 21:25). The church is now the true Israel, entitled to whatever rights Israel once had in the Empire.

G. B. Caird (p. 14) notes that Christians were blamed by Nero for the fire which burned half of Rome in July of A.D. 64. Up to this point, Roman officials seem to have made little distinction between Christians and Jews. Christians rode in on the legal coattails of the Jews, so far as their treatment by the Romans was concerned. Caird believes that Luke-Acts was "the first great apologia for Christian faith," intended for publication and written primarily for readers outside both synagogue and church. Luke, according to Caird, wanted to show that Christ and his followers at every turn in the story were treated with deference by Roman officials and declared innocent of political subversion by Roman law: the procurator Sergius Paulus lets himself be converted (13:12); Gallio dismisses a Jewish complaint against Paul (18:15); the Ephesus town clerk defends the Christians against the charge of profanation (19:37); Claudius Lysias (23:29), Felix (24:22), and Festus (25:4) refuse to convict Paul on the basis of charges brought against him and allow him to carry on his work "unhindered" (28:31). This word "unhindered," the very last word in Acts, could serve as a statement of the purpose of Acts and an appeal to the Empire to leave Christians alone (Haenchen, p. 102; Frank Stagg, "The Purpose and Message of Acts").

Haenchen's and Caird's depictions of Acts as an early apology or defense for the church to Rome reflect their own interpretive biases about the place of the church within society. The characterization of Acts as an apology to Rome is based more on liberal theology's attempt to reduce all theology to the task of translation and apology to culture than on the New Testament itself. Confronted by the powerful, self-confident culture of the modern world, liberal interpreters assumed that the major task of the church was to interpret itself to this culture, to make itself comprehensible and therefore acceptable to a world that did not recognize Jesus Christ as Lord. A favorite technique of liberal apologists for Christianity was to argue that religion is really at the core of all great civilizations, and since Christianity is demonstrably the greatest of all religions, it can contribute to the development of the very best of cultures. Christianity is thus defended on the basis of its utility in producing true civilization. In our own era theologians as diverse as Walter Rauschenbusch and Reinhold Niebuhr spoke of Christianity as a valuable contributor toward the development of a more democratic America.

But is this a purpose of Acts? The church of Acts holds no brief for Hellenistic culture. Luke's arguments are thoroughly Jewish. His audience is not the culture but the church which struggles to be faithful, even within a beautiful and seductive culture. Furthermore, Luke's church was not (despite the possibility of governmental persecution) on the defensive but on the offensive. Accommodation to Rome's "cultured despisers" (Schliermacher) was not the name of Luke's game. Greek culture would not become significant for Christian writers until the third century, when men like Clement and Origin, products

116

of the best that the culture had to offer, attempted a transposition of Christian categories into térms more comprehensible to the Empire. Luke however had no interest in their enterprise, no concern to clean up the church for Caesar, nor should we later interpreters of Luke-Acts.

An appeal for the church as a tolerated religion could be a subsidiary purpose of Acts, but it is unlikely. The arguments which Luke sustains in Acts, with tireless citation of texts from the Hebrew Scriptures and continuous assertion of who is the real faithful Israel, would have been incomprehensible to any outsider who had not devoted his or her life to a study of Israel and its Scripture. Besides, it is doubtful that Felix's counterparts in the imperial bureaucracy would be flattered by the portraits of official Rome in Luke-Acts.

Luke's church is persecuted and misunderstood by a wide array of adversaries: Sadduccees, Pharisees, Herodians, merchants with vested interests, as in Philippi and Ephesus, as well as Romans. The Roman officials in Acts do not actively go out and seek Christians for persecution. No doubt, the Romans could not have cared less about internal Jewish theological squabbles as long as they did not threaten Caesar's version of law and order. Whenever Jewish infighting bubbled over into civil disturbance, Roman governors had to step in, and usually did so in typically Roman imperial fashion—with ruthless brutality. A young Rabbi named Jesus was one of the many victims of the Roman desire to keep their brand of peace and justice within occupied territories.

By the time Luke wrote Acts, possibilities for the wholesale conversion of Israel were over. The future of the church and its impact on history (for Luke was having to struggle with the significance of the church in ongoing history since there was no immediate parousia) lay with gentiles like Cornelius in places like Rome. So we do see Luke struggling with the place of the gentiles in the unfolding story. It is a struggle, not because the church must somehow usurp Israel's legal status in the eyes of Rome *but because the very nature of the gospel renders problematic and subservient any relationship other than the relationship of the believer to Christ.* The church had a real problem with the authorities, whether they be Jewish authorities trying to keep power and peace within the synagogue or Roman bigwigs bent on keeping Jews in their place, because the church demanded so much of its converts.

117

In the Roman world religion was the servant of the *res publica*. The emperor cult was thought to be essential for the stability of the state. Academics and intellectuals like Marcus Aurelius, Lucian, and Celsus heaped scorn on Christianity as silly irrationality mainly because they feared that it would have a divisive effect upon the Empire. Even before the days of government research grants, the intelligentsia could be counted upon to provide a rationale for the political status quo.

The church became a new *polis*, a new nation for those who were baptized. In comparing the church to other voluntary associations in the Roman world, Wayne Meeks says that "Christian groups were exclusive and totalistic in a way that no club or even any pagan cultic association was . . . to be 'baptized into Christ Jesus' . . . signaled . . . an extraordinarily thoroughgoing resocialization, in which the sect was intended to become virtually the primary group for its members, supplanting all other loyalties" (p. 78).

The church reconceived Israel's concept of the covenant people. Covenant people are those who are called by God to be part of divine destiny. Even as God had chosen Abraham, Isaac, and Jacob to be recipients of a promise, to know something, to be "a light to the nations" (Isa. 42:6), so God had chosen a gentile, Cornelius. The dearly held social, ethnic, and sexual differences that dominated the Roman world were eliminated in this new covenant community which told its converts that "There is neither Jew nor Greek, there is neither slave nor free, there is neither male nor female; for you are all one in Christ Jesus. And if you are Christ's, then you are Abraham's offspring, heirs according to promise" (Gal. 3:26–29). Joining this new *polis* overturned all older politics.

What was Cornelius supposed to do after his conversion? Did he go back to his soldiering? We know from Hippolytus' picture of life in the church at Rome of the second century that soldiers or anyone else (philosophers, whores, artists) who helped to prop up the accoutrements of the pagan state were not admitted for baptism until they forsook their questionable occupations. But Luke does not say that Cornelius dropped out of Caesar's army. When soldiers asked John the Baptizer what they should do, John tells them to "Rob no one by violence or by false accusation, and be content with your wages" (Luke 3:14). When Jesus healed another centurion's slave, Jesus commented that he had not seen such faith "even in Israel" (Luke 7:9).

Perhaps these centurions are worthy of special note in Luke-Acts because they were so exceptional. Here were men who had pledged their highest allegiance to Caesar—to die for him and to kill for him as the god he claimed to be. And yet they were having their loyalties rearranged by the gospel. If faith can be found among *even* a powerful, arrogant army officer who says "Go" and "Come" to a hundred soldiers (Luke 7:8) and if another centurion can be converted and gifted with the Spirit (Acts 10:1—11:18), then *anybody* can be saved, *anybody!*

Then, as now, it would be difficult for Luke's church to imagine a more powerful adversary and competitor for the gospel than the state. Conversion of these who once made their living from the state and who derived their identity from service to the state would be spectacular indeed, even more spectacular than today when some convicted killer (or Hollywood movie star!) becomes a Christian. Rather than putting forth a rosy view of relations between the church and the Empire, Luke shows why the Empire is coming apart at the seams because of this new movement called "church." It is no small thing that the first gentile convert is a Roman soldier. Rather than depict the evangelization of the Empire as a gradual, cautious, respectful enterprise, Luke pulls out all the stops and slaps his readers in the face with the stunning assertion that the first convert was one of Caesar's finest—a centurion named Cornelius. Thereby we know that the church has every intention of going head-to-head with the Empire. The gospel will go to all and will change everything—even despised centurions.

We do not know where Cornelius went after his conversion. That concern is not part of Luke's story. It cannot be that he returned to business as usual because nothing the Spirit touches can do that. Change, reorientation is the name of the game. This is due to the nature of the gospel. Once a person is able to confess that Jesus Christ is Lord, to turn over his or her life to the direction of the Spirit, then Caesar and all that his world is built upon is in peril. Even though Luke appears to have no great animosity against Roman functionaries like Felix or Festus, and even on occasion shows them to be useful in the protection of Christian missionaries, he depicts them as rather

119

dumbfounded and perplexed by what they hear from the Christians. As Paul said, "None of the rulers of this age" understood who Jesus was, "for if they had, they would not have crucified the Lord of glory" (I Cor. 2:8). Poor Felix and Festus lack the political imagination to conceive of a world other than that ruled by Caesar. There is a sense of foreboding behind the testimony in their courts, as if they are part of a world beginning to crack. They are more sophisticated than some of the adversaries on the council at the temple, but they are in the final analysis about as stupid, cowardly, and inept as any other powerful official. They keep passing Paul along, like the political hot potato he is, unable to silence him or to figure him out. Even though Luke portrays positively the benefits of the *pax Romana* for missionaries like Paul (see the discussion of Acts 21:27—22:21), the church does not need Roman toleration to do its work, for the witness will continue whether Caesar sorts it all out or not. Caesar and his functionaries provide a mere backdrop, a stage set for a drama which has many more cosmic and global implications than even the bounds of his far-flung Empire. When Jesus stood before Pilate, the Jews charged that Jesus had set himself up as Caesar's rival, "an anointed king" (Luke 23:2); and in Acts 17:6–7 Paul's enemies charge that Paul has upset the whole world and violated Caesar's decrees, declaring that there is another emperor. Of course, these charges are made by opponents and are false. Yet there is more truth in them than the opponents knew. In Christ, Caesar has met his match.

Wherever the church finds itself today, it acts its drama before a similar backdrop. Since Luke's day, the state has assumed power and influence, efficiency and control Caesar would envy. The state has become, for millions of moderns, the ultimate source of identity. As the significance of the individual has decreased, the power of the state has increased proportionately. We look to our government to provide for our security, our safety, our comfort, our identity. The millions of persons who have been sacrificed to this alternate deity in this century alone—in wars of national pride and conquest, in the gulag and the concentration camp, in "resettlement programs" and the quest of the "Thousand Year Reich"—make an ancient Roman Caesar seem contemporary. We long for peace, yet the modern nation-state makes war inevitable, a consequence of national values like "self-determination" and "sovereignty." Violence is a function of the state, any state, democratic or totalitarian; for no state, of the right or of the left, can long tolerate counter claims of sovereignty, alternate structures of meaning, persons who, like Peter and Paul, would die rather than do what is best for the fatherland. Both Jesus and Paul were eventually executed as threats to the *pax Romana.*

Christians in our part of the world may have convinced themselves that Christ and Caesar can happily coexist, as long as Caesar tends toward democracy. We wonder what Luke would think of such arrangements. Would Felix, Festus, and Pontius Pilate be any less themselves, any less baffled by the claim of a kingdom other than Caesar's, any less deadly to the witness of the church if they were a bit more democratic? It is difficult to believe that Luke, the one whose witness is bracketed by the death of Jesus at the hand of Pilate and the death (presumably) of Paul under the justice of imperial Rome, would think well of our present willingness to give a pinch of incense at the altar of Caesar and allow the Empire to go its own way unmolested by the claims of Christ.

Luke's church was not trying to be credible to the Empire or to assure Caesar of its apolitical status. It sought to create an alternative political entity, which became a monkey wrench thrown into the clanking machinery of Caesar's systems. Christianity defeated the Empire, in great part, because it outorganized the Empire. The church gave the decaying classical world a vibrant, tightly knit, exclusivistic organizational alternative to other secular arrangements. Theophilus' church appreciated not only God's involvement in the world through the Spirit but also God's apartness from even the Empire's best cultural achievements. The *Didache,* our oldest catechism, prepared candidates like Cornelius for baptism by instructing them that they would not kill, would not have sex with other people's spouses, would not abuse young children, would not abort fetuses. In so doing the church put itself on a collision course with some of the Roman world's most widely accepted practices. But our current North American church—as well as some churches in the midst of revolution in Third World countries—so wants to be recognized as culturally significant (as Caesar defines significance), so wants to have the power to change and improve society without converting and evangelizing it, that we gladly adapt the foolishness of the gospel to the world's standards of wisdom and reduce our social witness to

121

the back-seat status of a general civilizing influence on the empire rather than form a new kingdom loyal to a King who is not Caesar.

In his first book to Theophilus, Luke tells a story which begins in a thoroughly political context when "a decree went out from Caesar Augustus that all the world should be enrolled . . ., when Quirinius was governor of Syria" (Luke 2:1–2). This is the way all significant history proceeds, with accounts of what Caesar was doing at the time, whose party was in power where, and who sat in the Kremlin or in the White House.

Yet Luke's readers note a strange irony in this story. By the time this Gospel was written, Augustus and Quirinius, such mighty men in their day, rulers who could speak and make the whole world shake, were now rotting in their graves, relegated to the dusty, forgotten footnotes of history. But the babe at Bethlehem, the one whose advent no one noticed, that baby has overturned the world of Augustus, Herod, and Quirinius, as his followers would upset the world of Felix and Festus. It was that babe at Bethlehem who was to have the last word, a word which has come full circle in the conversion of one of Caesar's own, a centurion named Cornelius. Acts, far from being a humble appeal to Caesar for a little recognition and respect, is a revolutionary manifesto addressed to a church determined to show Caesar that God, not nations, rules the world.

Theophilus' church had to re-learn the radical political, social implications of belief in the sovereignty of God, before whom the nations are as but a drop in a bucket, and so must our own.

Acts 13:1—14:28
The Gentile Mission Confirmed:
Paul and Barnabas at Work

When Paul was commissioned on the road to Damascus (9:15–16), he was told three things: (1) He was to be an instrument to carry the name of Christ (2) before gentiles and kings, and (3) he will be shown how much he must suffer for the sake of Christ. The narratives contained in 13:1—14:28 are dramatic confirmation of this commission. The unit begins in a way that we have come to expect in Acts—nothing begins without the initiation of the Holy Spirit (13:2–3). Barnabas and Saul are "set apart" for a new stage of mission. As usual, they are not "free agents" moving at their own initiative. This new step in outreach has been declared by the Spirit and confirmed by the church through fasting, praying, and laying-on-of-hands. The Spirit and the community work together to set apart some Christians for leadership (see discussion of 6:1–7).

Then begins a breathless itinerary which includes Seleucia, Cyprus, Salamis, and Paphos—far-sounding places which indicate the universal scope of this new stage in the mission. Now the evangelists take long journeys upon ships to far away islands as the gospel continues to spread. (It is estimated on the basis of the accounts in Acts that Paul traveled over ten thousand miles [Meeks, p. 20]). When they arrive at Paphos, they encounter a magician named Bar-Jesus, who is in the retinue of the proconsul Sergius Paulus. Sophisticated Romans were fond of keeping sorcerers and astrologers to help them make important decisions.

This display of pagan naïveté might have been insignificant had not the sorcerer sought to turn Sergius Paulus away from Christianity (v. 8). Paul squares off in a confrontation with the magician which is definitely reminiscent of the beloved contest between Elijah and the prophets of Baal on Mount Carmel (I Kings 18:19–40). In the story of Elijah and the prophets, there is a contest to see whose God has the most power. By the Holy Spirit working in him, Paul is able to show that the sorcerer is a fake. After Paul's scathing rebuke ("You son of the devil, you enemy of all righteousness, you . . .")—the words of true prophets are not kind to those who are false—the once influential Elymas is reduced to the level of a stumbling, mystified nincompoop who must be led by the hand (v. 11). Such a display of power was enough to make a believer out of Sergius Paulus (v. 12). In keeping with Luke's interest in the miraculous power of the Spirit, the proconsul is converted (cf. the accounts of miracles followed by conversion in Luke 4:31—5:11). Although Christianity is not magic, the gospel does not mind squaring off with the alleged gods and powers of the world because the power of God can manage quite well in open conflict with counterfeit deities (cf. 8:9–13; 19:18–20).

The next section (13:13–52) takes Paul all the way to Pisidian Antioch—no small journey considering that it requires

123

our missionaries to journey through more than a third of Asia Minor. The pace of the narrative is picking up speed, the entire world is being covered like wildfire. At Antioch, Paul does not encounter another superstitious pagan like the proconsul but, rather, Luke puts him within a synagogue service. Invited to speak a few words, Paul launches into a long speech meant to be an example of the appeal Paul made to his fellow Jews (13: 15–41). When Jews argue with one another about true and false faith, they do it not so much by appeals to miracle and power (Paul's contest with the sorcerer before the proconsul) but by appeals to history.

The speech can be divided, into three parts: Part 1 (vv. 16*b*–25): Jesus is a member of David's royal lineage and is the fulfillment of God's promises (cf. Rom. 1:3). The implication of this selective summary of the history of Israel is Paul's assertion that even as God liberated Israel, helped Israel conquer the promised land, and gave them a leader like David, God is acting in a similar way to liberate, conquer (the Romans?), and lead in Jesus.

Part 2 (vv. 26–37): Even though those who were in the synagogue every Sabbath were pouring over the Scriptures, when the time came for the fulfillment of those very Scriptures, "they did not recognize him nor understand the utterances of the prophets" (v. 27). Unlike some of the earlier speeches in Acts, which harshly depict the guilt of the Jews, here the emphasis is upon the innocence of Jesus rather than the guilt of his people.

In quoting Psalm 2 (13:33) we hear one of Luke's strongest assertions of what would later be called "adoptionist" Christology (cf. 2:36). But it is the resurrection which is decisive of Jesus' divine status in 13:33.

As is typical of Luke's understanding of the cross, there is no substitutionary atonement here (Luke omits the statement of Mark 10:45 that "the Son of man also came . . . to give his life as a ransom"), no glorification of the death of Christ per se; rather the cross is depicted as a result of ignorance, evil, and collaboration with the Romans (vv. 28–29). Statements such as "Christ died for our sins" (I Cor. 15:3) are unknown to the Paul of Acts. Jesus died in obedient fulfillment of his divinely bestowed mission (Luke 24:26, 46). He suffered and died (as Luke depicts the disciples suffering and dying) because he sought to reach the lost and the outcast. God's purposes for the world are realized through servants (like Jesus, like the disciples) who are obedient to the purposes of God, even when obedience means death. The resurrection/ascension of Christ is divine confirmation that Jesus' obedience is part of the purposes of God. While this warns us against dismissing Luke-Acts' theology of the power and exaltation of Christ as a complete denial of the historical Paul's theology of the humiliation and crucifixion of Christ, it also highlights what Luke believes is significant about the story of Christ. The resurrection is the interesting thing about Jesus, the divine response to human ignorance and rejection, a confirmation that Jesus was indeed the fulfillment of God's promises (cf. Rom. 1:4). Salvation is here and now.

Part 3 (vv. 38–41): Through this Jesus, forgiveness and deliverance are offered (literally, justification to God; cf. Rom. 6:5). The speech concludes with a solemn warning about the peril of unbelief. The hearers may not know what dread "deed in your days" (v. 41) God may have in mind for them, but we know: If they reject Jesus, the gospel will go elsewhere.

A short interlude tells us that Paul's words had effect—many Jews as well as gentile converts to Judaism were curious and begged to hear more (vv. 42–43). A week later "almost the whole city gathered together to hear the word of God" (v. 44). Luke does not give us the text of this speech, only its effects. The Jews, out of jealousy for his success in attracting a crowd, reject Paul's words. Then Paul and Barnabas, the new disciple and the old, boldly utter the fateful words we knew were eventually to come: "It was necessary that the word of God should be spoken first to you. Since you thrust it from you, . . . *we turn to the Gentiles*" (author's itals.).

Luke probably means for us to recall the initiation of the gentile mission when Cornelius was converted, a story which ended with the declaration that "Then to the Gentiles also has God granted repentance unto life (11:18); so the climax to this story comes in 13:46 with, "we turn to the Gentiles" and is reiterated finally in 14:27 that God "opened a door of faith to the Gentiles." The dramatic account ends with gentiles being converted (v. 48), but with Jews inciting persecution (v. 50) against the missionaries, who in obedience to Jesus' earlier command (Luke 10:11) "shook the dust from their feet against them" and departed with joy (vv. 51–52).

Somewhat surprisingly, chapter 14 opens with the evangel-

125

ists back in the synagogue. The movement toward the gentiles does not mean forsaking the Jews. Luke wants us to believe that the missionaries did all they could to convert their kinfolk. At Iconium the verdict upon the Christians was mixed. There is success, but persecution as well. Luke has graciously compressed the work of many months, or even years, into this interlude of 14:1–7. We are reading a theological work meant to say and do something to the church of Theophilus' day and our day, not a logbook of Paul's journeys. What Luke tells us is that while there is joy over the acceptance of the gospel there is also pain at its rejection and the constant threat of its extinction—such is the movement of the gospel.

At Lystra, Paul encounters a man who was "a cripple from birth" (v. 8). In reading the account we hear distinct echoes of Luke 5:18–26 and Acts 3:1–10 and 9:32–35. The miraculous powers of compassion and healing exercised by Jesus and Peter are now displayed by Paul. The crowd, as crowds often do, woefully misinterprets the healing power they witness. They think Barnabas is Zeus and Paul is Hermes. (Ovid tells of Zeus and Hermes visiting a pious old couple not far from Lystra, appearing to them in the disguise of humans. The couple offered them hospitality, even though they did not know they were entertaining gods, and were rewarded [*Metamorphoses*, VIII].) A pagan priest even initiates a service to pay homage to these two "gods." The humor of all this pagan commotion is self-evident.

Barnabas and Paul are not amused. They are not gods but rather bearers (in word and deed) of good news. The goodness the crowd has witnessed in the healing of the crippled man is typical of the many acts of goodness which God has graciously shown toward humanity from the beginning (14:16–17). The crowd misses the point: preparation for the worship of these two "gods" continues (v. 18). While Luke affirms the power of Christ to heal those who suffer and the divine power available for the world through these followers of Christ, Luke knows that that power is an ambiguous phenomenon. The gospel is not simply about power but about the *power of Christ*. Power, even power for good, is liable to misinterpretation and misunderstanding. Both believers and non-believers (the Jews and gentiles of Luke's story) may mistake the gospel for magic or divine omnipotence. Dramatic healings are sure to draw a crowd in Lystra, or on

126

Sunday morning television—for all the wrong reasons. Bearers of Christ's power are always in danger of being mistaken as the sources of power in themselves. Therefore they must be prepared to correct misapprehension of their good work and to point beyond themselves and their good work to Christ. Christian healers must also be teachers.

There is controversy, and after a nasty stoning, the opponents leave the apostle for dead (14:19). How could poor Paul, left for dead by the mob, suddenly spring up and offer consolation and organizational advice to the followers who found him? This is not a matter of interest to the teller of this tale. Luke lingers but briefly over the account of the stoning, for his story is not chiefly about the suffering of Paul but about the power of the gospel to break all barriers and overcome all obstacles. Once again, persecution and violence only serve to help "make many disciples" (v. 21).

Making disciples is the job of disciples in Acts. Mainline North American Protestantism, faced with steady decline in membership over the most recent decades, tends to waver between superficial techniques for church growth or unconvincing alibis for church death—"We are not really dying; we are tightening our ranks for service." "Only the reactionary, conservative churches are growing. We are too liberal and socially progressive to attract new members." Luke would not know what to make of a church no longer in the business of making more disciples. While the mission of the church is more than growth, it is not something other than growth. It is certainly not decline. We live in the gracious interim for witness (1:8). In Luke-Acts, any church bold enough to preach the Word, which dares to challenge the cultural status quo, which refuses to accept present political arrangements as eternally given, which is convinced of the truth of its message, which is willing to suffer for the truth will grow. God gives growth to such churches.

The Christian rabble rousers return to Iconium and Antioch, "strengthening the souls of the disciples, exhorting them to continue in the faith, and saying that through many tribulations we must enter the kingdom of God" (v. 22). If Luke's theology is one of growth, success, and victory, it is a success wrought on the hard anvil of suffering and peril. The account ends with the organization of new congregations, making provision for their governance, and a report of how God "had

127

opened a door of faith to the Gentiles" (v. 27). Tribulations are but seeds for the sowing of new congregations.

Success in Mission, Trouble at Home
ACTS 15:1–35

"But some men came down from Judea. . . ." With that abrupt insertion, the narrative shifts direction. The joy and peace which ended the account of the first stages of the gentile mission (13:1—14:28) is broken with this story of "no small dissension and debate" over the issue of whether gentile converts should be circumcised and become Jews before they could be Christians.

How many Christians have had their enthusiasm smothered by the bickering of the church? A member comes forward with an exciting idea for a church-sponsored after-school program for the children in the neighborhood. Put the gospel into practice! Reach out to the little ones who need us! The Board rejects the idea because the children might damage the church's new carpet. These church meetings with people crowding the microphone, bickering over budgets, basing their vote on their personal prejudices rather than on the Word of God—how many Christians have had the fire of their initial enthusiasm extinguished by unpleasant church meetings? Why can we not all act like Christians and agree? Why does there have to be such contentiousness within the Body of Christ? Who seated the Judean delegation anyway? Things were going so well for the church before they called for the microphone and opened the can of worms otherwise known as the mission to the gentiles. Why do they not just sit down and be quiet and leave the church in peace? How is this church ruckus going to appear when the newspapers hear of it?

Lest we be too quick to label these adversaries of Paul as conservative reactionaries, let us be sure that we know their motivation. None of them object to preaching to gentiles. They know that Israel's covenant included blessing to all the families of the earth (Gen.12:3). The sign of that covenant and that blessing was circumcision, a sign in which Jesus himself participated (Luke 2:21). Without circumcision, how could a gen-

128

tile possibly participate in the blessings promised to the covenant people; in short, how could they be saved? The concern is
not over racial exclusion but covenant inclusion. Although Paul
labeled these opponents as "false brothers" (Gal.2:4), let us
grant the legitimacy of their concern faithfully to include gentiles within all of the promises to Israel and all of the beauty of
a life lived by the Torah. Adherence to the beloved Torah is the
way in which a Jew remains a Jew. How dare Paul, Barnabas,
and the church at Antioch take it upon themselves to abrogate
these sacred demands? A delegation is sent to "the apostles and
the elders at Jerusalem" to settle the issue. Once again, when
there is a dispute about innovation or new twists in the task of
applying the gospel to contemporary challenges, our missionaries touch base with apostolic authority in Jerusalem, with normative tradition.

At Jerusalem, "they declared all that God had done with
them" (15:4). But some of the "party of the Pharisees" were
unconvinced and demanded that gentiles be circumcised and
keep the Torah. After much debate Peter speaks (vv.7-11),
alluding to his own experience in the Cornelius episode
(10:1—11:18). In his vision Peter learned that God "made no
distinction between us and them" (v.9). Realization of God's
inclusive grace (cf. Rom.2:11) has led Peter to the stunning
conclusion that "we believe that we shall be saved by grace,"
a conclusion that would have pleased the Paul of Romans as well
as Luther. Peter bases his argument upon new revelation (the
vision) as well as the gift of the Holy Spirit and the actual
experience of gentiles coming into the fellowship. Peter's evidence is confirmed by Barnabas and Paul, who narrate the
"signs and wonders God had done through them among the
Gentiles" (v. 12), another argument from experience. As if to
seal their argument, James (someone we have not met before)
rises to cite *Scripture* in support of the gentile mission, claiming
prophetic agreement (vv. 15-18). James quotes Amos 9:11-12
(Septuagint), a text which refers to the restoration of the true
People of God (v.16) and of the inclusion of "Gentiles who are
called by my name" (v.17), a wise choice of Scripture since
Amos says nothing about the need for these gentile converts to
follow the requirements of the law.

The method of debate in 15:7-21 is a useful guide for how
the church ought to argue. For one thing, the church listens to
its leaders. Paul's comments in his epistles about troubles with
Peter on the subject of gentile circumcision suggest that Peter

129

was not as agreeable as he is depicted as being in 15:7–11. Nevertheless, the church depends upon its leaders to be more than mere managers or bureaucratic functionaries. The church needs people of bold vision who know what is at stake in our arguments and who argue with clarity and courage. Yet, when the church decides on a proper course of action, feelings, sentiment, the power of caucuses, ethnic or gender considerations, the opinions of leaders, or the majority vote of the members (the ways the church often adjudicates its disputes today) count for little. New *revelation* along with confirmation by *experience* and with testing by *Scripture* are the proper measurements for the church. A church without these three standards is unable to have a good argument. All differences must be suppressed, and we dare not admit them for fear that the church be destroyed by our debate, since we have no commonly recognized authority for adjudicating our disputes. Congeniality and open-mindedness become the only values for a church without authority, values which ultimately prove inadequate for keeping the church faithful. Appeals to revelation, Scripture, and experience do not settle the church's inner differences. But these three criteria determine the boundaries for our debates. They are the ultimate court of appeal.

Based upon the evidence of experience and Scripture, James proposes that "we should not trouble those of the Gentiles who turn to God" (v.19). Luke's Jesus has separated salvation from Torah, or at least has found a way to include gentiles without first making them Jews. Yet Christian love and the concerns of community temper this inclusive spirit. Out of care for the sensibilities of Jewish Christians (a major concern of Gal.2:11–21), gentile Christians are asked to observe four things: eat nothing sacrificed to pagan gods, abstain from incestuous marriages, eat no meat of strangled animals, abstain from partaking of blood (15:20–21). Leviticus 17—18 applies these rules to both Jews and to aliens who reside within Israel. James seems to regard these gentiles as analogous to "strangers" in the Hebrew Scriptures. Thus, gentile Christians are compelled to observe the minimum requirements that had been set for strangers wanting to enjoy fellowship with conscientious Jews. At the table of the Lord, we gentiles continue to be the guests of a Jewish host.

130

Converts into the church are welcomed, but not without limits. Even as change was required of Jewish Christians to include converted gentiles in their fellowship, so converted gentiles must change for the good of the fellowship. Luke, in his enthusiasm for the gentile mission, does not claim that old Israel is replaced by a new Israel, the church. Rather, gentiles are welcomed into a reconstituted Israel which demands that they adhere to certain basic Levitical standards for the good of all.

Nowhere does Luke suggest that Jesus abrogates the Torah. Even gentiles are to keep that part of the Torah which applies to them as non-Jews. Our Protestant tendency to equate Torah with legalism deters us from seeing the Torah as Luke sees it. In Judaism, Torah was not a means of winning salvation. Jews knew that God is gracious and forgiving. For Luke, the law is not a means of salvation but rather is a means of signifying ones identity as a member of God's people—although, strictly speaking, no Jew would have understood a separation of salvation by God through the gift of the Torah and identity as God's people. Ceremonial rules for eating were just as important as ethical rules for marriage, money, and murder. Jews must be witnesses in the midst of a pagan world of God's gracious determination to have a people. As other signs of Jewish distinctiveness were destroyed, like their king, their land, and their temple, Torah held the people together. Torah was the Jews' joyful witness to the one true God in a world full of idols (E. P. Sanders).

This was Luke's view of Torah. God's people will live by God's law. To fail to do so would be to risk the disintegration of the community of the elect into another co-opted cult of the Empire. Paul solved the Jew-gentile problem in one way, Luke in another. Luke would never have said, "Christ is the end of the law . . ." (Rom. 10:4). Gentiles must be included in God's family, but on the family's terms—through belief in the Word and gift of the Spirit.

James' proposal "seemed good to the apostles and the elders, with the whole church" (v.22). A letter is sent from the Jerusalem mother church to Antioch (vv. 22–29) outlining the plan. The new congregation in Antioch was much pleased (v.31), and the work among the gentiles continued. The young church which has had to prevail against external adversaries, both Jew and gentile, as well as internal infidelity has demonstrated that it can prevail against perhaps the toughest foe of all—disagreements with fellow Christians about church policy. Rather than do what churches often do on such occasions—flee from the fight, submerge our differences, or else storm off in a

131

huff—the apostles demonstrate that the gospel has given them the resources to confront controversy without being destroyed by it. There are congregations who are too weak, too fearful of possible fragmentation, too bereft of any common, binding faith to have a good argument. Luke does not discuss those churches because their timid and supercilious stories could not give courage to anyone.

Why all this fuss over such archaic prejudices as not eating blood? Against our tendency to see Paul and Barnabas as the good, open "liberals" at the Jerusalem conference and their opponents as reactionary "conservatives," let us remind ourselves that Luke wants to demonstrate that the gentile mission and all of its exponents acted in fidelity to the true and historic faith of Israel. In Luke's story Paul could not have been faithful to the historic witness (represented in James' citation of Amos 9) had he refused to be a light to the gentiles. In our own decidedly anti-traditional, antinomian, "if-it-feels-good-to-you-then-do-it" environment, we may wonder why Paul and the apostles went to all the trouble to pacify the concerns of the circumcisers. For us, the church is more concerned with inclusiveness, openness, and affirmation rather than with fidelity to the historic faith of Israel. We are quick to lay aside historic standards of doctrine and morality as being historically conditioned and culture-bound and thoroughly irrelevant to our more progressive world view.

The apostles commended Paul and Barnabas to the new mission churches as "men who have risked their lives for the sake of our Lord Jesus Christ" (v.26). Before we arrogantly dispose of their witness in our contemporary debates over church policy, we ought at least to recognize the authority of their credentials, written as they are in blood.

Work Among the Churches

ACTS 15:36—19:20

132   After the Jerusalem Conference Luke depicts Paul and Barnabas on a return visit to all of the churches they have founded (15:36). This gives Luke an opportunity to organize a

number of stories about Paul's work among the gentiles, stories which will take Paul to the great cultural centers of the Greco-Roman world: Athens, Corinth, Ephesus. There are four major moves toward the gentiles in Acts: (1) Peter's move toward Cornelius in chapter 10, (2) the work of those in Cyprus and Cyrene in 11:19–21, (3) Paul's and Barnabas' work in chapters 13—14, and (4) the work of Paul and Silas in Acts 16—20. You will note that in each of these moves the work among the gentiles is confirmed by Jerusalem. Also in each of the last three there is a gesture of fellowship on the part of the gentile Christians toward their fellow Jewish Christians (11:27–30; 15:31; and 21:20–24, 26). In careful structuring of his narrative, Luke keeps reinforcing his central theme of expansion of the church into the whole world across every barrier, while at the same time dealing with numerous practical difficulties faced by the church of Theophilus' day. Luke hopes that we will be able to identify with his accounts of the dilemmas within early congregations by comparing them with our own congregations and attempt to live out the faith in our day.

Acts 15:36—16:10
The Gentile Mission Continues: On to Macedonia

The reason that Luke gives for the breakup of the Paul and Barnabas team does not square with Paul's version in Galatians 2:11–13. Paul's own assertion that he had doctrinal differences with Barnabas does not fit into Luke's purposes, so he transformed a theological dispute between Barnabas and Paul into a personal quarrel concerning the quitter, John Mark, who had withdrawn during the first missionary journey (13:13). Paul chose Silas, a prophet (15:40), and also Timothy—son of a Jewish-Christian woman and a Greek father (16:1–2). Paul even demands that Timothy be circumcised (a requirement somewhat surprising after the decree of the Jerusalem Council) so as not to offend Jewish-Christian sensibilities. By choosing Silas and Timothy, and by insisting on the circumcision of Timothy, Paul once again shows himself to be a loyal Jew who securely

133

yokes himself to the tradition before he launches any missionary thrust.

It would be difficult to reconstruct a "journey" out of the material Luke gives us, since he has obviously summarized a journey of well over two thousand miles and condensed it into a few verses. We are not told how churches were founded in Galatia and Phrygia—rather puzzling since in 16:6 Paul was forbidden by the Holy Spirit to preach there. These omissions and condensations, as well as Luke's reworked account of the split between Barnabas and Paul, remind us that while Luke is working with historical materials his main concerns are theological rather than geographical or historical. Historical details are not nearly so important to Luke as the theological assertion that "the churches were strengthened in the faith, and they increased in numbers daily" (16:5).

New challenges to the church require new leadership. Earlier, we saw how the church chose Matthias (1:15–26) to complete the number of the disciples in order to bear witness to Israel's twelve tribes. Seven were chosen in 6:1–6 to set right the injustices in the distribution to widows. Barnabas sought out Saul (11:25–26) as just the right person for work with the new church at Antioch. Now we see Paul choose Timothy to accompany him for the mission to Europe (16:3). Earlier, Matthias was chosen to complete the number of the Twelve because he had been with Jesus throughout his ministry. Saul was chosen for the work with Hellenist Jews and gentiles in Antioch because he had been a Hellenist himself. Now Timothy is chosen, not only because he is well thought of but also because in his background he unites both Jew and gentile. Leadership in the church is a function dependent upon what the church needs to have done. One is chosen by the church as a leader not as a matter of privilege or personal right or of individual status but as a function of the church's mission. The church determines that one has what it takes to facilitate the church's mission. We see this principle at work again in the choice of Timothy.

This section also calls our attention to the continual ability of the Spirit to overcome every barrier put in the way of the gospel. Earlier barriers included gentile scorn and Jewish hostility, as well as internal weaknesses within the fellowship itself (the lies of Ananias and Sapphira). In 15:1–35 we encountered the barrier of dissension within the church. Through the Jerusa-

lem conference, that barrier was overcome in a solution which
"seemed good to the Holy Spirit and to us" (15:28). Now two of
the church's leading missionaries quarrel over John Mark (15:
37–38). Squabbles among a movement's founders have destroyed more than one fledgling organization. Will this leadership disagreement destroy the young church? Will this be the
end of the gentile mission? No indeed! Now there are *two* mission thrusts to the gentiles rather than one. Even dissension
among the church's leaders only serves to double the church's
mission work. Almost anything, even squabbles within the
church, can be transformed by the Spirit into a means whereby
"the churches were strengthened in the faith, and they increased in numbers daily (v.5)." Nothing, including human limitations and the need for new young leaders can stop the
movement of the Spirit.

The work of Christian mission is not merely one of founding new churches. Young congregations, like young Christians,
must be carefully nurtured into the faith. So Paul, Silas, and
Timothy set out to nurture the congregations which had been
founded. After a while, Paul receives a visionary commission:
"Come over to Macedonia and help us" (16:9). As this section
ends, without warning, we note a startling shift in Luke's manner of narration. Use of the first person plural begins in 16:10.
These "we" passages comprise a total of ninety-seven verses in
Acts: 16:10–17; 20:5–15; 21:1–18; and 27:1—28:16. Scholars
have advanced three possible explanations of these "we" passages: Perhaps the author of Acts was a traveling companion of
Paul for certain portions of his journey and drew upon his diary
at those points when he shifts into the first person plural. Others
have suggested that "we" was found by the author of Acts in
one of the sources and it was incorporated into his book, even
though he had not been an actual companion of Paul. The other
possibility is that the "we" is a literary device used by Luke as
a subtle means of bridging the gap between the period of the
church when Paul's journey's actually took place and the time
when these journey stories were later assembled in accounts
like that of Acts.

It is unlikely that the "we" passages have come from another source because they are virtually indistinguishable from
the rest of Acts. We cannot say for sure whether or not the
author of Acts was a traveling companion of Paul, but we do

135

know that by using "we" the author gives the stories a sense of drama and immediacy which makes them particularly compelling narratives, as we shall soon see in the next account of those who have concluded that "God had called us to preach the gospel" in Macedonia (16:10).

Acts 16:11–40
Capitivity and Release in Philippi

If there is one virtue on which we can all join hands, it is freedom: freedom of speech, freedom of religion. Freedom is the blessed treasure of academia—freedom to think, teach, and publish. Freedom is also a blessed treasure of the pulpit—freedom to speak as one feels led by God to speak.

Freedom? Surrounded by our burglar alarms and medicine cabinets and our fears—heart attack, impotency, insanity, insolvency—this is freedom?

We Americans have built a society which has given an unprecedented measure of freedom to its citizens. I am given maximum space aggressively to pursue what I want—as long as I do not bump into you while you are getting yours. What we call culture is a vast super market of desire where citizens are treated as little more than self-interested consumers. I have freedom of choice, but now what do I do with my freedom? We are free but also terribly lonely, terribly driven. The nine-to-five job, monthly mortgage payments, over-programmed children, dog-eat-dog contests for grades at the university—this is our freedom.

There is freedom, and then there is freedom. One of our problems in this matter of freedom is that we may not even know what true freedom is. Acts 16:11–40 tells stories about people in Philippi who were in bondage and people who were free. Who in the story is free?

First we meet Lydia (v.14), a rich businesswoman and worshiper of God. God opens her heart to the gospel and she immediately demonstrates the Christian trait of hospitality, opening her home. The conversion of Lydia is interesting for a number of reasons. *First,* the narrator makes clear that her conversion is due to *the work of God,* not Paul's skill. *Second,*

Lydia is *a woman*. We need not be startled that Paul and Silas, Near-Eastern males though they be, are talking to women in public (v.13). Twice in his Gospel, Luke mentions the women who followed Jesus from Galilee (Luke 23:49,55). The detail is typical of a writer who shows throughout his Gospel and in Acts an interest in "those of low degree." Women, low on the social scale, were the first evangelists who ran to tell the male disciples (who were hiding!) that Jesus had risen from the dead (Luke 24:9).

When compared to conventional Jewish and Greco-Roman ideas about women, the church must have seemed radical in the way it welcomed women and featured them as leaders and prophets (I Cor. 11:2–16). Women could be members of this movement without the permission of their husbands, and they may, though Paul advised against it, initiate divorce from a pagan husband (I Cor. 7:13). The early church had women leaders like Lydia even though it seems to have struggled to square the cultural presuppositions about women with the experience of the gifts and leadership of women within early congregations—as, for example, in Paul's rather confusing words on the issue of women as leaders (I Cor. 11:2–16; 14:33–36). Perhaps Luke gives prominence to the role of women like Lydia to assure Theophilus' church—a church which may have regressed to more conventional cultural morés regarding the status of women—that the leadership of women had apostolic precedent.

Third, Lydia is a *rich* woman. In the opening of his Gospel, in Mary's *Magnificat* (Luke 1:51–53), Luke sounds a warning to the rich. Throughout both the Gospel and Acts, Luke portrays possessions as a special danger. "For it is easier for a camel to go through the eye of a needle than for a rich man to enter the kingdom of God" (Luke 18:25). Yet Luke never lapses into divisive notions of Marxist "class struggle" or simplistic "preferential option for the poor" of some theologies of liberation. Jesus redeemed the wealthy Zacchaeus (Luke 19:1–10), with the result that Zacchaeus gave over half of his wealth to the poor. The parable of the Good Samaritan illustrates the good that can be done through the right use of wealth (Luke 10:30–37). In the church wealthier members give for those who have less (Acts 2:44–45; 4:32–35). Cornelius, the first gentile convert, is depicted as a philanthropist (10:2), and now a rich woman named Lydia demonstrates her conversion through hospitality. That

137

Paul consented to stay in her house as the recipient of her hospitality indicates that barriers which sometimes divided male and female or divided Jew from gentile Jewish convert within the synagogues do not hold in the church. Lydia is now free to be hospitable, and Paul is now free to welcome her as a sister in Christ (v.15).

This mixing of classes is particularly interesting, given the context of the Roman world where there was virtually no movement out of the social class to which one was born nor any expectation of movement. Classes were hereditary, fixed at birth. Only the Roman army (and sometimes marriage of women into the ranks of the socially privileged) offered much hope of movement towards the more economically advantaged classes. Acts' picture of relaxed familiarity and warm hospitality between social classes in the church would not have been missed by Luke's readers (Meeks, pp. 19–26).

Celsus, the first pagan author who took the trouble to write a book to discredit Christianity, alleged that the church deliberately excluded educated and wealthy people because this faith appealed only to "the foolish, . . . slaves, women, and little children" who gathered at "the wooldresser's shop, or to the cobbler's or the washerwoman's shop, that they may learn perfection" (Meeks, p. 51). Many modern scholars feel that Celsus' description of the church was inaccurate—though it has been a favorite of Marxist historians or those who romanticize poverty. There is good evidence that early congregations attracted a surprising cross-section of first and second century society. Was this because the early church—unlike our church's all-too-frequent application of economic determinism to explain everyone's situation in life—failed to take either a person's poverty or wealth with ultimate seriousness? Wealthy Lydia as well as the improverished beneficiaries of Dorcas' generosity (9:32–43) worship together in the church.

Paul and Silas were going to the place of prayer and were accosted by a slave girl. Because this girl could tell peoples' fortunes she made money for her owners, who hired her out to read palms and provide entertainment at business conventions. She was possessed by a demon; mentally unbalanced, we would say. She took to following Paul and Silas around, shouting at them, saying things about them. Here is a picture of enslavement—the grip of mental illness, schizophrenia, some "demon" which holds the victim in bondage.

Paul has enough of the young woman's raving and in the name of Christ cures her. Thank God, she is free! Yet no, she is not free. She is a *slave,* someone who is not a person but a piece of property. "When her owners saw that their hope of gain was gone, they seized Paul and Silas and dragged them into the market place before the rulers" (v.19). The Philippian chamber of commerce moves into action.

One day Jesus healed a mentally deranged man by casting his demons into some swine (Luke 8:37); for this act of charity he was promptly escorted out of town by the local Pork Dealers Association. At Ephesus, Paul had a big revival and many were converted and it was all wonderful—except for the members of Local 184 of the International Brotherhood of Artisans of Silver Shrines to Artemis (Acts 19:23–41). They did not like it at all.

Here is a young woman, chained her whole life to the hell of demon possession, and now she is free; there ought to be rejoicing. But no, her owners are not free enough to do that. It was fine to give a dollar to the Mental Health Association drive last fall, but this is another matter. Religion has somehow gotten mixed up with economics here, and so her owners do what the vested interests always do when their interests are threatened.

The girl's owners say to the judge, "We're not against a little religion—as long as it is kept in its place." But "these men are Jews and they are disturbing our city. They advocate customs which are not lawful for us Romans to accept or practice" (vv.20, 21).

No, we do not come right out and say that our financial self-interest is threatened; we say that our nation is threatened. "These missionaries are foreigners." Buy American!

Besides, they are Jews. And we all know what they are like, money grabbing, materialistic. If the *nationalism* and the *anti-Semitism* fail to work, we will throw in an appeal for *old-time religion* saying, "They advocate customs not lawful for us to practice." Nation, race, tradition—all stepping into line behind the dollar.

Then the crowd, *democracy* in action, falls into line behind the business leaders of the town; and they attack and beat Paul and Silas. Paul and Silas are put into the back cell of the town prison and the jailer takes their feet and locks them in the iron shackles. The liberators have become the imprisoned. Jesus has helped set a pitiful young woman free, but two of Jesus' people get jailed in the process. That Jesus who preached, "You shall

139

know the truth and the truth shall make you free" (John 8:32)—you know where he ended up.

Paul and Silas end up in prison, languishing there (v.24). No, the story says, "about midnight Paul and Silas were praying and singing hymns to God, and the prisoners were listening to them, . . ." (v.25). Wait, these men in chains, legs locked in shackles are singing, praying, having a sort of rally in jail.

The earth heaves, the prison shakes, the doors fly open and everyone's chains fall off. The jailer wakes, and when he sees that the doors are open, he is horrified. Knowing what happens to jailers who permit their prisoners to escape he draws his sword and prepares to do the honorable thing for disgraced jailers. Having the key to someone else's cell does not make you free. Iron bars do not a prison make.

Paul shouts, "Don't do it. We're all here, just singing." The jailer says, "But you were bound in chains, now you are free to escape." Paul says, "No, we prisoners are free and you, our jailer, were chained but now you are free to escape."

And the jailer asks, "What do I have to do to be saved" (v.30)? What do I have to do to be free? And he was baptized.

What is freedom? By the end of the story, everyone who at first appeared to be free—the girl's owners, the judges, the jailer—is a slave. And everyone who first appeared to be enslaved—the poor girl, Paul, and Silas—is free.

After I spoke at a conference on women in the church, someone rose and said, "The federal government has done more for the cause of women in this country than the church ever thought about. At last, because of government help, women are enabled to be on an equal level with men in the workplace." And I had just heard on the radio that for the first time in history the rate of lung cancer among women is as high as it is among men. The rate of hypertension, heart disease, and other stress-related diseases is climbing among women, and some feel that in not too many years the life span of the average American female will have shrunk to that of the average American male.

You have come a long way—to get where you have gotten to today? There is freedom, and then there is freedom. Earlier, Jesus had said, "If you continue in my word, you are truly my disciples, and you will know the truth, and the truth will make you free" (John 8:31).

They stiffened their necks, held their heads high, and answered, "What is this 'will make you free' business? We are descendants of Abraham and have never been in bondage to anyone" (cf. John 8:33).

They lied. The ones who spoke so pridefully of their freedom spoke with the heel of Caesar upon their necks—slaves of Egypt, Assyria, Babylonia, Rome, anybody big enough to raise an army and blow through town. In truth they were not free.

Then Jesus said, "If the Son makes you free, you will be free indeed" (John 8:36).

At Philippi it was demonstrated that there is freedom and then there is freedom.

Acts 17:1–15
Empire in Uproar: Thessalonica and Beroea

"These men . . . have turned the world upside down . . ." (17:6) is a charge well documented throughout Acts. The trumped-up charges which jealous Jews in Thessalonica bring against Paul and Silas have more than a grain of truth in them. Even though the disciples are not the political threat the people and the authorities fear, the Empire is not secure with these Christians on the loose, Christians who teach "that there is another King, Jesus" (17:7) (see *Reflection: The Politics of Luke*).

Paul and Silas receive a better reception at the synagogue in Beroea (17:10–14), whose members were "more noble than those in Thessalonica" and examined "the scriptures daily to see if these things were so" (17:11). The implication is that if their fellow Jews had taken the effort to search the promises of Scripture like the Jews in Beroea, they would have discovered that the proclamation of Silas and Paul is true to the Scriptures of Israel. All went well until the Thessalonian Jews stirred up trouble in Beroea as well.

Even at this rather late stage in the gentile mission, we note that (1) Paul continues to go first to the synagogues, to those who ponder the Scriptures and that (2) not all Jews reject the gospel;

141

the reception continues to be mixed. We are not, at least at this point, to give either response prominence. When the word is taught—even for three Sabbaths in succession (v.2)—we must realistically acknowledge that some will reject. Yet our realism is combined with the optimistic confidence that many believe— even not a few leading Greek men and women! Is Luke bragging about Paul's success in attracting influential people to the faith or is he marveling that the Spirit is able to convert *even* people of "high standing"?

Acts 17:16–34
Paul in Athens Before Cultured Idolaters

We have seen the power of the gospel to reach rich and poor, Jew and gentile, slave and free, male and female. But can the gospel hold its own in the sophisticated intellectual environment of a university town? Luke takes Paul to Athens, to the heart of the very best of pagan culture, the town of Pericles and of Plato.

Frankly, Paul is unimpressed. The sculptures of Phidias move him not. Good Jew that he is, Paul sees Athens as little more than a wasteland "full of idols" (17:16). He argues with Jews, Epicureans, and Stoics, even those who look down their academic noses at this "babbler" (v.18). Others, after much research and careful investigation, come to the stunning discovery that "He seems to be a preacher of foreign divinities" (v.18), perhaps thinking to absorb whatever new gods Paul brings them into their pantheon of exotic divinities. Their legendary Athenian curiosity leads Paul into the Areopagus, where the Athenians spent their days doing what intellectuals enjoy— relieving their boredom by searching for new ideas. Novelty attracts their attention more quickly than truth. So much for pagan intelligence.

The setting gives Luke an opportunity for an attack upon and an evangelistic appeal to Christianity's cultured despisers. In a well constructed piece of classical rhetoric, Paul, a virtual Christian Socrates, first flatters his audience (vv. 22–23). Idolaters they may be, but at least they are searching; their impulse to worship is right even if the objects of their worship are wrong. He has seen their altar to "an unknown God" (v.23). Their religious yearning, even though a bit of a scandal to a monotheistic Jew, is the inarticulate and uninformed yearning of the pagan for the God whom only the Scriptures can disclose.

Sometimes believers look with scorn upon the religious infatuations of Christianity's cultured despisers. Pagans criticize the Christian faith as being "simplistic," "pre-scientific," "superstitious" and then rush to the strange consolations of astrology, transcendental meditation, parapsychology, esoteric cults, or happy hearted humanism. And they have the nerve to call Christians simplistic! Yet Paul might say, as he said on Areopagus, that at least they are searching. They at least know that something else is needed to make sense out of life, to give coherence to the world. The church, rather than standing back from pagan religiosity, pointing our fingers in righteous indignation, should, like Paul in Athens, minister to their searching.

Paul continues. Appealing to their knowledge of creation (for he could not simply recite Scripture to pagans who were ignorant of Scripture) and to our common humanity, Paul asserts that his God "made the world and everything in it" (v.24). This great God cannot be captured in "shrines made by man" (v.24) but exists over the face of the whole earth that we all may find our true purpose in his service alone (vv.28–29). Until now pagan ignorance was overlooked, but now is the time to turn toward the one true God who has not only created the inhabitants of the world but will also judge them (v.31).

In reasoning from the natural world toward faith in God, Luke's Paul borders upon a "natural theology"—our observation of the natural world and its wonders is a forerunner of faith. How can people look up at the stars or ponder the mysteries of the world without imagining a real, though still unknown, divine force behind it all? In citing the verses of a pagan poet (17:28), in drawing upon the pagan's experience of the world, Paul hopes to move them toward faith by way of the natural world. (The historical Paul used natural theology, not to appeal to pagans but to condemn pagan sinfulness—Rom. 1:18–23.)

Yet Paul cannot convert his audience through an exclusive appeal to their observation of the world. Revelation takes us where observation alone cannot go. Too many people look at

143

growing grass and see only cells dividing, or into the sky and see masses of matter and swirling gas. Natural theology is hardly more than preliminary instruction. Something else is needed. Paul mentions the resurrection—a fact completely contrary to our observation of the way the world works. In nature things die, decay, decline. Death is death. What is done is done, over and finished, ended. Yet Paul concludes his speech with the assertion that for Christians the resurrection of Jesus is our "assurance." Not grass growing in spring, the return of the robin, the opening of the cocoon, or any other naturalistic drivel; the resurrection, something beyond the natural, is the final assurance that this one is "Lord of heaven and earth" (17:24).

In mentioning the resurrection, Paul risks rejection by his audience. They may agree to a created world and to our common humanity, but there is no possible "natural theology" evidence for an assertion of the resurrection. Appeals to reason and to observation of the natural world can only be taken so far in the proclamation of the gospel. Eventually revelation must be invoked and the scandal of faith to reason and experience must be made plain.

There are limits, limits imposed by the nature of the gospel, on the evangelist's ability to "become all things to all men, that I might by all means save some" (I Cor. 9:22). The response to Paul's address is much the same as he encountered elsewhere: Some mocked (v.32), others believed (v. 34)—including two prominent Athenians.

Christian proclamation is not to be judged merely by its success in winning an approving response. Where the Word is faithfully preached, some believe, some mock—for even the oratorical skill of Paul cannot remove the offense of the gospel, in fact it accentuates it.

Calvin charged that "the human mind is a perpetual factory for idols." Idolatry is not necessarily the pastime of the ignorant and the simple. Intellectuals play the game quite well. Natural inquisitiveness and delight in the novel and the strange, so prevalent in the academy, can be little more than the itch for some new graven image. The God whom Paul proclaims is not just another option for human devotion, not an accommodating God content to be one among many. The God who sent the Christ is still the Holy One of Israel, a jealous deity without rivals, an exclusive lover who tolerates no competition—money, sex, philosophical ideals, institutions—who fiercely judges all idols made by hands or minds of men.

Acts 18:1—19:20
Success and Opportunity for Paul

From Athens Paul journeys to another great city of Greece—Corinth, where he is the guest of two Jewish refugees from Rome, Aquila and Priscilla. (When Luke later puts Priscilla's name before Aquila's, it suggests that she had become a leader of the Corinthian Christians—consistent with Luke's emphasis upon the role of women in the early community.) While in their home, Paul practices his tentmaking trade (18:3, cf. I Thess. 2:9; II Thess. 3:7–8), though his work does not hinder his preaching in the Corinthian synagogue (18:4), particularly after the arrival of Silas and Timothy (with a gift? II Cor. 11:9; Phil. 4:15). Paul regards his tentmaking work as an opportunity for evangelization: "... You remember, brothers, our work and toil. It was while we were laboring night and day, in order not to burden any of you, that we proclaimed to you the gospel of God" (I Thess. 2:9; author's trans.). Christian witness is not only for the synagogue or place of Sunday worship.

When Corinthian Jews oppose him, Paul washes his hands of them, declaring that he is no longer responsible for their fate. Now, he will "go to the Gentiles" (18:6), moving in with a gentile God-fearer named Titius. This move is confirmed, not only by the conversion of the ruler of the synagogue but also, as is the custom of Acts, with a vision which reassures Paul that he is not alone because (1) "I am with you," and (2) "I have many people in this city" (v.10). Reassured by this promise of support from the Lord and the Lord's people, Paul stays and teaches there for a year and a half (v.11).

Eventually, Paul is dragged before the proconsul, Gallio, but Gallio judges the matter to be an internal Jewish problem and says, "I refuse to be a judge of these things" (18:15). The converted ruler of the synagogue is then beaten by a mob—whether by non-Jews or Jews, we are not told, and Gallio could

145

not care less. Even the newest convert is vulnerable to the same persecution which afflicts the eldest apostles themselves. The promise of the vision to Paul (18:9–10) has been fulfilled, for he is allowed to continue his work. The prophecy-fulfillment scheme, so prominent throughout Acts, becomes even more frequent and obvious for the remainder of Acts—Luke's way of instilling our confidence in the trustworthiness of the plans and purposes of God.

When Paul declares, "from now on I will go to the Gentiles," it does not mean that he no longer attempts to convert his fellow Jews or that he will cease going to the synagogue first. He is simply moving his base of operations in Corinth. Christianity is still a sect within Judaism—as even Gallio knows. The new movement must not be severed from its roots, as Paul's vow in conformity with ancient tradition shows. The claims of Christians make sense for Luke (and for us?) only within the context of the hopes of Israel.

In Ephesus, Paul repeats his pattern in Corinth of going first to the synagogue (18:19) but then moving on. This journey gives Luke the opportunity to let Paul instruct us on the nature of *Christian baptism* (18:25—19:5). It seems that one Apollos—described in glowing terms as "eloquent," "well versed in the scriptures," "fervent in spirit," "accurate"—having every possible Lukan attribute of the ideal disciple, lacked one thing: he had never heard of Jesus' baptism, knowing only the baptism of John (18:25). Priscilla and Aquila sought to set Apollos straight (demonstrating that the strictures against women preachers and teachers in I Tim. 2:12 did not hold for all churches). Like John the Baptist, Apollos "confuted the Jews in public" through Scripture (18:28). Yet when Paul encounters Apollos' converts, he is shocked that they say, "we have never even heard that there is a Holy Spirit" (19:2). He baptized them and layed on hands that they might receive the Spirit. Paul explains that John's baptism, like John's ministry as a whole, was concerned with preparation for the one who came after him, the one whose presence would signal the new age of the Spirit (Luke 3:16). The descent of the Spirit at Jesus' baptism (Luke 3:21–22) added a significant new dimension to John's preparatory baptism of repentance—the Spirit. "When Jesus also had been baptized and was praying, the heaven was opened, and the Holy Spirit descended upon him in bodily form, as a dove . . . (Luke 3:21–22). At Pentecost (Acts 2) the Spirit descended upon all of

146

Jesus' followers, signaling that the long-awaited age of the Spirit is now.

Later commentators who saw in this story of Apollos' baptism an affirmation of *two* baptisms—that is, baptism in water followed by baptism of the Holy Spirit—misread Luke's intentions. In the only instance of "rebaptism" in the New Testament, Paul baptizes Apollos' people in Jesus' name *in order that they should receive the Holy Spirit.* It would have been inconceivable to Luke that someone could be "in" Jesus and not be also "in" his Spirit. Baptism "in the name of Jesus" is baptism in the Holy Spirit. In a sense, two baptisms are being reported here; (1) the baptism of repentance practiced by John, which is preparatory and preliminary, and (2) the baptism of Jesus, which is with water and the Holy Spirit and is a sign that one has been initiated into the new age. Luke would not have understood any conception of discipleship without the Spirit. The Spirit, as Paul assures the followers of Apollos, is not optional equipment for Christians, not some advanced degree which separates "Spirit-filled Christians" from the run-of-the-mill nonspiritual Christian proletariat. By virtue of baptism in the name of Jesus and laying-on-of-hands, all Christians are "charismatic" (19:6).

Lest anyone think that the power bestowed through the gift of the Spirit is mere magic, Luke inserts a vignette about "extraordinary miracles by the hands of Paul" (19:11–20). Paul is so close to this healing power that even bits of clothing which touch his body effect healing. Assuming that his power is a sort of magic, some itinerant Jewish exorcists attempt to invoke the name of Jesus to heal. "Jesus I know, and Paul I know; but who are you?" asks the evil spirit who then jumps upon them and they flee naked away (19:15–17). While Luke considers magic to be a serious issue, he is not above treating it in a comical way. The healing power of Paul is no commodity to be seized and used (cf. the discussion of magic and Simon Magus in 8:18–23), not some miraculous force to be channeled at will. *Power* is part of a relationship with the Lord *who is personally known by the believer.* Seeing their black arts, astrology, and voodoo thus derided, once superstitious Jews and Greeks forsake their foolishness; and again, "the word of the Lord grew and prevailed mightily" (19:20), but not without the careful teaching and nurture of leaders like Priscilla, Aquila, and Paul. This faith is not simply about conversion nor is it only about wonder-working

147

power; it is conversion into and power derived from a relationship with the risen Christ. No muddle-headed enthusiast, saying "It doesn't really matter what you believe as long as you are sincere," Luke insists upon correct belief and careful nurture of new converts.

The Final Journey
ACTS 19:21—28:31

About half of Luke's Gospel (from Luke 9:51 to 19:37 or even 22:10) is an account of a journey, a final journey, a kind of exodus for Jesus (according to Luke 9:31). Jesus called his disciples to "follow me" (Luke 9:59). In Acts the Christian life has been called "the Way" (9:2; 19:23; 24:14). Now Paul shall imitate Christ's way as he journeys toward Rome. We wonder if the motif of the journey appealed to Luke, since at the time he wrote expectations for an imminent parousia were receding. Now Christians must cultivate the virtues of patience and perseverance for the long haul (Luke 8:15; 21:19).

In Luke's account of the journey to Emmaus on Easter evening, the despondent disciples walked in blindness, gloom, and abandoned hope. Their mysterious companion charged them with lack of faith and then persuaded them that all that had happened to Jesus, even his suffering and death, was a prelude to glory. Their eyes were opened and their hearts were warmed (Luke 24:13–32). In recounting the last journey of Paul in Acts, Luke surely intends to convince Theophilus that the Christian way, though not without suffering, is no solitary, melancholy journey but a walk with Christ, who has not abandoned his faithful ones, like Paul, but will lead them through grief to glory. For now, there is a sense of growing peril, beginning at 19:21 when "Paul resolved in the Spirit to pass through Macedonia and Achaia . . . , saying, 'After I have been there, I must also see Rome.'" Paul's determination to take Christianity to the capital of the Empire reminds us of Jesus setting his face toward the Holy City (Luke 9:51). Like Jesus (Luke 9:52), Paul sends helpers on ahead of him (Acts 19:22). In fact we now begin a number of close parallels between the career of Paul and that of Jesus. In his ministry and journey toward Rome, Paul demonstrates that he follows Jesus not only in *power* but also in suffering, for this is the way it is in the kingdom—evangelistic success is never without cost (Luke 9:23). Luke's alleged "theology of glory" is constantly tempered with the recognition that discipleship is a matter of cross-bearing (Luke 14:27). The Lukan portrait of Christ may stress the power, glory, and triumph of God's anointed, but the risen One is also the crucified One who is known by the nailprints in his hands and feet (Luke 24:39). Disciples of this Messiah will be known by their scars. Like the tower-builder in Luke's parable (14:28–30), Paul counted the cost of discipleship and determined to be faithful even unto Rome.

Encouraging the Congregations
ACTS 19:21—21:16

Paul's resolve to go back through Macedonia and Achaia is connected with his work of *strengthening congregations for the struggle ahead.* Far from being some itinerant evangelist who blows through town, preaches, converts some, and then packs his bags and moves on, Paul is also a nurturer. Young plants must be cared for if they are to survive (18:23; 19:21–22; 20:1–2). Within American Methodism, George Whitefield was the great preacher and supreme evangelist who ignited one of early America's "great awakenings." Whitefield preached from Georgia to Massachusetts, converting thousands. Francis Asbury, while not remembered for his preaching, is honored as the father of American Methodism because of his organizational ability. Whitefield made converts, Asbury founded—and continued to nurture—churches. American evangelical Protestantism has been accused of producing "still-born Christians." The first stages of faith are reiterated with scant attention to the next step. The result can be Christians of stunted growth who never take root. Such infantile discipleship may be enough for a church where accommodation is the name of the game, a church which never challenges the status quo or the powers-that-be, yet it is no match for the great threats to the gospel which are presented by both culture and life itself. The Body of Christ must take visible, institutional form. It must be strengthened and edified.

The ministry of teaching and strengthening the church may not be so glamorous or so satisfying as preaching before mobs, winning new converts, founding new churches. The day-to-day mundane tasks of administration, counseling, teaching, and going to church meetings borders on drudgery. No one forgets Paul's conversion or the riot at Ephesus or his sea voyage, but who remembers the months of patient day-to-day teaching and nurture in which Paul engaged during his ministry of strengthening the churches? Paul's epistles are testimonial to his determination to be attentive to even the smallest details of daily life within the church. Writing letters to strengthen a struggling congregation, patient instruction of new converts—these are not among the most dramatic or exhilarating tasks of ministry. Yet we know enough of the needs of congregations and the challenge of discipleship to believe that Paul's tireless efforts in Christian nurture were among his most lasting contributions to the church and his worthy example for succeeding generations of Christian leaders.

Acts 19:23–41
A Riot in Ephesus

The new pastor became concerned about the problem of illegal beer and wine sales to minors in the community. After a sermon on the responsibility of the church to protect the young, a crusade was launched to clean up the town and to prosecute those businesses violating the law on alcohol sale to minors. Good! No, bad. How was the young pastor to know that one of the most prominent members of his church owned the convenience store across from the town's high school? He is now the *former* pastor.

We saw in 19:26–27 what happens when disciples dare to disturb the vested business interests. Religion is fine, kept in its place, we say. There is the "real world" of practical, no-nonsense business concerns and then there is the world of religion. Unfortunately, things are not that neatly divided, as Paul's troubles with the Ephesian Silversmiths Union, Local 186 show.

The silversmith's argument against Paul's monotheism is revealing (19:25–27). First they appeal to the Ephesian's greed and financial sensibilities—if Paul's religion catches on, we will

151

be out of work. Then, as if by afterthought, they add that his deprecation of polytheism will also be bad for dear beloved Artemis (v. 27). Alexander's efforts to dissociate Judaism from the Way are fruitless (19:33–34). This not only shows the intimate linkage between Christianity and Judaism, even in the minds of the pagan crowd, but also the threat that both monotheistic faiths pose to polytheism. The mob scene is vivid testimony to the power of economic self-interest to sway a crowd. In the confusion "some cried one thing, some another; . . . and most of them did not know why they had come together" (v. 32). Luke's portraits of the behavior (to say nothing of the intelligence) of pagan idolaters is never too flattering. In this story devotion to Artemis is dismissed as a cover for simple greed.

Artemis had an honorable history in the ancient world. Her temple was regarded as one of the seven wonders of the world and part of the Roman banking system. Artemis, the multibreasted, bountiful earth mother, was a goddess of banking and protector of debtors; and thus her worship was a syncretism of idolatrous religious devotion and economic interest—a wonderful opportunity for Luke to comment upon the peril of vested interests to the gospel. Artemis has her devotees in every town, even today.

Acts 20:1–12
The Comforting Gospel

In Macedonia, Paul gave the disciples "much encouragement" (20:2)—an activity which occupied a large portion of Paul's ministry in Acts (16:5; 18:23). The saints must persevere through many trials, so the task of comforting them (literally: *with strength*) is always a big part of faithful ministry. This *ministry of encouragement* takes many forms, a number of which are in evidence in this section. *Exhortation* (20:1) by Christian teachers and preachers enables disciples to discern between true and false gospels, authentic tradition, and spurious imitation. "It doesn't really matter what a person believes, as long as he or she is sincere," is not a slogan devised by Paul. Weak, inarticulate, unexamined beliefs lead to weak disciples. The Christian faith is considerably more than a mere intellectual exercise. But it is not less than an intellectual challenge. There are facts to be mastered, truths to be discerned, stories to be told right; thus a major part of any faithful congregation's life will be spent in exhortation. Joined to this "ministry of the Word," as it is sometimes called, is the ministry of the table. "On the first day of the week, when we were gathered together to break bread" (v. 7), reminds us of the centrality of common worship for the church.

This is one of the New Testament's earliest definite references to weekly *Sunday worship.* The Christians have continued to gather in the synagogue—unless they have been expelled. But they also apparently gather on Sunday, the first day of the Jewish work week, the day which is for Christians a day of resurrection. The church Luke describes is thus moving toward a distinct day of worship of its own, a day symbolizing clearly that while there is much uniting the church with Judaism there is also much dividing it from Judaism. The day of worship, as well as the stories and actions which occur around the table, constitutes the church as a distinct entity, gives it an identity, keeps reminding the church of who it is. Sunday is the Lord's Day when Christians gather to celebrate the Lord's Supper. Around the table in the gathering for worship, in the *breaking of bread* (2:42,46), Christians sustain one another through the presence of God as experienced at the table. As the Reformers agreed, word and sacrament belong together. Here is where the Body of Christ is made visible (I Cor. 11:17–32). Here is where the Body re-forms, receives nourishment and encouragement in this weekly rhythm of renewal and reiteration of our identity as God's family.

The church of Acts is not always pushing out, on the move, opening its doors, appealing to unbelievers. The church also gathers for worship and fellowship. Without the sustenance received at its Sunday gatherings, the church might lose itself in mere busyness, might forget who it is and whose it is, might lose heart amidst the myriad of demands and assaults upon it by the surrounding world. The things which happen when the church "gathered together to break bread" (v. 7) simply do not happen for the church anywhere else. While we are busy praising God and exploring the ways of God in our worship, something happens to us—the ministry of encouragement.

153

A church with no prophetic thrust, which does not challenge the status quo, has little need for the weekly rhythm of worship. So relaxed and at home in the world, this church needs no encouragement. Or does the problem arise from the other side of the equation? A church without vision, without power flowing from its gathering around the Lord's Table, has little energy or insight and thus no basis for a prophetic challenge to present arrangements in the world. The evangelical activist Jim Wallis has said:

> The greatest need in our time is not simply for *kerygma,* the preaching of the gospel; nor for *diakonia,* service on behalf of justice; nor for *charisma,* the experience of the Spirit's gifts; nor even for *propheteia,* the challenging of the king. The greatest need of our time is for *koinonia,* the call simply to be the church, to love one another, and to offer our lives for the sake of the world. The creation of living, breathing, loving communities of faith at the local church level is the foundation of all the other answers. The community of faith incarnates a whole new order, offers a visible and concrete alternative, and issues a basic challenge to the world as it is. The church must be called to be the church, to rebuild the kind of community that gives substance to the claims of faith (p. 109).

As sometimes happens on occasions when the church gets together, the preacher for the day in Troas went on a bit too long. In fact, Luke says, "he prolonged his speech until midnight" (v. 7). Young Eutychus—whose tribe was to increase throughout Christendom during lengthy sermons—"sank into a deep sleep as Paul talked still longer" (v. 9). The humor suddenly turns to tragedy when the young man "fell down from the third story and was taken up dead."

Tragedy tends to come upon us like that. We are at church, things are going along as usual, then someone slumps forward or a cry goes up, there is the shock, and tragedy engulfs the flow of the ordinary. A once vibrant young disciple is dead—the word is like a gavel coming down, a door banging shut, the end, dead. We are suddenly rendered speechless, immobilized. Death does that to people.

"But Paul went down and bent over him and embraced him," saying to the grieving church, "Do not be alarmed . . ." (v. 10). Into the fixed immobile deadness of things comes a tender embrace. The embrace is modeled after the dramatic stories of Elijah (I Kings 17:21–24), where the prophet embraced and resuscitated the dead son of the widow of Zarephath (a story invoked by Jesus in his Nazareth sermon [Luke 4:24–

27]), and Elisha's reviving of the Shunammite widow's son (II Kings 4:34). Even as these premier prophets of Israel exercised divine power to wrest life from death, so Paul interrupts the accustomed fixed flow of things to reverse the flow of life to death. Like the prophets before him, Paul has demonstrated an alternative reality that destabilizes our expectations for the way the world ought to work. Where we expected the embrace of death, we encounter the embrace of life. Where we expected a church service to turn into a funeral, Paul confidently breaks bread, eats, continues to talk "until daybreak" (why let a thing like death stop a good preacher?) and then the boy is presented alive. Luke's rather laconic comment concludes the drama: they "were not a little comforted" (v. 12).

Prophets like Elijah, Elisha, and now Paul comfort God's grief-stricken people by confronting the status quo, by assaulting the givenness of reality with their prophetic gestures of defiance. God is sovereign. Let not your hearts be troubled. God has no greater adversary than death, no greater enemy who is able to control the thoughts, imaginations, and decisions of humanity. Death is not to be granted a monopoly on the future. The theme of Luke's sermon about Paul's sermon is (in a brevity that might have been good for Paul to practice!) "Do not be alarmed" (v. 10) because there is life. This word and act of life rehabilitates the church, brings it back to life, transforms the church from the fearful little band huddling behind closed doors to a confident, brash band of prophets who are able to confront the world's arrangements with death by shouting the words, "There is life."

Sure, it was a long sermon, but what more could a church ask of its Sunday worship than to return into the world on Monday morning alive and "not a little comforted"?

Acts 20:13–38
Leadership in the Church: Paul's Speech to the Ephesian Elders

Paul the pious Jew wants to be in Jerusalem in time for Pentecost (20:16)—even though he is now in constant contact with gentiles, Paul in no way forsakes his own tradition. Would it not have been easier for Paul to go to the Ephesian elders than for them to come to Paul in Miletus? Was he forbidden as a troublemaker from entering Ephesus (cf. II Cor. 1:8–10)? Luke's major concern is not with these matters but with the lengthy speech to the elders (20:18–35) in which Luke is able to make an authoritative statement about *the nature of the church's leaders* and about Paul as the model leader.

Recalling how Jesus, as he moved toward his own death, delivered a farewell speech (Mark 13; Luke 22:14–38; and most extensively in John 13—17), we sense that we are to overhear a most important pronouncement. As the Master leaves, the questions of the disciples are those of little children as their parents leave for an evening—Where are you going? What is going to happen? Who will stay with us? In the farewell discourse around the table in Luke, Jesus tells his disciples that he will suffer, that "Behold," there are those among them who will betray him, and that there will be misunderstandings among them about the nature of leadership in the community he leaves behind; but the disciples should emulate him as the "one who serves" (Luke 22:14–38). Then, after they go out to the Mount of Olives, he warns them about coming temptations and dangers and tells them to "pray that you may not enter into temptation" (Luke 22:40). The parallels between Jesus' farewell speech to his disciples and Paul's farewell speech to the Ephesian elders are too numerous to be merely coincidental.

Here is one who deserves to speak because all know that he has served the Lord "with tears and with trials" (Acts 20:19). Now, he sets his face (like Jesus) toward Jerusalem, knowing only that "imprisonment and afflictions await me" (v. 23). Even as the storm clouds gathered during the last chapters of Luke's Gospel, the clouds gather for Paul. We know that his life will come to some somber end, even though the true disciple is able to say that "I do not account my life of any value nor as precious to myself," because the only thing significant about his life is his fidelity to "the ministry which I received from the Lord Jesus, to testify to the gospel of the grace of God" (v. 24).

Paul has suffered, now will come the elders' turn to suffer, because after his departure "fierce wolves will come in among you" (v. 29; cf. I Tim. 1:3; II Tim. 1:15). Those who feed the church must guard it as well, because there are those who would pervert the apostolic faith for their own ends (v. 30).

A bit surprisingly, Paul moves from concern about heresy

156

to assert that he "coveted no one's silver or gold or apparel" (v. 33) and that he supported himself with his own hands (v. 34), a fact attested by his work as a tentmaker with Aquila and Priscilla. Somehow, when it comes to duties of the church's leaders, heresy, infidelity, and love of silver and gold go hand-in-hand. Money can corrupt the witness of a preacher as quickly as bad doctrine. In writing about the challenges of leadership in the contemporary church, Richard Neuhaus has said:

> . . . Sinclair Lewis's Elmer Gantry still casts a shadow of suspicion over Christian ministry. . . . There are few decisions that a young pastor or pastoral couple make that are more important than the attitude toward money. One should as early as possible determine the top income one would ever want or strive to have. . . . Otherwise the desire ineluctably grows, avarice feeds upon itself, and one ends up as the victim of an appetite that is in fact insatiable and consumes by worry, guilt, and discontent the hours and days that were once consecrated to ministry . . . there is today a happy reawakening to the liberation of living in simplicity of life, of breaking free from consumerism's grip. Very early we must determine whether we are going to live "the good life" of our own design, worked out in fear in trembling toward our destiny and our calling from God, or whether we are going to live the massified "good life" proffered on television . . . (pp. 191–192).

In his farewell speech at the Last Supper, Jesus contrasted the leaders "of the Gentiles" with leadership among disciples (Luke 22:25–27). In the company of the disciples, the leader is "one who serves," not one who seeks privilege, power, and authority. Paul makes a similar point in discussing leadership and the love of money by noting that when it comes to evaluating the church's leaders, "It is more blessed to give than to receive" (20:35). There is a marked difference between the way the world judges leadership and the way leadership is sought in the church.

Paul not only gives advice to the Ephesian elders but dares to offer himself as an example. Contemporary clergy may be uneasy offering themselves as models for faithfulness, but Paul had no such scruples. "I urge you, then, be imitators of me" (I Cor. 4:16). Paul spoke so boldly because of his conviction, "as I am of Christ" (I Cor. 11:1). The one who "did not shrink from declaring to you the whole counsel of God" (v. 27), despite the suffering it brought to him, and who now heads toward Jerusalem for his final journey felt that he had reason for boldness. The

157

elders in their feeding, care, and vigilance for their flock do well to follow Paul's example.

When it comes down to it, without examples to follow Christians really have very little to offer the world. Jesus did not come preaching a new philosophy. He came preaching a new way of living and dying. Holy ideas were not his main concern, at least in the light of Luke-Acts. *Holy people* were the subjects of his teaching and witness, people who in the words of Paul had been built up and sanctified (v. 32). Examples of holy living and dying make a great difference to the church in every age. If we Christians are unable to point to some Teresa of Calcutta or Desmund Tutu or Martin Luther King or Paul, we have very little to preach. The world is quite right in assuming that if the gospel of Jesus is true it will receive embodiment in the lives of people who follow Jesus. Lacking such people, we turn the Christian faith into an intellectual problem, a matter of academic debate, a thing of deep, inarticulate emotions, or some other invisible exercise which excuses us from the task of making people who really do look, think, and act differently from the rest of the world. Unable to stand and say to the church and the world, "You yourselves know how I lived among you all the time . . . ," as Paul was able to say (v. 18*b*), we say that we are too modest, too self-effacing to offer ourselves as examples to the flock or anyone else. In reality, we are too proud to submit to the change of life and heart required to "testify to the gospel of the grace of God" (v. 24). Leadership in the church would be a simpler affair if we were able to say, "Who cares what a preacher does when he or she is off duty?" or "It doesn't really matter how a priest lives during the week as long as he speaks well in Sunday sermons."

Paul's speech to the Ephesian elders would be a fine text for an ordination sermon or for a reconstruction of our theologies of ordination. In its interplay between the *action* and the *being* of church leaders, its focus upon the *duties* of the elders for the support, care, and protection of the flock, in its frank admission of the *possibilities for pain* within the Christian ministry it provides us with a model (as Paul himself was a model) for thinking about Christian ministry. Perhaps that is why most services of ordination draw directly upon many of the images and concerns of Acts 20 in their frank exposition of the duty of contemporary pastors to be "examples to the flock." The question to a candidate for the priesthood in the *Episcopal Book of Common Prayer* (pp. 531–532) is typical: "Will you do your best to pattern your life in accordance with the teachings of Christ, so that you may be a wholesome example to your people?"

Acts 21:1–16
The Cost of Discipleship

"Ask, and it will be given you; seek, and you will find; knock, and it will be opened . . . how much more will the heavenly Father give the Holy Spirit to those who ask him!" (Luke 11:9, 13). The saying is a beloved one, found in Luke's collection of Jesus' sayings about prayer. It seems to typify Luke's emphasis upon the empowerment of disciples through the Holy Spirit to receive all that they ask of the abundant life. This is Luke's alleged "theology of glory," which stresses the benefits, gifts, and power of the Holy Spirit available to disciples if they will just ask.

Yet it was also Luke who told the story of Jesus in Gethsemane (Luke 22:39–46), where Jesus asked his father to "remove this cup from me" (v. 42). Jesus received a "No" to that request, for "No" is also an answer to prayer even if it is not the answer we hoped to hear. Yet in Gethsemane Jesus' prayer was answered that "not my will, but thine, be done" (v. 42). Disciples in Acts do not merely receive empowerment and healing miracles, great signs and wonders. They ask and find God's will. For the disciple sometimes that will involves suffering. Take Paul for instance.

In a tearful scene Paul leaves the Ephesians (Acts 20:36–38). From town to town he travels on his way to Jerusalem, upheld by the Christian communities in places like Tyre and Ptolemais. The church has become a counter-cultural, global network of communities caring for their own subversive missionaries who are now traveling to and fro throughout the Empire. Prayer and fellowship (20:36; 21:5) keep Paul going along each step of his foreboding journey toward Rome. In Acts 18:21 Paul told the Ephesians, "I will return to you if God wills." His journey is not of his own volition but under the guidance of God, for his concern is to do God's will rather than his own. Agabus in his act of prophecy (21:10–11) warns Paul of his destiny. Even as Jesus was warned (Luke 9:44; 18:32), so is Paul. The servants of God may be empowered and gifted with the Spirit, but this in no way ex-

159

empts them from suffering for the cause of truth (9:17; Luke 3:21–22; 4:16–19). In Luke's Gospel Jesus accepts suffering and death as part of the way he must walk (chaps. 9—23). Paul's journey toward Jerusalem parallels Jesus' passion, for Jesus is the "leader" or "pioneer" who goes before the disciple in every way, including the way of pain (Acts 5:31). Whatever prayer "in Jesus' name" may mean, whatever it means to be "in the Spirit," it does not mean exemption from pain.

In the realistic and somber interlude of Acts 21:1–16, the writer of Acts, with his stress upon the empowerment of the Spirit, corrects misconceptions which might have arisen about the cost of discipleship. The age of the Spirit has begun at Pentecost in the resurrection and ascension of Jesus. Yet this does not end sickness, suffering, evil, injustice, ignorance, and rejection. That would be to fall into a "realized eschatology" which acts as if the kingdom has already come in its completeness. Nor does Luke act as if in Christ nothing has happened and we are still awaiting deliverance. Those who are "in the name of Jesus" know that the decisive victory against the forces of evil and death has been won, yet there are still battles to be fought. Suffering per se has little redemptive meaning in Luke-Acts. Pain is not glorified in itself. Rather, the suffering of disciples like Paul has meaning as a sign that they are indeed participating in the will of God to encounter evil and to defeat it through the mysterious yet certain increase of the word and its effects.

The world where disciples must witness is an inhospitable place. The world did not see who the babe in the manger really was, and when it did, the trouble began. Scarcely did Jesus finish his first sermon in Nazareth before they cried for his blood. As Jesus warned his followers:

> . . . they will lay their hands on you and persecute you, delivering you up to the synagogues and prisons, and you will be brought before kings and governors for my name's sake. . . . You will be delivered up even by parents and brothers and kinsmen and friends, and some of you they will put to death; you will be hated by all for my name's sake (Luke 21:12–17).

Throughout Acts we have followed the fulfillment of these grim predictions—from the martyrdom of Stephen to the troubles of Paul. The message of Acts is not about embracing and loving the world, but rather about teaching the world to repent. Here is a ministry which casts fire upon the earth (Luke 12:49) and turns parent against child.

Paul can face his coming suffering with confidence because of his assurance that in his life "The will of the Lord be done" (Acts 21:14). This assurance comes to us—as it came to both Paul and to Jesus—in prayer. Jesus wrestles with God's will for him in prayer in Gethsemane. Paul is in constant prayer with the churches. As in the case of Jesus, Paul's friends fear for his safety and attempt to dissuade him from his mission (21:12). Like Jesus, Paul is determined that God's will be done. This is what it means to pray "in Jesus' name." To be empowered by the Spirit cannot mean to be shielded from all heartache and pain. The notion that only good things happen to faithful people was put to rest on a Friday afternoon at Calvary. Rather, to be gifted by the Spirit must mean the gift of meaning in our struggles, the conviction that God can use whatever abuse, heartache, and tragedy we encounter in our attempts to be faithful to bring about God's purposes.

> Likewise, the Spirit helps us in our weakness; for we do not know how to pray as we ought, . . . the Spirit intercedes for the saints according to the will of God. . . . If God is for us, who is against us? He who did not spare his own Son but gave him up for us all, will he not also give us all things with him? Who shall bring any charge against God's elect? . . . Who shall separate us from the love of Christ? Shall tribulation, or distress, or persecution, or famine, or nakedness, or peril, or sword? . . . No, in all these things we are more than conquerors through him who loved us (Rom. 8:26, 27, 31–33, 35, 37).

The bread was broken and laid upon the altar and the blood-red wine was poured out in the cup. The priest spread out his hands in blessing. A child, seeing the gesture, cried out, "Look, Mommy, he's trying to look like Jesus on the cross."

That is not a bad thing to say about a Christian.

Paul's Arrest and the Journey to Rome
ACTS 21:17—28:28[29]

Throughout the last chapters of Acts the clouds have been gathering. Paul has been warned of the trials which await him in Jerusalem. Yet, led by the Spirit, Paul has determined to go back to the home base, back to the mother church of the Way.

We know that we are at the beginning of the end for Paul.

Yet we say it with too much finality, as if we were merely reading the last chapter of the novel, the conclusion of the story. Luke means for these final chapters in Acts to do much more for us. There will be grave dangers ahead. Jerusalem was where Jesus gathered his friends to be strengthened by them but also where he met his fate at the hands of his enemies. It will be much the same for Paul in the closing chapters of Acts. Yet there will also be the great adventure of a sea voyage and a long and eloquent summation and defense of Paul and his work. A number of trajectories, which we have been following throughout Acts, will meet in these final chapters: The unhindered gospel will be vindicated and Theophilus and his church, as well as our own, will hear Luke's final word on the "truth concerning the things of which you have been informed" (Luke 1:4).

Acts 21:17-26
Return to Jerusalem

Luke's main concern in this account of Paul's final trip to Jerusalem is to solidly ground Paul's work in the blessing of the apostles in Jerusalem. Throughout Acts we have seen efforts to preserve the authority of the community at Jerusalem, having them approve of each new thrust of the gentile mission. In the diaspora which followed the murder of Stephen (6:8—8:3), believers were scattered far beyond Jerusalem—everyone except for the Twelve. Luke cannot allow them to leave, since they represent the eyewitness link with the facts of Jesus' ministry and resurrection. Jerusalem is for Luke the tradition, the facts, the apostolic faith, which is always the final test for the church's fidelity. The Lukan Paul must be in congruence with the tradition represented by Jerusalem. Perhaps this explains why the collection Paul was to deliver from the gentiles to Jerusalem as a sign of solidarity between gentile and Jewish Christians (see Rom. 15:25–31) is not mentioned in this section. Did Jewish Christians at Jerusalem reject gentile beneficence? We do not know. At any rate, Luke does not mention the collection, perhaps because it was a source of some controversy between Paul and Jerusalem and Luke wants to show the unity of Paul with the home church rather than disagreement.

162

The pattern within chapter 21 is a familiar one we have encountered elsewhere in Acts. Outreach to the gentiles is legitimated by the blessing of Jerusalem; then the gentile converts respond with conciliatory gestures toward Jerusalem— (see 10:1—11:18; 11:19–30; chaps. 13—15 and 16:1–4; chaps. 16—21). Acts 21:17–26 is a culmination of the stories of work among the gentiles we have been hearing in chapters 16—20. Paul returns to Jerusalem to gain the approval of the elders there.

The Christians in Jerusalem "received us gladly" (21:17), glorifying God at Paul's report on his work among the gentiles (21:20). They also reaffirm the earlier Jerusalem conference agreement on fellowship between gentile and Jewish Christians (21:25).

Paul takes steps to reassure Jerusalem of the error of the charges against him. Paul is unjustly accused of teaching "all the Jews who are among the Gentiles to forsake Moses, telling them not to circumcise their children or observe the customs" (21:21). Through his taking of a Nazarite vow (21:24), Paul demonstrates that like all the church leaders in Acts he is thoroughly orthodox and faithful to the historic faith of Israel. We are reminded again of Luke's insistence that members of the Way like Paul are faithful Jews, while those who oppose him are not.

We do a great injustice to the Paul of Acts if we transform him into a first-century "liberal," the great innovator who sought to drag his conservative friends toward his more open and inclusive ideas. In Luke's mind Paul's loyalty to the faith of Israel is the source of his radical move toward the gentiles. As is often observed, "radical" comes from the Latin *radix*, "root." Luke implies in passages like chapter 21 that if we will dare to get to the roots of Israel's faith, we will see the validity of each turn in the early church's journey. Many modern people have forsaken both memory and history in favor of their fascination with the existential self. Why worry about the witness of the ancestors when the only truth worth trusting is the truth of *me?* We think of tradition as inherently conservative, archaic, and antiquarian. Yet sometimes the invocation of tradition is a means of returning to our origins, not in time but in substance. Our culture conditions us to think of tradition as something we must put behind us in order to progress. Yet sometimes memory is the source of radical new thrusts in ministry. We not only hold on to what is important through

163

our tradition but also through memory gain imaginative new constructions for the future. A church without memory, without some "Jerusalem" to return to for guidance and blessing, is destined to become the prisoner of the status quo, a people without vision who can see no further than merely present arrangements, slaves to the opinions of those who happen to be walking about.

Hans Mol has noted that the charismatic biblical leader is not so much a ground-breaking revolutionary as a reformer, a renewer of tradition. The prophet is the one who recalls the tradition and recalls the faithful to the tradition. The prophet repristinates rather than innovates. Although the religious establishment may have perverted the tradition, may have ignored certain aspects of the faith to suit its own purposes, the prophet does not jettison the tradition (pp. 45–46).

In his obedience to the heavenly vision, in risking everything to be true to what he had seen, in casting aside all concern for his personal well-being and safety to follow the divine leading, Paul is demonstrating his "Jewishness," his membership within a people who down through the ages have endeavored to listen to God and to be obedient, even when the world was busy traveling in a different direction, even when faithfulness to God meant great suffering for them. Luke has nothing whatsoever against "traditionalism." The issue is not whether we shall honor the tradition of the past. The issue is, *Which tradition is worth our whole mind and soul and strength?* Luke has no problem with the church being "conservative." Our modern separation of open-minded liberals from closed-minded conservatives is a false dichotomy of no concern to Luke. The issue is, Is the tradition we are conserving *true?*

Acts 21:27—22:21
Being Zealous for God: Paul's Speech at the Temple

The alarm goes out, "Help! This one teaches against the people, the law, and the temple." Someone teaching something new? Someone defiling the tradition, our holy places, mixing everything up and turning everything upside down? Such charges are sure to draw a crowd and the crowd quickly becomes a riot.

With a few bold strokes, Luke paints a scene of confusion and violence with everyone shouting, pushing one another about, and beating Paul. The civil confusion enables Luke to introduce into the narrative the one before whom Paul will give his testimony, the tribune, the commandant of the Roman garrison at Jerusalem. The tribune arrives with his soldiers to break up the confusion. Unable to ascertain what has happened, he has Paul bound in chains and rescued from the mob. Paul has been saved from the fury of the mob so that he may give his speech before the Roman authorities, a speech he will give in chains. This subtle detail of the chains (v. 33) contributes to the increasingly ominous tone of the narrative, for as we see Paul bound by the tribune something tells us that we shall not see him free again (cf. 26:29). This section introduces a series of trial scenes that culminates in Acts 26.

We are not to ponder how a man, nearly beaten to death by a lynch mob, could now give a moving speech from the tribune's stairs or how the howling mob became quiet and attentive. The location and the audience for the speech are what merit our notice. We are standing before the temple, listening to a man who has come close to being lynched because of accusations that he has defiled the religion of Israel. The context gives meaning to Paul's speech. In elegant Greek, Paul informs the tribune that he is not the Egyptian revolutionary but a devout Jew of Tarsus, a citizen of no mean city of Cilicia (21:39). The tribune discovers that Paul is not the troublemaker whom the authorities expect. According to Acts 1:11, the first Christians were in expectation that their Messiah would form a new kingdom. The Romans knew that they must be ever-vigilant against Jewish national and messianic hopes. The tribune seems to be put at ease in learning that Paul is not the Egyptian Jew who tried to overthrow the Roman yoke. The issue between the Jews and these Jewish Christians like Paul is one of religion—or so the tribune reassures himself. He allows Paul to make his case before his fellow Jews, content that this Jew poses no harm to the security of his grip on Jerusalem. Paul is non-political—or so the tribune assumes.

It is significant that Paul asks the tribune to allow him to speak "to the people" (21:39). He uses the word customarily employed in Acts to refer to the *Jewish people* (3:23; 4:8; 7:17).

165

INTERPRETATION

In 21:39 Paul asserts, "I am a Jew." To a great extent this speech will be a defense of that assertion. When a mob wanted to kill him (and eventually succeeded), Stephen defended himself by recounting Israel's history. Paul defends himself by recounting his own history. The speech in 22:1–21 is addressed, in Aramaic, to "brothers and fathers"—here is one of their own attempting to testify to his own family about what has happened to him, pleading that he is still a member of the family, even when his actions appear to have removed him from the family's values and traditions.

We can identify four basic units within the body of the speech:

1. *A description of Paul's training as a zealous Jew* (vv. 3–5)
2. *Paul's encounter with Jesus* (vv. 6–11)
3. *Ananias and his help* (vv. 12–16)
4. *Paul's vision in the temple* (vv. 17–21)

1. Note that Paul uses the present tense to describe his relationship to Judaism. "I *am* a Jew." Whereas those who have beaten him are zealots for the tradition and law and order, Paul describes himself as a zealot for God (v. 3). Like them, Paul knows what it means to persecute others in the cause of religious righteousness, for this is exactly what he did to "the Way" (v. 4). By language, upbringing, and zealotry Paul has established a link with his audience. If someone does not believe him, all he has to do is to ask the chief priest and the council (v. 5).

2. Thus far, we have heard evidence that Paul was a conventional, devout believer with peerless credentials. Everything about him makes him one with his audience. Now comes an account of the reversal worked in Paul on the Damascus road. While there are many parallels between this account and that of 9:3–9, there are a couple of striking differences. For one thing there is more talk here about *light*. The vision is said to have occurred "about noon," when the sun would be most intense; so if Paul was blinded by a greater light, it must have been a great light indeed. Careful comparers of 22:9 with 9:7 notice that in the first account Paul's companions heard a voice but saw nothing (9:7). Now Paul tells us that his companions "saw the light but did not hear the voice" (22:9). In this speech verse 9 once again calls attention to the great power of the light. It also heightens the drama of the encounter by emphasizing that though many saw the light only Paul heard what was said,

particularly the words which told him what he was to do. Luke is doing something different in this speech than he was doing in the conversion account of 9:3–9.

We also note that Paul appears to be a more active participant in this recollection of the Damascus road experience. Before, Paul was struck down and had little to say but, "Who are you?" Now, Paul says that he asked, "What should I *do?*" Before, Paul was led by the hand. Now, Paul says that he waited for the fulfillment of Jesus' words concerning what he is appointed to do (22:10).

3. The visit of Ananias (vv. 12–16) helps Paul to see what his commission is to be. In Acts 9 Ananias functioned mainly to underscore that the community's old enemy had been transformed into a friend. Here, that emphasis is dropped. We are told that Ananias is pious and respects the law—someone whom Paul's audience should respect. Ananias' role here is to deliver the call: "The God of our fathers appointed you to know his will, to see the Just One and to hear a voice from his mouth; for you will be a witness for him to all men of what you have seen and heard" (vv. 14–15). "God of our fathers" is the traditional way of referring to the God of Israel (e.g., Gen. 43:23; Exod. 3:13; Deut. 1:11). The God of Israel's past has chosen Paul to be a "witness" to what is happening in the present.

4. This section puts Paul at prayer in the temple (22:17). Here is the heart of faithful Judaism and this is where Paul is placed, where Paul is delivering this speech at this moment. Verse 18 introduces the first indication of conflict between Paul and his fellow Jews. Up to this point they have been in agreement. Ironically, Paul says to the Lord that it is because of his record of persecution and zealotry that his fellow Jews should believe him (vv. 19–20). But no, the Lord has other things in mind for Paul. If he is to be faithful, he must obey the surprising commission: "I will send you far away to the Gentiles" (v. 21).

The crowd, which had listened up to this point, is sent into a rage. This is the climax of Paul's speech and the audience knows it. Instead of the overthrow of the enemy, which we said characterized the account of Paul's conversion in Acts 9, Acts 22 may be summarized as *the call of the loyal and zealous Jew.* There was a calling of Paul in Acts 9, but that call was not the driving force behind that account. Here in Acts 22 the call of Paul by Christ is both his defense for his actions and the cause of his rejection in Jerusalem. He attempts to justify his actions

167

by claiming that he has gone to the gentiles, not because he has forsaken Judaism but because he was trying to keep up with the movements of the God of Judaism. It is a defense—a fulfillment of Christ's prediction that "they will not accept your testimony about me" (22:18).

As usual, Luke is dealing with a number of themes at the same time and working on a number of different levels in this section. The passage suggests reflection upon questions of *the Christian's relationship to the state and the role of the governmental authorities.* A Roman tribune, despite what a Christian might think of his profession or of his presence in an occupied Judea, has intervened in a religious dispute and saved the life of Paul, now he can again testify to what has happened to him. In 18:12–17 and 19:23–41 the pagan authorities have been most helpful in keeping believers from tearing one another to shreds! In denying that he is the Egyptian revolutionary (v. 38), Paul has said that he is not a political revolutionary—at least in the sense that the tribune may take him to be. Revolutionary violence does not seem to be the path advocated by Christ or his followers; in Luke's story they are able to be law abiding citizens of a pagan state (cf. Luke 2:1–7; 20:21–25). In 22:24–29 Paul appeals to his Roman citizenship as a protection against examination by torture, thus suggesting that Christians may be free to use their legal rights, even those bestowed upon them by pagan governments, as protection against injustice and as a means of enabling them to witness to the truth of Christ. As Paul advised the church at Rome, "rulers are not a terror to good conduct, but to bad. Would you have no fear of him who is in authority? Then do what is good, and you will receive his approval, for he is God's servant for your good" (Rom. 13:3–4). Luke's story of Jesus opens with the holy family's journey to Bethlehem as required by Roman law. God used Caesar's decree to accomplish his purposes. Now God uses even a Roman tribune to further the spread of the gospel.

The primary emphasis of Paul's address to his fellow Jews is the theme of calling. His account of his "conversion" is, as we read it in Acts 22, *an account of Paul's vocation.* Here is an account of someone who in the light on the Damascus road was called "out of darkness into his marvelous light" (I Peter 2:9). There Paul says he saw something he had not been able to see; he heard something he had not heard. Our "vocation" as Christians, the story suggests, is not something we merely "do for a living," but rather the way in which we respond to the commission of God upon our lives, the things God asks us to do as part of God's work in the world. The story also suggests that we need not expect our attempts at being faithful to our call to be without trouble or pain. Not everyone "sees" the call the same as we see it. The light we see, which shines upon us and helps to make sense out of our journey, only baffles or blinds others. In our attempts to live out our vocation, we may be misunderstood, even hated, by those who have not been so called or have not heard as we have heard or seen as we have seen. The tough part of living our "call" may not be only in our attempts to be faithful to God but in our efforts to account for ourselves before our brothers and sisters who do not understand. The same light which enlightened Paul on the Damascus road blinded many and broke the hearts of many more in Luke's world. It is capable of doing the same today.

Aside from the theme of the mission to the gentiles being of divine initiative, this section also suggests reflection upon the question of *tradition versus traditionalism*. The mob sought to kill Paul because of their zealous adherence to "tradition." But Paul's defense was that he was the real adherent to tradition, because he attempted faithfully to be obedient to God's leading—even when that leading led him into areas of surprising divine graciousness, such as to the gentiles. To be a faithful member of Israel, Paul's speech suggests, is to be willing to be surprised, to be led into strange areas of God's grace. This is the *tradition* worth defending, worth living out in our own day, as opposed to the dry and often dead *traditionalism* which merely appeals to blind obedience to what we have always done. Today's church, like the faithful who gathered at the temple before us, is subject to new divine calling and revelation. Knowing this debate over tradition versus traditionalism, we should listen carefully and take note—our beloved tradition, our accustomed ways of doing things, can make us deaf to the call of Christ and blind to the light of new revelation.

Acts 22:22—23:11
Defense Before the Council

There are many different ways of doing theology. One popular method is to glean from Scripture certain abstract propositions and principles and then systematically to develop them, applying these propositions to contemporary concerns of the church. Theology in this way is the sibling of philosophy; it consists in the reflection and application of ideas. Luke tackles theological problems with another method. Through stories problems are explored in their complexity. Assertions are made, but always within the context of unfolding drama. Readers are left to draw their own conclusions, to see things in a new way, to become part of the stresses and ambiguities within an issue. As a result, we not only gain information but we also undergo conversion. A story about Paul becomes our story. We go back to our lives with a different *perspective* (meaning literally: *to see through*) because the story has enticed us into viewing and reviewing the world in a way that would have been difficult without the story.

If we look for "information" in Acts 22:22—23:11, we may be disappointed. The scenes are chaotic, cryptic, at times illogical. Why did Paul wait to tell the tribune that he was a Roman citizen (22:25)? Why is the tribune convening a meeting of the Jewish council (22:30)? Did anyone else speak at the council hearing?

Yet these questions do an injustice to Luke's dramatic art. The scene opens with the mob's cry, "Away with such a fellow from the earth! For he ought not to live" (22:22). Paul's declaration of his mission to the gentiles (22:21) has sent them into a frenzy, echoing their cry against him in 21:36. The Jewish leaders and the people want Paul out of the way, silenced. They would prefer him dead rather than to hear him continue to challenge their view of God's will.

A curious Roman tribune is now inserted into the story. Through a good flogging he hopes to get to the bottom of this Jewish commotion (22:24). Jews may argue about theology; Romans have their own way of getting to the truth—torture. Yet Paul is no mere victim of religious hostility or governmental oppression. Even in his chains, he is still in control of the situation, a fact Luke beautifully depicts by having Paul bring the torture to a sudden stop with an (almost casual) inquiry: "Is it lawful for you to scourge a man who is a Roman citizen, and uncondemned" (22:25)? Theophilus must have thoroughly enjoyed this delightful twist in the narrative, thinking of Paul sending the soldiers into confusion with the revelation that his Roman credentials are more impressive than even those of the tribune himself (22:28). The tribune is a dime store Roman, whereas Paul, the man whom the tribune would teach a lesson in civics by use of the whip, is a citizen by birth. Who is laughing now? In his ministry Paul has been the bridge between the faith of Judaism and the people of the Empire, so in his own life Paul is not only a Jew (22:3) but also a Roman citizen (22:28).

Paul is crafty, shrewd, humorous in the face of Caesar's power, the master of his would-be oppressors. For a people accustomed to seeing things always work out the other way, this story must have been a delight to hear. Good stories, like the parables of Jesus, often have a subverting function. They set up the accustomed flow of history; then they throw it in reverse. We are lured into the conventional, expected, predictable only to have the story transform it into the surprising. Humor arises in the Acts narratives from time to time because humor results when we encounter the gap between the way things are and the way they are supposed to be, the space between the fixed world as it is and the movement of the world toward the purposes of God. A preacher like Luke delights to play within this space, using narrative to open such spaces so that we may be surprised, may smile at the incongruity between Caesar's power and God's power, may delight that a man in chains has more control over the situation than a man with a sword.

When faced with tragedy—the persecution of the church, the suffering of disciples, the cruelty of tyranny—what is a faithful response? Theophilus could weep over the situation, which is alright as far as that goes. With Acts so full of consoling, strengthening words for Theophilus, many tears must have been shed within his church. Or Theophilus could laugh. Laughter occurs when we go on the offensive against despair, when we take the initiative against tragedy, determined not to relinquish tomorrow to the powers of evil and death. There is more than one way for the church to "take courage" (23:11). Caesar's legions are powerless against such holy humor. Tyrants of both the political left and the right hate humor, despise satire for this reason. Most of our really good comedians come from the ranks of people who know what it means to be on the receiving end of injustice. There are much worse sins for Christians than to be laughing in church.

171

Now the tribune, "desiring to know the real reason why the Jews accused" Paul (22:30), convenes the Jewish council. Paul addresses them as "Brethren" (23:1). The high priest acts in much the same conniving, deceitful way that he acted at the trial of Jesus. Paul is adamant, but in fidelity to the law (23:5) gives the priest the respect Scripture says he is due. Paul appeals to his Pharisaic heritage (23:6), an appeal which immediately sends the Sadducees and the Pharisees into a shouting match. The conservative Sadducees square off with the more progressive Pharisees over issues of the spirit and the resurrection (23:7–8). The Pharisees are quite pleased by what they hear from Paul. If he has acted under the direction of an angel or a spirit, that is fine with them. Note that Paul does not say that he has now become an enlightened Christian who has put his Pharisaic heritage behind him. *"I am* a Pharisee," he says. Luke has thus linked Christianity and Pharisaic Judaism. With the temple destroyed (by the time that Luke wrote Acts), why can the Pharisees and the Christians not get along with one another; they already agree on so much? Unlike the unprincipled assassins whom we meet next in 23:12–35, these knowledgeable and devout Pharisees say "We find nothing wrong in this man" (23:9). The main theological point of the scene is a recurring one in Acts: *Christianity is in continuity with the best of Judaism,* more specifically here, Pharisaic Judaism. Judaism is not some archaic faith that more progressive Christians have outgrown. The claims of Christ are intelligible as the fulfillment of the hopes of Judaism. The difficulties the Way encounters are those of an impassioned intramural debate between Jew and Jew.

Paul is rescued from being the victim of the debate by the tribune. Sometimes Christians may rely upon the order and power of the state to preserve them, even though the purposes of Paul and those of the tribune are diametrically opposed. Perhaps Luke is a bit chagrined that sometimes in the fierce debates between believers it takes a non-believing pagan to keep believers from tearing one another to bits! No doubt the tribune was less than impressed by the spectacle of this Jewish intra-family feud—as little impressed as the contemporary world is with current Christian name-calling and interdenominational jealousy. That night, Paul is visited by the Lord who has directed him throughout his ministry; this same Lord urges him to "Take courage," and now directs him to "bear witness also at Rome" (23:11).

Acts 23:12—25:12
Accounting for the Hope That Is in You

It is typical of Luke to work on a number of levels in his narrative. Acts 23:12—25:12 is no exception. Themes reappear, are reiterated, expanded. Events are echoed by other events. The same idea is treated, but from a different perspective. Let us lift out some of the major themes in this rich section of Acts' account of Paul.

Paul is always in mortal danger. The Lord told Ananias that he would "show him how much he must suffer for the sake of my name" (9:16). *Paul must follow his call through many tribulations,* including three attempts on his life by opponents in Jerusalem (21:31, 36; 23:12–15; 25:3). The Christian faith is borne into the world in a very personal way, through persons whom God chooses to speak the truth. It is quite natural then for the enemies of the gospel to try to stop its spread by killing those who bear the gospel. Paul's would-be assassins are dedicated, their oaths sealed by fasting. They will fail because Paul is God's chosen instrument (9:16). The account of Paul's protection by the tribune is an example of Luke as a master of adventure narrative. The planned ambush is thwarted through the intelligence work of the son of Paul's sister as well as by the intervention of the tribune. As we have noted *(Reflection: The Politics of Luke),* Luke took a generally dim view of the imperial Romans, although it was not completely negative. Even the Romans can be useful in protecting a disciple. That the tribune protected Paul is more than support from Luke for the Roman state. It is rather an affirmation that even Caesar's legions can be useful as God protects his endangered messengers and enables them to accomplish their purposes.

The tribune Claudius Lysias writes a letter to Felix declaring Paul's innocence as far as Roman law is concerned (23:26–30). The letter enables Luke to reiterate his point that *Paul can*

173

be accused of no crime for which the State is responsible. Claudius Lysias, Felix (by implication; 24:23, 26, 27), and Festus (25:25) declare Paul's innocence. The debate about Paul is a matter of theological contention between Jews (23:29; 25:18), a debate about the resurrection (24:15; 26:6–7). Luke's claim is that Paul is guilty of treason against neither Judaism nor Rome. Of course, Paul's real audience in Acts is neither Roman nor Jewish officials but the church of Theophilus' day—a church of Jews and gentiles. First, Luke wants to say, our movement is best understood as a branch of faithful Judaism which, like the Pharisees, believes in the resurrection. Secondly, Luke says, we can work within the Empire to accomplish our purposes.

Ananias the high priest, when he argues before Felix through Tertullus, bows and scrapes before the Roman governor, flattering him and saying that he accepts his rule "with all gratitude" (24:3). As for Paul, Ananias calls him a "pestilent fellow" who is a "ringleader of the sect of the Nazarenes" who tried to "profane the temple" (24:5–6). As in the trial of Jesus (Luke 23:2), Paul's opponents attempt to present this as a political problem rather than a theological debate. Paul is a threat to law and order, a menace to the security of the Empire. We have heard these false accusations before. They give Paul the opportunity to defend himself before a high Roman official, Felix the governor. The speech is, like the others in Acts, a carefully constructed statement to the church of Theophilus' day, having as its end the shaping of contemporary Christian identity.

The charges of political subversion are false, says Paul, for he had been in Jerusalem twelve days prior to his arrest and incited no one to riot (24:10–13). Paul says, "I worship the God of our fathers, believing everything laid down by the law or written in the prophets," who also hoped in the resurrection (24:14–15). The Way is not some radical new innovation but something that stands in line with the central affirmations of historic Judaism. It is the Way's claim of the resurrection of the dead which is at issue in the debate and is the cause of contention between the Way and the high priest (24:21). Contemporary scholars may be unconvinced that the Christian affirmation of the resurrection is affirmed by "the law or written in the prophets" (24:14), but this is a central contention of Luke.

174

Felix postpones a verdict and places Paul in custody. In allowing the case against Paul to drag on, Felix is being no friend to his prisoner. His apparent kindness toward Paul, in allowing Paul's friends to attend him, is clouded by Luke's comments about Felix in 24:24–27. As it turns out, Felix kept Paul in prison in hopes that "money would be given him by Paul" (24:26). We have encountered this pagan confusion about Christians before. Christians have power, but it is not the power of the purse. Furthermore, Felix' wife Drusilla enters the story. She is a Jew who has married this functionary of Caesar. It is her second marriage. Paul boldly speaks to the imperial couple about "justice, self-control, and the judgment to come," subjects which could not have amused Felix or Drusilla. Paul switches from the political to the personal. Who cares what a politician does in his bedroom as long as he votes for the right things on the floor of the Senate? That may be our way, but not Paul's. Is there no limit to the impudence of these Christians? They not only challenge the theological establishment but the political establishment as well. Even in custody, even with his fate in the hands of the procurator, Paul is God's faithful prophet, who like the prophets of Israel boldly proclaims the truth of God, despite the possible cost. He is able to speak bluntly to the high priest and he will not curb his tongue before the unprincipled Felix. In his prophetic boldness and concern for ethics, Paul does represent the best of the faith of Israel.

Acts 25:13—26:32
Defense Before Agrippa

Upon the Damascus road, Paul was commissioned to "carry my name before the Gentiles and *kings* and the sons of Israel" (9:15; author's ital.). Throughout the latter part of Acts, we have watched Paul fulfill Jesus' words that "they will lay their hands on you and persecute you, delivering you up to the synagogues and prisons." Now it is time for Paul to fulfill the rest of that prediction: "you will be brought *before kings and governors* for my name's sake" (Luke 21:12–13; author's itals.).

Before Luke has Paul leave Jewish soil for the fate that awaits him in Rome, the stage is set for one final dramatic scene. Poor Festus, perhaps well meaning but woefully inadequate to understand what Paul is about, is blessed by a visit from none other than King Agrippa II and his sister Bernice (25:13–27).

175

The surprise visit enables Luke to have Festus ask his royal visitors their opinion of what he ought to say to Emperor Nero about this odd prisoner. Festus tells Agrippa that there is a muddle among Paul's accusers who "disputed with him about their own superstition and about somebody called Jesus who was dead, but whom Paul claims is alive" (author's trans.; 25:19). Festus clearly has an equally low opinion about Jews and these Christians. The strange Jewish squabble intrigues Agrippa, who says "I should like to hear the man myself." With blare of trumpets and great pomp, Bernice and Agrippa enter the hall. The audience becomes hushed. All eyes are upon Paul. For one last time he rises in his own defense. Luke has skillfully drawn together a number of personalities and themes and set the stage for a dramatic presentation in Acts 26 of Paul's final defense before his Jewish adversaries and the baffled representatives of the Empire.

We heard Paul defend himself in Acts 22 against the charge that he teaches against the law and the people. His defense there was that he was a loyal Jew who did only as he was directed by God. In the intervening chapters we have heard additional charges brought against Paul: He has been called a "pestilent fellow," and "an agitator," whose cohorts have sought to defile the temple (24:5–6). Paul has appealed to Caesar (25:11), so now the judicial process must do its work. Festus suggests that Agrippa hear Paul for himself, asserting that in his opinion Paul does not deserve death. Since he has no charges to send to Caesar regarding Paul (25:23–27), Festus hopes that Agrippa will help him decide upon the accusations. Paul speaks for himself, summing up his defense against all of the accusations brought against him.

Paul stretches forth his hand in the traditional pose of the classic orator as he begins his defense. He credits King Agrippa with knowing all the customs of the Jews, a remark causing some to speculate on the possibility of whether or not Agrippa might be a Jew himself. But this speculation deters us from hearing the remark as being Luke's subtle statement of the purpose of this particular defense speech. Paul is about to present himself as victim of an internal Jewish squabble about the resurrection from the dead, an issue of "customs and controversies" that is hardly deserving of the sentence of death.

176

Gaventa suggests that we ought to compare this introduction with that of Paul's earlier speech in Acts 22 (pp. 79–80).

There Paul begins by addressing his "brothers and fathers" in Hebrew. Here he speaks of controversies among "the Jews" as if he is somehow distinct from that group. When he describes his Pharisaic life (26:5), he speaks almost as an outsider, describing the Pharisees as a party or sect. Everything in Acts 22 was designed to demonstrate that Paul is a loyal and faithful Jew. Here in Acts 26 we get the impression of more distance and detachment from Judaism, the sort of phrases one might use in speaking of ones faith to an uninvolved observer like Agrippa.

"And now" (v. 6) indicates a pivot in the speech. From here on his old manner of life is past and something new has begun. "The promise of my Father upon you" earlier stood for the promise of the gift of the Holy Spirit (1:4; Luke 24:49) with the coming of the Messiah (2:39; 13:23), but now it refers to the promise of resurrection, indicating that the resurrection is the central problem between Paul and his adversaries (cf. 22:22—23:11).

This assertion is followed by a lengthy description of Paul's activity as a persecutor, repeating and elaborating on the material in Acts 9 and Acts 22. At verse 12, we come to Paul's encounter with Jesus, a description different in some interesting ways from the earlier accounts. No mention is made of Paul's blindness (cf. 9:8; 22:11) or to the help of Ananias. We do hear of a bright and powerful light, so strong as to be impressive even in the midday sun (v. 13). The voice Paul hears is the same except for the assertion that "It hurts you to kick against the goads" (26:14). Gaventa notes that this is a common expression in Greek literature referring to the futility of pushing against a greater power. Using a familiar Greek expression, Luke indicates that Paul cannot resist the power of Christ.

The result of the encounter is that Jesus tells Paul what he is to do:

> ". . . for I have appeared to you for this purpose, to appoint you to serve and to bear witness to the things in which you have seen me and to those in which I will appear to you, delivering you from the people and from the Gentiles—to whom I send you to open their eyes, that they may turn from darkness to light . . ." (26:16–18).

This grammatically difficult sentence raises questions. How can Paul bear witness to the things he has seen when he has not yet seen very much? From what Jews and gentiles does he need deliverance? We must be reminded that this speech stands as a final defense, a summation in gentile categories for a gentile audience, a climax of Luke's defense of Paul. We are looking back across many events and struggles which, in Luke's view, make sense only when viewed from the standpoint of the divine commission.

What is the nature of the commission? Paul is to be a "servant," someone who is given a job to do, not someone who has some privileged possession of his own. He is to be a "witness," a term Luke regularly employs for the apostles (e.g., 1:22; 2:32; 3:15). Although Luke cannot quite call Paul an apostle, he nevertheless is engaged in the same work as apostles: to tell in words and to demonstrate in works what has happened in Christ. Paul must go to whom he is sent, Jew and gentiles alike, even when their reaction requires God to deliver a persecuted Paul from their violence.

Isaiah heard God say, "I have given you as a covenant to the people, / a light to the nations, / to open the eyes that are blind" (Isa. 42:6-7). Luke picks up on this imagery about giving sight to the blind in Paul's commission "to open their eyes." Just as the risen Christ has opened the eyes of Paul (v. 16), so Paul is sent to open the eyes of others. This movement from "darkness to light" is standard in describing conversions (I Peter 2:9), a move which implies also turning from Satan and evil (Eph. 2:2; Col. 1:13), a turning which is made explicit in Acts 26:18.

At the end of Paul's description of his commission, we realize that we are reading an account of conversion which differs from those found in Acts 9 and 22. In this account the work Paul is to do, the work of turning and enlightening, is the central focus of the narrative. It was this commissioning vision that Paul obeyed (v. 19), a commission involved with both turning (conversion) and repentance, acts which constitute a unified movement in this account (v. 20). The mention of repentance leading to the performance of deeds "worthy of their repentance" is reminiscent of John the Baptist's call to sinners in Luke 3:8.

The defense concludes with the assertion that Paul has always had the help of God in being obedient to his commission (vv. 22-23). His witness has not differed from that of the prophets and Moses. He is innocent because he has dared to proclaim only what faithful Israel has always proclaimed.

178

Luke says that the response to Paul's earnest appeal was mixed. Festus thinks Paul is mad (v. 24), Agrippa is incredulous that Paul expects to make him a Christian in so short a time (v. 28). These cultured despisers of Jewish squabbles will not be so easily persuaded. They are intellectually sophisticated, smug, powerful persons. They do not turn and repent. Yet they do agree that "This man is doing nothing to deserve death or imprisonment" (v. 31). They had hoped to uncover some credible charges against Paul, but instead they can only acquit him. Paul heads for Rome only because he has appealed to Caesar.

Unlike the defense in Acts 22, this speech has not been given to fellow Jews but before representatives of the Empire. Paul speaks not as one speaking within the house of Israel but as one attempting to persuade by more philosophical means. Paul sought in Acts 22 to place himself firmly within the tradition of Israel. Here, he presents himself as a victim of intramural factionalism (26:3), a person who is rejected because of his belief in the resurrection of Jesus. The risen Lord has told him that he is to be a "servant" and a "witness"; so, like Acts 22, it is a story not so much of a conversion as of a *call.*

Although Paul's defense has objective content—something has happened to him to which he must be obedient—his technique for delivering his defense is *a subjective account of personal experience.* His speech in Acts 26 has given a pattern for generations of personal testimonials by Christians, a testimony in themselves to the power of Luke's dramatic creation. In fact this manner of "accounting for the hope that is within us" makes such an impression upon us that many later-day Christians have come to feel that this is the *only* means of witnessing to the power of Christ in our lives (see *Reflection: Conversion in Acts*). Generations of believers have followed that healed man who was told by Jesus to "Return to your home, and declare how much God has done for you" (Luke 8:38–39).

Today, many contemporary Christians are either suspicious of or bored by the hackneyed, stereotypical accounts of personal conversion experiences tirelessly reiterated at testimonial services in some churches or exhibitionistically narrated on the Christian talk shows of the electronic church. After hearing the ten-thousandth account of "What Jesus did for me when he came into my life," can we blame those who flee from this radically subjectivized and relentlessly experiential approach to the Christian faith? "I was miserable." "Then I found Jesus." "Now my life is fulfilled and I am happy." We have heard this testimonial pattern a thousand times. Note that when compared to Paul's "testimonial" before Agrippa this pattern comes up short. First, nowhere does Paul say that he was miserable or felt the need for anything else in his life. Unlike modern people, Paul did not conceive of religion before or after his Damascus road experience as primarily a matter of self-fulfillment. Secondly, Luke goes to great lengths to demonstrate that nobody "finds" Jesus. *Jesus finds us.* Paul was not on his way to Damascus searching for anyone other than Christian heretics. The initiative in all these stories of change and turning around is God's. Luke would know nothing of our rather smug declaration of spiritual expertise which believes that I found Jesus, I took Jesus into my life, or I gave my life to Christ. For Luke, most of the traffic on the bridge between us and God is moving toward us. Finally, there is the question of happiness as a result of conversion to Christianity. Well, Paul must have felt joy at being God's instrument and at being part of the good news to Israel and the gentiles. Yet the man who testifies before Agrippa does so in chains. He has been beaten, stoned, imprisoned. It would be difficult to claim that meeting Jesus has solved all of Paul's problems—in fact meeting Jesus has been from the very first the beginning of problems Paul would surely have avoided and would not have wished upon himself.

The "Christian Talk Show" host smiled and said, "We are so thrilled to have a famous Christian with us today to share his testimony with us—Saint Paul!" *(Enthusiastic applause.)*

"Tell us, Paul—or should I call you 'Saint', which do you prefer?"

"Paul, just Paul the Pharisee would be fine, Jim."

"Great! Paul, tell us about all the wonderful things that happened to you when the Lord Jesus came into your life."

"Well, let's see. First I was struck blind. I got over that but then somebody tried to kill me and I had to escape in a basket. Then they stoned me and. . . ."

Granted the inadequacy of some contemporary definitions of witness, there can be no doubt that Luke believes that *a personal experience of the risen Christ is the bedrock upon which faithful witness is built.* It is this Christ who comes to Paul saying, "I have appeared to you for this purpose, to appoint you to serve and bear witness to the things in which you have seen me and to those in which I will appear to you" (26:16). The Paul whom we meet in Acts (regardless of how he may differ from the Paul whom we meet in the Epistles) offers personal

180

testimony to personal and ongoing experience of the risen Lord as an unanswerable argument for his position. Of course, this personal and ongoing experience is itself answerable to Scripture and tradition, even to the scrutiny of the Christian community itself. Yet there can be no denying that the witness of Paul, as we encounter it in Acts, is driven by the power of personal experience.

Always be prepared to make a defense to any one who calls you to account for the hope that is in you; yet do it with gentleness and reverence, counsels I Peter 3:15*b*. What, according to Acts 26, makes for effective witness before both our contentious fellow believers and our skeptical pagan neighbors? Certain *facts should be known,* for the Christian faith is not about feelings, even very deep feelings, but about something which has happened, something which has happened to us: the fact of the risen Christ. Yet, as we have said above, this faith is validated through our personal experience of the reality of Christ. Paul did not simply know *about* Christ; he knew Christ. Until the fact of *the risen Christ becomes part of our lives, something motivating and empowering us,* we have little to say, even if we know the facts. Finally, Acts 26 suggests that we must *know and respect the recipients of our witness.* Paul heard himself called not simply to speak the truth but to speak the truth to those whom the risen Christ loved enough to send a witness to turn them toward the light. Paul's speeches are tailored to their audience. Although the content of his testimony is amazingly consistent, his style, approach, language, and goals are different within different contexts. He flatters his fellow Jews by calling them "brothers and fathers" as he begins his defense in Acts 22, but he also knows how to act when standing before a self-important pagan like Felix or Agrippa in Acts 26. A contemporary communicator of the Christian faith (which should include everyone in the church) would do well to ponder Paul's speeches in Acts 22 and Acts 26 as models of Christian testimonial.

We cannot read this account of Paul standing before these sophisticated representatives of the Roman legal system without hearing echoes of Jesus' trial and passion. Both Jesus and Paul go to Jerusalem ready to suffer and die in obedience to the will of God (cf. 19:21; Luke 9:51). Both appear before the Sanhedrin and a Roman procurator and governor. In both cases their fellow Jews cry "Away with him!" (21:36; Luke 23:18). Both

181

were beaten and both were at several times declared to be innocent (v. 31; 23:29; Luke 22:63; 23:4, 14–15, 22). The pain and trial suffered by Jesus was also suffered by his servant Paul. Jesus promised that "everyone who is fully taught shall be like his teacher" (Luke 6:40). Paul exemplified how closely the ministry of the witness and servant would resemble the life and trials of the Master.

Yet there the parallels between the trial and death of Jesus and the trial and death of Paul end. Unlike the death of Jesus, the death of Paul has little interest in Luke's story because this story of a servant named Paul is, in reality, a story about the risen Christ. Unlike his Master, Paul did not die in Jerusalem. Jesus spoke only once or twice, and then very briefly, during his trial (Luke 22:67–70; 23:3) while Paul testified constantly. Unlike Paul, Jesus did not need to speak constantly during his trial, for he was the content of his defense. The death of Jesus is narrated in gruesome detail, whereas Luke has no report of Paul's death at the end of Acts. Was this because, unlike the death of Jesus, the death of Paul was not the vindication of God's purposes through the resurrection, not God's act of redemption but was merely the culmination of Paul's ministry in behalf of Christ? Luke's failure to narrate the death of Paul is an unsolved mystery of Acts (unless Luke wrote before Paul's death).

Perhaps the real issue at Paul's trial is the vindication of his message, whereas the issue at Jesus' trial was the identification of God's Messiah. Paul's death, unlike that of his Lord, is not narrated because Paul is the instrument for the resurrected Lord. His life and death are the vehicle to proclaim the truth of Christ. It is Christ who is the center of Paul's trial, the subject of his testimony, not Paul, who is content to be the obedient servant of Christ.

Acts 27:1—28:16
Perilous Voyage

From the time of earliest literature, human imagination has been gripped by stories of sea voyages—the travels of Sinbad the Sailor, Odysseus' legendary exploits on the wine-dark sea, Jonah swallowed by a great fish on his way to Nineveh, the disciples crying out to Jesus in the midst of a storm on the Sea of Galilee. Is it because of the dark perils the sea represents, the threat of watery oblivion? Or are we attracted to these tales of sea journeys because we know that we ourselves are wayfarers, voyagers upon uncharted seas, pilgrims at the mercy of the elements?

The Christian notion of a human being as a wayfarer in search of salvation no longer seems to inform Western culture. Is life still conceived of as a journey, a pilgrimage, or as only a rootless, incoherent exploration of the inner-self? We want security more than adventure, rewarding interpersonal relations rather than truth. If we can find a place to rest, we settle there. "Follow me," says the Christ. Dare the journey? Can we know what it means to be so gripped by a vision, a truth, a yearning to tell what has happened that we would be as willing as Paul to put to sea, going God knows where?

The sea gives both life and death. One can imagine the terrors the sea held for people in the ancient world. Is it any wonder that, for the Hebrews, the sea represented that watery chaos the Creator pushed back when the earth was formed from the void (Gen. 1:6–10)? That sea burst forth by God's anger with humanity, wiping out every living thing from the face of the earth in the days of Noah, the first sailor. For Noah and his family the sea was not only the source of God's judgment upon human sin but was also the place of gracious divine deliverance for God's faithful ones. The waters which destroyed were also those which purified and delivered. And when at last we are the recipients of a new heaven and a new earth, the sea, that great, threatening abyss, shall be no more (Rev. 21:1). Even today the sea represents a place of peril, of human vulnerability, the place where would-be sailors are at the mercy of the elements, held safe only by the hands of God.

"We put to sea," says our first person plural narrator of this section of Acts (27:2), and Paul's adventure begins. Read Acts 27:1—28:16 aloud before examining it more closely. Luke would want us first to savor the drama of the narrative, the movement of the story, the rich images before we attempt to glean theological implications.

This is the last of ten or twelve sea voyages to which Luke refers in Acts (e.g., 9:30; 11:25–26; 13:4, 13). The fast was already over (27:9). This is reference to the Jewish Day of Atonement in September-October. By that time of the year sailing was treacherous. Paul advises the centurion Julius not to sail, but he took the advice of the captain instead (27:10–11). Julius, who was kind to Paul (v. 3), learns to listen to Paul the next time (v. 31). Julius also prevents a massacre of the prisoners because "he wished to save Paul" (v. 43). Although Paul is the prisoner of this pagan soldier, Luke's portrait of Julius is (typically) not a simple one. Even though like most pagans Julius erroneously thinks he knows more than this ignorant Jew, kindness and compassion are found in this pagan soldier.

Pagan soldiers are not the chief protagonists of this story, however; Paul is the center of the action. He gives expert advice about weather and navigation, he maintains amazing calm in the middle of a raging storm, even delivering a sermon to the hardened sailors who had "abandoned all hope" (27:20–25), and he helps to head off a mutiny. He predicts that no lives will be lost (27:22), a prophecy fulfilled when "all escaped to land" (27:44). In the story of Jonah and his tough sea voyage, the presence of a reluctant prophet endangered the lives of everyone on the ship. Paul is no reluctant messenger of God, however, and his presence is the avenue of salvation for all on board. When Jonah refused to go preach repentance to the Ninevites, he nearly perished. Paul on the other hand obeys the divine command to go preach in Rome (23:11), so things will go differently for him and his fellow travelers in the midst of the storm at sea.

The winds and waves of the sea are in the hands of God (Ps. 95:5). Knowing that his life is involved in God's mission (27:24), Paul not only has courage but seeks to fill his shipmates with courage as well (27:25). Then, in the ultimate act of confidence, Paul urges his companions to eat. He took bread, blessed it, broke it, and began to eat (27:35). This repetition of the familiar fourfold table action by which the risen Lord was revealed (Luke 24:30–31) is a source of encouragement for all on board (27:36). What is the response of the church in the midst of discouragement and fear? Like Paul, the church takes bread, blesses it, breaks it, and begins to eat. "What good will that do?" the world may ask. In this sign of hope in the power and presence of God, this Eucharistic witness to our confidence in God's will to give us what we need even in the midst of the storm, the church not only feeds itself but witnesses to the world. Of course, we are not told that this was what we call the sacrament of the Lord's Supper. Nor are we told whether or not the pagans

on board joined with Paul in his blessed food. Yet surely Theophilus' church would make the connection between their
Sunday meals together in whatever "storm" they were ex-
periencing and this meal on a dark day at sea. *The Eucharist is
food of confidence shared in the middle of the storm.*

In earlier trials Paul is vindicated through argument or the
verdict of the judge or crowd. Now, as those on the ship reach
the safety of land, Paul is vindicated through deliverance from
the sea. In Homer's *Odyssey,* Odysseus' crew perished because
they had killed Helios' sacred cows. In the story of Jonah, the
voyagers knew that their troubles were due to the anger of God
at the reluctant prophet on board (Jonah 1:7–10). Now in their
salvation from perishing all know the blessing of God for this
faithful prophet, Paul.

If the dramatic and happy ending of the storm was not
enough evidence for the divine approval of Paul, Luke adds yet
another story of miraculous deliverance. When Paul is bitten by
a viper in Malta, the natives there come to the conclusion that
"No doubt this man is a murderer" (28:4). After all, conventional wisdom says that bad things happen to bad people, that
there is a definite cause-effect relationship between bad deeds
and the swift and just retribution of God. Yet when Paul shows
no adverse effects from the snake's bite, their theology swings
to the opposite extreme and they "said that he was a god" (28:6).
Bad theology is equally inept in both its assessment of the meaning of tragedy and in its ascriptions of good fortune. Paul is not
a god. He is a servant of God. The Maltese are correct in assuming that there is a divine aura about him. Just as the pagan
authorities have declared Paul innocent, these two stories in
Acts—the storm at sea and the viper—show that even the mysterious forces of nature bow before the servants of God.

Yet the powers which protect Paul are not merely for his
own enjoyment. Paul is preserved so that he may continue to
serve. The father of Publius, the chief on the island, was sick.
Paul visited him and prayed, laying-on-hands, and the old man
was healed (28:7–8). "The prayer of a righteous man has great
power in its effects" (James 5:16). Paul's righteousness is
confirmed by deliverance from an angry sea, by preservation
from the bite of a deadly viper, and by Paul's ability to effect
the healing of others.

185

Men and women of the ancient world were totally at the
mercy of the whims of the natural elements and the vicissitudes

of nature. They sought power over their destinies. Perhaps we modern men and women, who have gained such great control over the forces which once brought havoc to our ancestors, are no longer impressed by stories of the power to calm the waves and to heal the fevered brow. Our physicians and pilots do this every day. We think it is our right to be able to control all of the forces in our world, just like God, and feel terribly hurt, terribly betrayed when we cannot. We may smile at the naïveté of these stories of miracles and wondrous deliverance. Yet we live in a part of the world where great resources have been expended in attempts to predict the weather, to take the threat out of travel, and to insure life without sickness, pain, or disability. The largest buildings in most of our cities are not temples to gods, at least not to the traditional deities. The largest buildings are hospitals or government agencies that promise us control over our destinies, divine-like power over the world. As if in imitation of the ancient Maltese, we bow before the technocrat, for here is where our transcendence lies. Our machines shall save us by making life more like machinery—rational, predictable, dependable. Technology shall give us life everlasting on our own terms, without risk or pain or mystery. How dare we snicker at the religious naïveté of the Maltese?

This dramatic segment of Acts ends with the travelers at last making their way to Rome (28:14). Paul is welcomed into the city, not as a defeated captive in chains but almost like a triumphant general. When word reached the Christians at Rome (evidently, Luke knows of a community there before Paul arrived), they traveled over forty miles to meet Paul and welcome him to the city. "On seeing them Paul thanked God and took courage" (28:15). In a narrative filled with accounts of power, miraculous deliverance, and divine intervention, this is perhaps the greatest power the Christian faith puts at the disciple's disposal—the power of brothers and sisters in the church.

In struggles with injustice, cruelty, and life's difficulties, one of the church's greatest gifts to us is the church. If Luke seems preoccupied with the church, it is perhaps because Luke knows that the church has become the content of the gospel proclamation. Jesus came preaching, not simply a new philosophy of life but a new way of living. He formed a new people, a new community. The nineteenth-century historian Alfred Loisy is often quoted as saying, "Jesus proclaimed the Kingdom of God, and what came was the church." Loisy did not mean

186

this in the cynical way in which it is often repeated, as if the church were a later misunderstanding of the original, more individualistic teachings of Jesus. Jesus' message formed a distinct people. His message was about a new community. The Acts question is not merely the intellectual one of "Do you agree?" but the political and social question, "Will you join up?"

Paul spoke of the church as a colony of heaven (Phil. 3:20). A colony is a beachhead, an island in the midst of another kingdom. On their own, individual colonists could never survive in the alien culture. So they work and live together, come out to meet one another, give each other courage. The colony is not yet fully established, not out of danger, for it lives in the midst of a culture which bows to other gods. The North American church may not adequately appreciate the precariousness of its existence within American culture. The world has stopped giving us favors. People will not become Christian by living within this country, drinking the water, watching television. We are—like those brothers and sisters who ran out to Three Taverns to greet Paul—aliens, exiles, colonists more than we know. The power of the church to support us and to create a new counter-culture for us is bound to take on increasing significance in the future.

Paul is still in chains and must know the somber fate awaiting him (28:16). Nothing in the story relieves us of knowing that tragic end. Yet Paul is filled with courage because he is not alone. God has people even here. This new trans-national, global empire made up of "all who invoke the name of our Lord Jesus Christ in every place" (author's trans., I Cor. 1:2) upholds Paul in his time of trial. Not only is God demonstrably beside him but so also are brothers and sisters in Christ. They run all the way to Three Taverns to have the privilege of escorting their hero into the city. The gospel is taken to the heart of the Empire, brought by one who journeys not alone.

Acts 28:17–28[29]
This Salvation of God

187

"And so we came to Rome" (28:14). His perilous journey at last ended, we stand with Paul in the capital city. But note where Paul goes first—not to see the grand sights of the imperial city, not to the gates of Caesar, nor even out to convert gentile Romans. "He called together the local leaders of the Jews," (v. 17) and preached to them. As always, Paul goes first to the house of Israel. His sermon is a concise summary of his defense speeches in the past. It is a two-point sermon: (1) a concise defense of his actions in the past and (2) assertion that "I had done nothing against the people or the customs of our fathers" (v. 17). He stands now awaiting trial in Caesar's court because of the actions of his own people (vv. 18–19). Like Jesus, his own people have delivered him into the hands of the Romans and, like Jesus, he brings no charges against his nation (v. 19). This statement does not exactly fit what we were told about Paul's rescue by the Romans (21:31) but fits Luke's purpose in this sermon—a defense summation by Paul before his own people, a defense made in part by showing how Paul's trial parallels Jesus' trial. The Lukan Paul stands before his own people in Rome, a man in chains, not because he sought to play havoc with the historic faith of Israel but rather because he sought to live out "the hope of Israel" (v. 20).

The reaction to Paul's defense is threefold. *First,* the Roman Jews say that they have received no official directives about Paul but that they know this "sect" is "everywhere . . . spoken against" (v. 22). Will they think for themselves or only await official guidance or judge by popular hearsay? *Second,* the requested follow-up meeting lasting from morning until evening consisted of Paul's attempt to "convince them about Jesus both from the law of Moses and from the prophets" (v. 23). Paul takes a great amount of time to witness, and he witnesses on the basis of the tradition his hearers hold dear. *Third,* the reaction of his Jewish audience is typically divided. Some are convinced, others are not (v. 24). There is joy that some hear and receive the good news, but sadness that many do not. Isaiah 6:9–10 is used to explain their rejection. Some in Israel had always grown "heavy of hearing," unable to "understand with their heart." It had happened before, now it was happening again.

Behind this confrontation with Israel is the church's attempt to explain to itself the mystery of unbelief. Unbelief is always a mystery to those who believe. How can we explain that the truth which motivates us, which helps us to explain the world and to give meaning to our lives, does not move others? Why do some look at Christ and see the Light of the World and others see nothing? Eyes and ears see and hear differently. Rejection of our gospel is perceived as a threat. If the truth is so self-evident to us, why do not all believe? Rather than impute wickedness to the unbeliever, we must rejoice in those who do believe and allow the mystery to remain a mystery, hidden somehow in the inscrutable purposes of God. Like Paul, we must go to those who are able to listen (v. 30). The section ends with Paul saying that "this salvation of God has been sent to the Gentiles; they will listen" (v. 29). As Luke sees it, gentiles listen, not because they are better people than the Jews but because they have absolutely no possibility of salvation outside of these promises. Luke told a story of a great banquet where the original recipients "all alike began to make excuses" (Luke 14:18). The rejected host then sent his messengers to "bring in the poor and maimed and blind and lame" (14:21). These outsiders come, not because they are especially perceptive but because they have nowhere else to go. Unless someone else's invitation comes to them, they are without hope. The poor enter because in this kingdom populated by little ones only those who are poor, hungry, weeping, and reviled are empty enough to hear and accept the invitation that is offered. The gentiles respond because they have no other hope than that offered in fulfillment of the promises to Israel.

Paul's declaration that he will now go to the gentiles does not mean that God has at last forsaken the promises to Israel. From the beginning of Jesus' ministry, he encountered a divided Israel. That many in Israel still reject the message about Jesus does not negate their status as the chief beneficiaries of that message. The mission to Israel continues throughout Acts—Paul goes first to the Jews in Rome—and we could easily expect it to continue in the church of Theophilus. There is no indication that the promises of God to Israel, the promises in which Luke places such great meaning, have come to an end simply because of the rejection by most of the recipients of those promises. The God of Luke-Acts is a resourceful, persistent God who does not give up easily. The words from Isaiah quoted by Paul do not in their original context signal the end of God's work with intransigent Israel but its beginning. The mission to Israel was not a complete failure (21:20). Luke would not, as the church did later, have transferred the guilt of one generation's rejection to another. The Jews who rejected the gospel do not necessitate the end of appeals to them anymore than Pilate's actions lead to the discontinuance of the mission to the gentiles. Luke would not have advocated, as did some later Christian commentators, a new gentile particularism denying God's universal love for the Jew (see *Reflection: Luke and His Fellow Jews*). Among both Jew and gentile, the verdict upon the gospel is mixed. Therefore, Paul welcomed "all who came to him" (v. 30).

Preaching and Teaching Unhindered

ACTS 28:30–31

Perhaps Paul welcomed all who came to him at his lodgings (28:30) because members of the Way had been excluded from the synagogues (cf. 28:22). No impediment will silence Paul as long as he has breath from "preaching the kingdom of God and teaching about the Lord Jesus Christ" (28:31). In fact the last verse of Acts could be taken as a summary of the whole book. The Spirit that descended at Pentecost gave the young church its tongue to tell "the mighty works of God" (2:11). We have observed the church proclaiming those mighty works despite every hindrance and every obstacle. Bold proclamation to all who will listen is a mighty work of God.

Acts 20:25, 38 suggests that Luke knew full well the result of Paul's trial. Theophilus and his church also must have known that Paul finally died a martyr's death at Rome. Earlier we noted the parallels between the final trial and suffering of Paul and the passion of Jesus as recorded in Luke's Gospel. Why did Luke not also develop an account of the death of Paul to parallel the death of Jesus?

We can only speculate on why Luke chose to end Acts as he did. We know enough of his dramatic genius to be assured that his ending was not accidental. The Book of Acts began with Luke telling Theophilus that his second volume would be a continuation of "all that Jesus began to do and teach until the day when he was taken up" (1:1–2). The words and deeds of Christ continue in the work and proclamation of his disciples. They could not silence Jesus, because the Holy Spirit empowered Jesus' people to continue to speak of the coming kingdom of God. In Acts we have witnessed how that bold proclamation reached out to include all people (4:29; 28:31), anyone who would listen. Caesar cannot silence the gospel. The proclamation was not stilled at Calvary, not ended when Stephen was stoned, nor can the story end with the death of Paul in Rome. Paul has been delivered from the forces of nature (27:1—28:16). He has been pronounced innocent by the Roman courts. He has thus triumphed over the most dreaded powers. What can stop his witness? The risen Christ told his disciples, "You are witnesses of these things" (Luke 24:48), implying that the story had begun rather than ended. Acts is the continuation of that story of witness into "Jerusalem and in all Judea and Samaria and to the end of the earth" (Acts 1:8).

While in no way denying the real challenges the gospel must overcome, as well as the real suffering believers must endure, Acts is determined to encourage Theophilus by telling the positive story of the forward advance of God's truth. Three thousand were baptized at Pentecost. By chapter 21 the Jerusalem elders can report that tens of thousands of Jews now believe in Jesus (21:20). Philip out-performed Simon Magus (8:9–13); Paul outdid Elymas the magician (13:6–12). The stories of success—stories a persecuted, despondent church needs to hear—abound in Acts.

Though this world is often an inhospitable place for the gospel and its witnesses, real conversion is possible. Disciples are to be in the world, witnessing to a power unknown to the world. A simplistic division of the world into the children of light and the children of darkness is not found in Luke-Acts. Surprising converts are made. No one is without hope. Paul, who now bears the gospel to Rome, was once a dreaded enemy of God. The Ethiopian was an outsider. Cornelius was a foreigner. With the Spirit active, who can defeat this gospel? In the words of Gamaliel, a member of the high court who sought to silence these witnesses, "keep away from these men and let them alone; for if this plan or this undertaking is of men, it will fail; but if it is of God, you will not be able to overthrow them" (5:38–39). The future belongs to the Way.

To call Luke-Acts "triumphalistic," as some have done (D. L. Tiede, pp. 139–140), is to ignore Luke's intended audience—a persecuted minority fighting for its life. The basic optimism of Acts sometimes has been used by succeeding generations of Christians in a triumphalist fashion, but that is not Luke's prob-

191

lem. Luke's problem is Theophilus and his church—a tiny band of disheartened believers who are in danger of losing hope. A smug, self-satisfied, culturally significant church cannot easily understand Acts.

As the contemporary American church finds itself pushed to the periphery of the dominant culture, severed from its former props and social crutches, the encouraging words of Acts may take on a relevance unknown to Christians in our more "successful" days. A "triumphalist" gospel is a dangerous temptation for a "successful" church but an appropriate source of encouragement for the Lord's persecuted and oppressed.

You and I live in the continuation of the story of Acts. Acts must close in an open-ended fashion, with the door still open for work and witness rather than closed by death, because the Spirit is still active. Luke is not simply writing history. He writes the story of the Spirit, the Spirit incarnate in people like you and me. Theophilus' church asked, "Lord, will you at this time restore the kingdom to Israel?" (1:6). When will the story end and all the promises be fulfilled, when shall we receive the benefactions of God in their fullness, when will the power we glimpse in the miracles of the disciples be present forever (28:30)? Luke gives no answer except that the story continues. Living here between the times, as we always have, there is work for the church to do. We need not be gazing into heaven (1:11) when the Spirit is active here on earth. The period of the world mission of the church is now. There is still time to tell what has happened on earth. We need not cower from confrontation with the future, fearful of some cataclysmic nuclear end. There may be tribulation, and some of it may be at the hands of our own technology gone mad. Yet there has always been tribulation for disciples—even in times when the rest of the world felt quite peaceful and secure. Our security as believers lies, as it always has, not in the fulfillment of optimistic hopes for human progress, in either technology or super-power arms control. Our hope lies in the hands of a loving and powerful God. This knowledge enables us to speak, even when nuclear paralysis or fear of the future makes many stand in helpless silence. Since Pentecost nothing has been able to silence the tongues of God's faithful witnesses. In your church and mine the story continues.

192

The mandate of Luke 24:47 and Acts 1:8 is still in force for contemporary witnesses who must continue to be faithful and to proclaim the gospel "unhindered" (28:31). Even bound in

Caesar's chains, Paul continued to witness unhindered. Even when Paul is murdered by the state, the gospel continued unhindered in Theophilus' church. Now, nearly two millennia after Luke wrote to Theophilus, Acts reminds us that despite rejection, persecutions, setbacks, and our own lethargy or cowardice the gospel proclamation continues to the very end of the earth, by God's grace, unhindered.

BIBLIOGRAPHY

1. For further study

BRUCE, F. F. *The Book of Acts* (Grand Rapids: Wm. B. Eerdmans, 1956).

DIBELIUS, MARTIN. *Studies in the Acts of the Apostles,* translated by M. Ling (New York: Scribner's, 1956).

JUEL, DONALD. *Luke-Acts: The Promise of History* (Atlanta: John Knox Press, 1983).

KRODEL, GERHARD. *Acts* (Philadelphia: Fortress Press, 1981).

O'NEILL, J. C. *The Theology of Acts in Its Historical Setting* (London S.P.C.K., 1961).

TALBERT, CHARLES H. *Luke-Acts: Perspectives from the Society of Biblical Literature Seminar* (New York: Crossroad, 1984).

2. Literature cited

ADAM, ADOLF. *The Liturgical Year* (New York: Pueblo Publishing, 1981).

BAUR, F. C. *Paul, the Apostle of Jesus Christ, His Life and Work, His Epistles and His Doctrine* (London/Edinburgh: Williams and Norgate, 1873–1875).

BECKER, ERNEST. *The Denial of Death* (New York: Free Press, 1973).

BERGER, PETER and THOMAS LUCKMANN. *The Social Construction of Reality: A Treatise on the Sociology of Knowledge* (Garden City, N.Y.: Doubleday & Co., 1966).

CADBURY, H. J. *The Book of Acts in History* (London: Black, 1955).

CAIRD, G. B. *The Gospel of St. Luke* (Philadelphia: Westminster Press, 1963).

CONZELMANN, HANS. *The Theology of St. Luke* (Die Mitte der Zeit [1953]), translated by Geoffrey Buswell (New York: Harper and Row, 1960).

CULLMANN, OSCAR. *Baptism in the New Testament* (London: S.C.M. Press, Ltd., 1950).

DIDACHE, THE. *Teaching of the Twelve Apostles,* ANCIENT CHRISTIAN WRITERS, translated James A. Kleist (Westminster, Md.: Newman Press, 1948).

DODD, C. H. *The Apostolic Preaching and Its Development* (New York: Harper and Row, 1937).

EUSEBIUS. *Historia Ecclesiastica* (New York: G. P. Putnam's Sons, 1926–1938).

FARLEY, E. *Ecclesial Man: A Social Phenominology of Faith and Reality* (Philadelphia: Fortress Press, 1975).

FIORENZA, ELISABETH SCHUESSLER. *In Memory of Her: A Feminist Theological Reconstruction of Christian Origins* (New York: Crossroad, 1983).

FREND, W.H.C. *Martyrdom and Persecution in the Early Church: A*

Study of a Conflict from the Maccabees to Donatus (Oxford: Blackwell, 1965).

GAVENTA, BEVERLY R. *From Darkness to Light: Aspects of Conversion in the New Testament* (Philadelphia: Fortress Press, 1986).

HAENCHEN, ERNST. *The Acts of the Apostles,* translated from the 14th German edition (1965) by Bernard Noble and Gerald Shinn. Translation updated and revised by R. McL. Wilson (Philadelphia: The Westminster Press, 1971).

HARNACK, ADOLPH. *Luke the Physician,* NEW TESTAMENT STUDIES, I (New York: Putnam, 1907).

HAUERWAS, STANLEY. *Vision and Virtue: Essays in Christian Ethical Reflection* (Notre Dame: Fides Publishers, 1974).

———"On Taking Religion Seriously: The Challenge of Jonestown," *Against the Nations: War and Survival in a Liberal Society* (Minneapolis: Winston Press, 1985).

HENGEL, MARTIN. *Acts and the History of the Earliest Christianity,* translated by John Bowden (Philadelphia: Fortress Press, 1979).

JEREMIAS, JOACHIM. *The Eucharistic Words of Jesus* (Philadelphia: Fortress Press, 1977).

JERVELL, JACOB. *Luke and the People of God: A New Look at Luke-Acts* (Minneapolis: Augsburg Publishing House, 1972).

JOSEPHUS. *Antiquities* (New York: Putnam's Sons, 1926–1943).

JUEL, DONALD. See 1. For further study, above.

JUSTIN MARTYR. I *Apology* (New York: Christian Heritage, 1949), 14:2–3.

KELSEY, DAVID H. *The Uses of Scripture in Recent Theology* (Philadelphia: Fortress Press, 1975).

KUENG, HANS. *The Church* (Garden City, N.Y.: Doubleday & Co., 1976).

MEEKS, WAYNE A. *The First Urban Christians: The Social World of the Apostle Paul* (New Haven: Yale University Press, 1983).

MOL, HANS J. *Identity and the Sacred* (New York: Free Press, Division of The Macmillan Publishing Co., 1977).

MOULE, C.F.D. "The Christology of Acts," in Leander Keck and J. L. Martyn, editors, *Studies in Luke-Acts* (Nashville: Abingdon Press, 1966).

MUNCK, JOHANNES. *The Acts of the Apostles* (Garden City, N.Y.: Doubleday & Co., Inc., 1967).

NEUHAUS, RICHARD JOHN. *Freedom for Ministry* (San Francisco: Harper and Row, 1979).

O'CONNOR, FLANNERY. *The Habit of Being,* Sally Fitzgerald, editor (New York: Vintage Books, 1979).

SANDERS, E. P. *Paul and Palestinian Judaism* (Philadelphia: Fortress Press, 1977).

SNOWDEN, F. M. , Jr. *Blacks in Antiquity* (Cambridge: Harvard University Press, 1970).

STAGG, FRANK. *The Book of Acts: The Early Struggle for an Unhindered Gospel* (Nashville: Broadman Press, 1955).

———"The Purpose and Message of Acts," *Review and Expositor,* XLIV (Jan. 1947), pp. 3–21.

STEINMETZ, DAVID. "Reformation and Conversion," *Theology Today*, 35 (1978), pp. 25–32.

TALBERT, CHARLES H. *Acts* (Atlanta: John Knox Press, 1984).

——*Luke and the Gnostics* (Nashville: Abingdon Press, 1966).

TIEDE, DAVID L. *Prophecy and History in Luke-Acts* (Philadelphia: Fortress Press, 1980).

TRACY, DAVID. *The Analogical Imagination: Christian Theology and the Culture of Pluralism* (New York: Crossroad, 1981).

WALLIS, JIM. *Call to Conversion* (New York: Harper and Row, 1982).